Illuminating Humor
of the BIBLE

STEVEN C. WALKER

 CASCADE *Books* · Eugene, Oregon

ILLUMINATING HUMOR OF THE BIBLE

Cascade Books
A Division of Wipf and Stock Publishers
199 W. 8th Ave., Suite 3
Eugene, OR 97401

www.wipfandstock.com

ISBN 13: 978-1-62032-148-5

Cataloging-in-Publication data:

Walker, Steven C.

Illuminating humor of the Bible / Steven C. Walker.

xiv + 242 p. ; 23 cm. Includes bibliographical references and indexes.

ISBN 13: 978-1-62032-148-5

1. Wit and humor in the Bible. 2. Wit and humor—Theology. I. Title.

BS680.W63 W344 2013

Manufactured in the U.S.A.

ILLUMINATING HUMOR OF THE BIBLE

Alice in Wonderland *has it exactly right—*
some things get "better and better and better":
Scott and Rebecca and Emily
and the King James Version of the Bible.

"Man thinks, God laughs."
HEBREW PROVERB

Contents

Preface

Humor in the Bible?

GIVEN HOW PERSISTENTLY HUMOR smiles and chuckles and sometimes laughs right out loud in virtually every book of the Bible, it's remarkable how consistently readers manage to overlook it. It's also unfortunate. Humor graces biblical texts so pervasively that to miss the humor is to miss not only much of the emotional impact of the Bible, but much of its meaning.

Illuminating Humor of the Bible reveals how—and how much—comic elements contribute to understanding the most vital book in our culture. Biblical humor has been so seriously underestimated that we have not even considered its function, have not begun to appreciate why humor winks with such unexpected frequency and understated significance from this revered text. This investigation shines a spotlight on scriptural wit that illuminates the ways humor manifests biblical meaning.

Unveiled by the frank perspective of humor, Bible texts reveal implications that will surprise the most informed readers. The "Bible as Literature" wave of the past thirty years has revolutionized time-honored traditions of biblical studies, reexamining familiar cultural material through a new microscope. The humor approach, by means of its close-up-and-personal perspective, accesses more of those literary insights more meaningfully, making Bible reading both richer and more relevant.

Because a pointed punch line can disclose the subtlest implications, reading by the reader-response lamp of humor lights up dark corners of biblical significance until now inaccessible. Recognizing biblical humor does more than alert us to deeper dimensions of biblical meanings. Awareness of the wit enables not just better readings, but better ways to read, ways of reaching where no Bible reader has gone before. *Illuminating Humor of the Bible* unveils eight fresh and relevant methods of reading the Bible better through the lens of its humor:

[Chapter 1]

"A Time to Laugh": Humor "More Abundantly"

So much humor shimmers from so many aspects of the Bible it's a miracle we haven't noticed. Maybe we're just not paying attention—reliable statistics indicate that nine out of ten Bible readers at any given time are asleep. Yet this text that lulls and lullabies us as soporifically as *Ambien* includes, for those with ears to hear, some of the wittiest narrative ever written. When it gets noticed, biblical humor reveals rich irony and sharp satire and intense sarcasm and penetrating wit and outright joke in the farthest reaches of the Good Book. We've only to see it to realize how meaningful that Bible humor can be.

[Chapter 2]

Jonah as Joke: Lightening Up the Orthodox

A crucial function of humor in the Bible is to persuade the self-righteous to laugh at themselves—a process that proves especially enlightening when the self-righteous turn out to be us. Jonah sasses God. Heathen Ninevites and scurrilous sailors prove more pious than the prophet, who is subjected unceremoniously to his comeuppance, upchucked by the biggest fish ever featured in a fish story. For readers who question whether divinity has a sense of humor, Jonah's God responds with an emphatic grin that back-lights narrative implications as edifying as they are entertaining.

[Chapter 3]

"Turned to the Contrary": Comic Reversal in Esther

Much traditional Bible reading is reactionary rather than revolutionary, concerned with consolidating what is already known rather than expand-ing possibilities. But the text itself tends more to novel insight than to stale certitude. Topsy-turvy poetic justice in the refreshing satire of Esther trains readers to resist a disposition to find in Scripture only what they have found before. The wit of Esther, by turning our usual expectations upside down, alerts us to expect the unexpected.

[Chapter 4]

Eve's Initiative, Sarah's Sassiness, and Jael's Nail:
Humor as Social Justice

Bible humor encourages the underdog as it pulls the rug out from under the arrogant. Its farcical social reversal is particularly pointed in matters of gender. For a book so frequently held up as the standard of patriarchal prerogative, the Bible features remarkably feisty females—women prove more dynamic in the Bible than men, initiating more than their share of narrative action. Those proactive females foster genial gender humor. Despite the paternalistic context, angels prefer to deal with females. And women get the last scriptural word.

[Chapter 5]

"Peter Stood at the Door Knocking": Slapstick in Acts

Acts lampoons the pecking order of the fledgling church by means of whimsical portraits of early leaders. Peter is satirized as a lovable bumbler, Paul as a man who can't shut up. Ecclesiastical eminence gets seriously questioned by slapstick, sometimes even gallows humor, as in the amusing mishap when Paul's sermon inspires young Eutychus to "slump down" into such deep slumber he falls fatally, bored to death by the apostle's "long speaking."

[Chapter 6]

"A Ruddy Countenance": David as Trickster

Traditionally viewed as a pantheon of perfect role models, the Bible actually reads more like a rogues' gallery of unlikely heroes. Such protagonists as Gideon the coward, Samson the bully, David the trickster surprise again and again with their always intriguing and sometime hilarious quirks and warts and peccadilloes. There is in all this unlikeliness of heroes the pie-in-the-face shock of humorous epiphany—implication of positive potential where we least expect it, in places where we would do well to learn to look for it. Discovering strengths disguised in the ludicrous oddities of others invites us to look for them in our own idiosyncrasies.

[Chapter 7]

"And Who is My Neighbor?": Odd Couples in Genesis

The convention of paired characters (Adam and Eve, Jacob and Esau, Peter and Paul, and almost everybody else biblical) juxtaposes dynamic duos who contrast and complement as intriguingly as Laurel and Hardy. Like Luke Skywalker and like us, Bible characters learn a lot about both their dark sides and their light sides from those apples-and-oranges contrasts. The matchmaking pattern encourages not just tolerance but self-awareness. People who appear different, even exasperatingly peculiar, surprisingly often turn out to be our shadow selves.

[Chapter 8]

"Man Thinks, God Laughs": Humor as Morality

The Bible's insistently understated smiles stretch far beyond entertainment value. Bible humor can dispose readers for the better. The thoughtful humor of the Good Book is capable of urging responsive readers in more positive directions, revitalizing lives, enlarging horizons, stretching souls. Humor can even discourage misconduct, particularly the darker dispositions like pride and self-righteousness. As the people of the book demonstrate delightfully, humor reaches beyond the enlivening of worship to the enrichment of life. Ultimately the humor of the Bible can inspire insightful readers to live "more abundantly."[1]

1. John 10:10.

Acknowledgments

Thanks to my friends my students,
who have opened my eyes to how much more there is in the Bible than has
yet been seen—"Blessed are your eyes, for they see."

Thanks to superb translations of the Bible:
The Jerusalem Bible. Garden City, NY: Doubleday, 1966.
The New American Bible. New York: P. J. Kennedy & Sons, 1970.
The New English Bible. New York: Oxford University Press, 1970.
The New International Version. Grand Rapids: Zondervan, 1989.
The New Revised Standard Version. New York: Oxford University Press,
    1989.
Tanakh. Philadelphia: Jewish Publication Society of America, 1985.
—and, always preeminently for me,
The King James Version of the Bible. Nashville: Thomas Nelson, 1982.

Thanks to Brigham Young University—for fifty happy years.

Thanks to Cascade editors Jim Tedrick, Christian Amondson, and particularly Robin Parry—
for their warm graciousness as much as for their impeccable competence.

Thanks, thanks, and ever thanks to my wife, Mary Walker—
for seeing me through this book, and my life.

1

"A Time to Laugh"

Humor "More Abundantly"

A REASONABLY SANE PERSON COMES to a consideration of humor in the Bible as to claims of Elvis appearances or reports of UFO sightings or rumors of unicorns glimpsed at the mall. It's not that you're the world's most enthusiastic fan of Bible humor, just curious to see whether there might actually be any. Despite insistent indications to the contrary, there really is humor in the Bible. We'll find some.

And we might find something even better. Scripture possesses power to shift our dispositions, holds even more than most literature the latent potential to change our minds, the potent literary capacity to alter our perspectives. At its best—and our best—its deep dreams and its revolutionary visions and its provocative questions can ferment in us yeastily enough to stretch our souls. Discovering humor in the Bible could change not just the way we see Scripture but the way we see. We may actually manage, by means of the happy expedient of appreciating Bible humor, to make ourselves capable of reading better. By the light of God's good word, we might read better everything we read, maybe even our own murky psyches. By reading its humor we're certain to read the Bible better, beyond reverently to relevantly.

The headlights of this venture into biblical humor will seem less theologically directed than typical Bible study, but the focus should actually explore biblical values more deeply. The undergirding doctrinal principle proceeds from the Will Rogers premise that God must have a sense of humor, since he made us. Humor may be the Bible's most direct access into human experience. "Whatever else you care to say" about these Bible characters, they strike a lot of us as "quintessentially human." "They are three-dimensional beings with a substance to them," not so much saints as "fellow pilgrims. Like me, they are flawed. They trudge along, step by step, just like most of us mortals. What they share in common is a sense that the call of God is the call to be human, to embrace our humanity in all of its ambiguity."[1]

D. H. Lawrence thought the novel "the one bright book of life."[2] Many of us think the Bible is—think it deserves to be read as life-affectingly as Lawrence read the novel. So the specific approach of this book will be enthusiastically literary. That does more than make the Bible easier to read, more accessible and invitational. Reading the Bible as literature makes the most of the best recent scholarship and at the same time taps into the reader-response methods of traditional midrashic close reading. It's a rewarding way to read. After almost half a century of teaching the Bible as literature, I know enough serious Bible readers well enough to know you are likely a first-rate reader of Scripture already. But I guarantee that insofar as we're missing the literature in it, and particularly the humor in it, we could read the Bible better. In the course of this volume, we will.

Bible Bloopers

Our cultural reluctance about biblical humor isn't helped much by the unfortunate fact that most of the funny things we *have* noticed in the Bible aren't really there. The drought of our awareness of any kind of mirth in Scripture is so severe it makes us read in mirages of humor, punfully. "Who was the most constipated man in the Bible? Cain—he wasn't Abel." "Who was the best financier? Pharaoh's daughter, when she went down to the bank of the Nile and drew out a little prophet." "Who was the greatest biblical comedian? Samson: he brought the house down." Yuk yuk. Maybe even *yuck*.

Part of the reason we resist the notion of humor in the Bible is that this sort of shameless punning is not just not funny, it's not in the Bible. Not even close. We are understandably reluctant to contribute to a chorus

1. Balmer, "Generation of Faith," 197–98.
2. Lawrence, *Works of D. H. Lawrence*, 195.

of laughter celebrating that kind of gross misunderstanding, especially when it points an accusing finger at our own obtuseness. We naturally resist chortling at concepts beyond our ken, wisely avoid the obtuseness of rednecks mocking British accents, or opera fans dissing rap music. That kind of uninformed laughter at biblical matters can be as demeaning to the scoffer as it is to the Bible. "For as the crackling of thorns under a pot, so is the laughter of the fool."[3]

We're nervous about biblical humor even when it's obviously there. We worry that the most arrogant Bible characters slipping most clumsily on the slickest banana peelings on the very steps of the temple right before our eyes might be funnier for us than for the Bible. Because our amusement is so often "based on the perception of an incongruity between something dignified and something mean,"[4] we worry we might be laughing at the Bible rather than with it. We're susceptible to that kind of uncertainty even in genuinely comic moments. Lack of appreciation of biblical humor makes us hesitant to smile at unmistakably amusing scenes—like Adam and Eve's embarrassment, blown so far out of proportion to their perfectly natural nakedness that the juvenile couple, blushing incandescently, tries to hide, fetchingly ineffectually, behind too-scanty leaves in Eden.[5]

Our kneejerk habit of looking away from biblical humor makes us miss moments as inherently funny as Noah planting vines first thing off the boat so he can grow grapes so he can get soused as soon as possible.[6] Or Abraham bidding down the Lord for the sake of those oversexed Sodomites: "Will you take fifty? Will you take forty?"[7] Or Jacob conning his twin out of the birthright through the burlesque travesty of irresistibly delectable boiled beans[8] (perhaps the only such beans in the history of legumes) and a silly goat disguise.[9] Or Leah slyly passing herself off as her prettier sister in the dark of the honeymoon bed of Jacob, the patriarch apparently too drunk to tell the difference.[10] Or Rachel claiming menstrual distress,

---

3. Eccl 7:6. Biblical references throughout are to the inimitable—and inimitably funny—King James Version, unless otherwise specified.

4. Telfer, "Hutcheson's Reflections upon Laughter," 360.

5. Gen 3:7.

6. Gen 9:20–21.

7. Gen 18:28.

8. Gen 25:29–34.

9. Gen 27:6–33.

10. Gen 29:21–30.

refusing to rise so her father can't find the filched household icons she sits on in disrespect not only of her father but of the gods.[11] Or Moses dredging up every excuse in the book to try to squirm out of God's majestic call out of the burning bush.[12] Or Aaron's interesting explanation of how the golden calf just happened to form itself from those golden earrings that just happened to be melting over his campfire—"I cast it into the fire, and there came out this calf."[13] Or the Hebrew midwives rescuing death-sentenced newborn babies by means of the zany excuse that their mothers deliver too Quickdraw-McGraw "lively."[14] Or solemn prophet Balaam lectured by his upstart politically incorrect ass.[15] Or Samson in juvenile delinquent mode torching Philistine fields in a flaming-foxes-tails scenario fit for a *National Lampoon* comedy.[16] Or mighty Philistine warriors smitten not by enemy sword in battle but by hemorrhoids.[17] Or David eluding clumsy Saul in the desert as cheekily as Brer Rabbit fooling Brer Bear.[18] Or Elijah ridiculing Baal's prophets on Mount Carmel.[19] Or Elisha calling down by the powers of heaven a hearty she-bear mauling on youths jeering "Baldy, Baldy."[20] Or Haman, in a poetically just result of his convoluted Wile E. Coyote machinations against Esther, hoist on his own gallows.[21] Or Jonah's[22] "absurd sulking."[23]

Laughing So We Won't Cry

Examples of that kind of biblical slapstick could be multiplied a hundredfold, and the droll details of the examples multiplied more. This sort of broad farce is ubiquitous in the Bible. Yet—and this is particularly typical of

11. Gen 31:17–35.
12. Exod 3–4.
13. Exod 32:24.
14. Exod 1:19.
15. Num 22:22–35.
16. Judg 15:3–5.
17. 1 Sam 5:6–12.
18. 1 Sam 19–24.
19. 1 Kgs 18:26–29.
20. 2 Kgs 2:23–25.
21. Esth 5–7.
22. Jonah 4:1–5.
23. Stinespring, "Humor," 662.

the more violent scenarios that dominate this oxymoronic genre—however familiar we may be with Hebrew vaudeville, we hardly know each time we meet it whether to laugh or cry. The burlesque scenes of the Bible invite the kind of guilty laughter provoked by watching a friend walk into a glass door. Because the comedy centers on pratfalls, involving as much embarrassment as wit, humorous reaction to such humiliating situations can feel condescending, even cruel. We're hesitant in these biblical contexts to enjoy too much of the kind of laughter generated by the misfortune of others, even when it is sparked by their own stupid mistakes, even when the stupidity is kindled by their pride.

Yet however accidental such comic situations may seem in the Bible, they are too persistent to be incidental, too numerous to be unintended. The humor is so determined a part of the Bible scene it can only be deliberate. Genesis generates an amusing scenario of this sort almost every chapter. Acts is a funnier book than Genesis. The book of Judges alone presents a complete compendium of unlikely heroes, a catalogue of clowns intended to include every character: We meet anticipated hero Gideon hiding in his shed.[24] Abimelech gets crowned king by default—like the bramble in Jotham's derisive parable of the trees, he is the least competent candidate, so the only one who can be duped into taking the job.[25] The bachelor Benjamites procure wives through a ruse rollickingly reminiscent of *Seven Brides for Seven Brothers* rather than the classical *Rape of the Sabine Women*.[26] Deborah dominates every male in sight, from the entire Assyrian war machine to the Hebrew general Barak, who's so henpecked it's a joke. His name, *Lightning* in Hebrew, snidely suggests he's always a day late and a dollar short, arriving at the ultimate battle scene only when Jael—yet another incongruous female standing out among these majorly incompetent males—has the pointedly discomfited Assyrian general safely nailed.[27]

Ehud sets the stage for that Judges comedy show with his assassination of King Eglon of Moab in a scenario whose buffoonery verges on the bizarre. Ehud's unexpected lefthandedness enables him to surprise the king with a cartoon-force dagger thrust that penetrates the royal obesity so deeply "the fat closed upon the blade, so that he could not draw the dagger out of his belly." And if that's not grossly blunt enough, throw in a

24. Judg 6:11–12.
25. Judg 9.
26. Judg 21.
27. Judg 4–5.

little biblical bathroom humor: "and the dirt came out."[28] That scatological loosening of the regal sphincter enables Ehud's comic escape. The courtly servants, noses in the air, steer clear of his highness's room (the room that features the less formal and more functional throne), assuming, quite likely from the smell, that the king is personally engaged, that "he covereth his feet in his summer chamber."[29] Mel Brooks would have played the scene less outrageously.

Even the tragedies of Judges, gruesome to the point of the grotesque, are backlit by a kind of quizzical comedy. When Jepthah's preposterous vow—to sacrifice whatever emerges first from his door—climaxes dramatically in the rushing out of his only daughter to congratulate him on his miraculous military victory, we feel deeply the tragedy of that victory won at the cost of her innocent life. But we feel irony as well. We cannot help shaking our heads over the reckless foolishness of the father's vow, can't help wondering what Jephthah was thinking, or if he was. Did he expect the family dog? A pet goat, maybe? Did the likelihood of an unfortunate retainer's untimely exit never enter his thick head?[30] The tone of Judges, like that of the Bible generally, is at heart tragic. But the systole that drives its diastole is the pulse of comedy.

That's true amid the grisliest brutalities. The Levite's concubine is gang-raped to death, her hacked-up body parts mailed across the country to incite a war of vengeance.[31] Even in this obscene scenario it's impossible to miss the irony. Atrocity that is so bizarre it can scarcely be imagined is precipitated by mundane husband deafness, the drolly familiar male failure to listen. The outrageous obtuseness of the Levite, snoring blissfully as his wife dies horrifically on his doorstep, is in its appalling exaggeration almost a parody of husbandly ignoring of wifely needs, so callous it's ludicrous. That ghastly irony targets the gross culpability of this minor aristocrat, a member of the privileged and probably educated priestly caste, who really, really should have known better. The very villains, the redneck rapists themselves, would have known better than to behave the way this heartless husband behaves. The deepest irony in Judges 19, and simultaneously and significantly the most tragic moral of the story, is that *anyone* should have known better.

28. Judg 3:22.
29. Judg 3:24.
30. Judg 11.
31. Judg 19:29.

Simple Samson

Samson's bawdy burlesque climaxes the crescendo of tragicomedy that enlivens Judges. His picaresque saga delights in toppling Israelite icons from their pedestals. The hero's miraculous birth, the dramatic entrance of the divinely-endowed marvel, gleefully parodies the sacrosanct traditions of biblical birth miracles. Whenever a faithful woman, long barren, has her prayer for progeny answered by an angel, Bible readers have learned to expect miraculous results—an Isaac, a Jacob, a Joseph. We may even be anticipating such a spiritual prodigy as Samuel. What we get in Judges instead—in anticlimax so blatant it approaches parody—is Arnold-Schwartzeneggerish Samson. That introductory skit lets us in on what we are in for. However profound a tragedy this may be, it will be tragedy informed by "extended passages of humorous intent."[32]

"Always brawling and excelling all rivals in muscular strength, this uncouth fellow is no match for feminine wiles"[33]—we savor Samson's unluckiness in love almost as much as his smart-aleck exploits in battle. His most spectacular actions are snickered at through undertones of humor—the idiosyncratic riddle contest where both riddler and riddled cheat outrageously,[34] the paying off of Philistine gambling debts by the sardonic expedient of slaughtering Philistines,[35] the unfortunate "fool me once" episodes with not one,[36] not two,[37] but three[38] risqué Philistine women, the unexpected and unsavory and—most scandalous for the Hebrew audience—ritually unclean picnic of honey from a lion's carcass,[39] the peace committee so nervous it dare not approach Samson with any less than three thousand members,[40] the decimation of an entire brass-armored Philistine cohort, bristling with technologically imposing spears and swords, by the most ludicrously insulting and laughably outmoded weapon imaginable, that obvious joke of a jawbone of an ass,[41] the instrument of jesters.

32. Stinespring, "Humor," 662.

33. Pfeiffer, *Introduction to the Old Testament*, 320.

34. Judg 14:12–18.

35. Judg 14:19.

36. Judg 14:1–3.

37. Judg 16:1.

38. Judg 16:4.

39. Judg 14:8–9.

40. Judg 15:11.

41. Judg 15:15–16.

Cecil B. DeMille himself couldn't turn this burly material into romantic comedy—it's clearly the stuff of action movies. But that high-octane narrative is fueled by humor. We relish the inevitability of the trickster's getting tricked almost as much as the gusto with which he turns the tables on his tormentors. Carrying off the Gaza Gate impishly as my uncle in his teenage day carted outhouses to the tops of farmhouse roofs, "Samson is a sort of irresponsible and uncontrollable Till Eulenspiegel or Peer Gynt."[42] Moffat's translation captures the mischievously macabre tone of this frolicsome murderous romp: "With the jawbone of an ass, / I have piled them in a mass."[43]

The Word of God, for all its seriousness even at this slapstick level, has funny stuff in it. The bottom-line implication of that pervasive presence of humor is clear—the Bible is funny, so funny we sometimes have to laugh, whether we like it or not. We can't help liking it a little even when the humor calls up those old movie moments when Oliver Hardy swings around with the rolled-up rug under his arm and flattens Stan Laurel into another disgusted reiteration of "this is another fine mess you've got us in." Such common human foibles, anything but funny to the people getting knocked down, can be hilarious to those of us looking on. That's because we can relate. We've been knocked down enough times, done enough dumb things ourselves, to be able to share in the experience of laughing our way through the loony things people do. "I wish I could find an etymological connection between the word *humor* and *human*. It's so apparent that if anything defines humanity it is a sense of humor."[44]

However hard we resist it, however much we misunderstand it, we're susceptible to Bible humor. We're even more susceptible to the implications, to the implicit meaning of the humor, however situational, however slapstick. As irrefutable evidence of the sensitive calibration of our biblical-humor radar, I offer my students' tongue-in-cheek marriage guide, with its facetiously realistic technique of fleshing out from a modern perspective—more precisely the perspective of a 1930s Hollywood screwball comedy—the comic implications of actual Bible how-to-get-married scenes:

---

42. Pfeiffer, *Introduction to the Old Testament,* 320.

43. Judg 15:16.

44. Waldoks, "Meditations on a Joyful Year," 59.

Top Ten Biblical Ways to Snag a Husband:

[10] Enlist an angel to twist the man's arm to marry you, like Mary.[45]

[9] Beat your little sister into the honeymoon tent. In the dark, keep your identity secret until it's too late for objections, like Leah.[46]

[8] Try watering the marital target's entire camel herd, like Rebecca.[47]

[7] Get your dad to set up a date with a homeless guy, like Moses's wife-to-be.[48]

[6] Get your dad to fix you up with your ex-husband's best man, like Samson's wife.[49]

[5] Trick your father-in-law into paying you for sex, get pregnant, then pressure him to do the honorable thing, like Tamar.[50]

[4] Bathe nude within full view of your intended, like Bathsheba.[51]

[3] Party hearty and, after your date has fallen asleep, crawl into bed with him. When he wakes up confused, encourage him to do right by you, like Ruth.[52]

[2] Have God create a husband from scratch so you have some chance of getting one that's "good," as Eve did.[53]

And the #1 biblical way to acquire a husband?

[1] A husband? Are you kidding me?[54]

No Laughing Out Loud

Most biblical humor is more subtle. The most meaningful humor in the Bible doesn't clamor for our attention. Biblical humor at its best is

45. Matt 1:18–24.
46. Gen 29:14–27.
47. Gen 24:1–58.
48. Exod 2:15–21.
49. Judg 15:6.
50. Gen 38.
51. 2 Sam 11.
52. Ruth 3:1–14.
53. Gen 1:26–27.
54. 1 Cor 7:32–35.

dramatically understated, the understatement concentrating the humor as it mutes it. The humor is often so implicit it's easy to miss, and that makes it not just funnier but more meaningful when we get it. It's rare in the Bible to find jokes straightforward as: "As a jewel of gold in a swine's snout, so is a fair woman which is without discretion."[55] Not that that kind of Don Rickles over-the-top insult can't be funny, even in its modern political incarnations: *a pig wearing lipstick is still a pig.*

More satisfyingly risible for most of us would be something more understated, something more along the lines of "let not him that girdeth on his harness boast himself as he that putteth it off."[56] In this more typical biblical instance we are engaged at least as much by the message of the proverb as by the humor of its expression. When the light goes on above our heads in recognition of the wit, the point of the irony underscores the warrior's jeer as much as the impact of the humor: *Enough talk. Let's see some action.* The humor is more than a spoonful of sugar that makes the message go down; it is part and parcel of the meaning. Playing on the incongruity of boasting before battle, the wit of the quip sharpens the edge of Ahab's cutting challenge to put up or shut up. As so often throughout the Bible, the implicit humor of the proverb amps up its conceptual emphasis: *Don't brag, trash talkers, until you have something to brag about.*

The compression of that typically laconic approach—all of that implicit in sixteen words, six in Hebrew—suggests we need to be alert to notice biblical humor. We will need to look closely to find it at all. The concentration further suggests that the more fun we are able to find in it, the more we are likely to find that the humor means. We alert ourselves to humor in the Bible not because we need to laugh more, though we do, but because the humor matters, pulsing at the heart of the meaning. The struggle to understand biblical humor is essentially a soul-searching with Carl Jung after "the laughter at the heart of things."[57]

Central as it is, crucial as it is, it's easy to overlook. It's easy to see why we miss the most important biblical humor. Bible humor at its best, like most Bible rhetoric, is quiet, understated, not "sounding brass or a tinkling cymbal,"[58] instead a stillness that runs deep. The antithesis of the brassiness

---

55. Prov 11:22.

56. 1 Kgs 20:11.

57. Luke, *Laughter at the Heart of Things*, 108, 110.

58. 1 Cor 13:1.

of standup comics, biblical humor is a "still small voice."[59] "Humor is slow and shy, insinuating its fun into your heart." "Wit," by contrast, "is abrupt, darting, scornful, and tosses its analogies in your face."[60] The Bible, from earliest Genesis to a surprisingly sarcastic Jesus, is not without wit, some of it stinging. But it invests most of its meaning in humor.

That may be why the humor tends to be tongue-in-cheek, wry. It has a kind of Woody Allen fumbling philosophic quality that struggles to confront the cosmic incongruities of our mundane lives—"I don't mind dying. I just don't want to be there when it happens."[61] In as plaintive a minor key as Middle-Eastern music, Bible humor is a personal defense against what can feel like an overwhelmingly impersonal universe. The humor is idiosyncratic, whimsical. And it is surprisingly practical. It can offer insights as imminently helpful as Jesus's sardonic proverb on why we might want to think twice about borrowing trouble: "Sufficient unto the day is the evil thereof."[62] That characteristic stress on realistic meaning makes Bible humor serious humor—the opposite of lighthearted, sometimes almost sad. There's a lot of laughing so we won't cry.

Insensitivity to tone isn't the only handicap that inhibits modern perception of biblical humor. A disposition to notice the most obvious joke makes us prone to missing the most meaningful humor in the Bible, which is almost invariably the most understated. That natural blind spot to the subtlety of biblical wit gets compounded by our severe worship habits, by blinders of sanctimoniousness. We're so straitlaced about the solemnity of our religiousness we convince ourselves "serious business is incompatible with laughter."[63] Our pride in our dour piety may explain why there's so much more humor in the Bible than we've noticed, why "the literary art of the Bible, in both prose narrative and poetry, reflects many more elements of playfulness than might meet the casual eye."[64] Our squinting piousness might even explain why we don't notice how much the humor matters. It's probably not surprising, having mostly missed the playfulness, we've missed most of its implications.

---

59. 1 Kgs 19:12.

60. Whipple, *Literature and Life*, 91.

61. Benayoun, *Films of Woody Allen*, 163.

62. Matt 6:34.

63. Trueblood, *Humor of Christ*, 15.

64. Alter, *Art of Biblical Poetry*, 203.

We've missed so much of that meaning it would be funny if it weren't so sad. We read about as perceptively as Matthew when, odd man out among the gospel writers, he misconstrues with somber literalness the poetic duplication of Zechariah's prophecy of a savior "riding upon an ass, and upon a colt the foal of an ass"[65]—for literal Matthew, separate mounts, two for the price of one. So for Jesus's triumphal entry into Jerusalem, in addition to "an ass tied," he provides a bonus "colt with her"[66]—dual steeds for the messianic ride, one presumably for each leg. We read as wrong-headedly literally as Matthew counts mounts. We read, in our insistent solemnity, about as insightfully as that normally masterful reader Luke when he transliterates Old Testament prophecy of a maiden giving birth[67] into a "virgin" forced to manage that feat under rather more remarkable circumstances.[68] Clearly, if it could clarify the readings of such experts as the gospel writers themselves, more alertness to the possibilities of humor might make us common readers more aware of scriptural meaning.

Perhaps the most profound contribution of Bible humor is the most surprising: its realism. Humor underwrites the psychological and often the historical reality of biblical events. Isaac gets named *Laughter* because his mother—with her usual shrewd skepticism—reads extravagant angelic promises about prospects of his birth as a joke: "Sarah laughed within herself."[69] She has good reason. Over ninety, postmenopausal by half a century, Sarah quite correctly declares herself and, more pointedly, her withered and wizened husband, "well stricken in age"—and, she might add, even in his prime none too helpful in the production of progeny. The sad fact that her eggs are long gone is compounded by the sadder fact that the happy couple is no longer making love—"shall I have pleasure, my Lord being old also?"[70] With a wryly realistic cleverness that would make the most urbane twenty-first-century teenager smile, Sarah frankly assesses her personal fertility probabilities as less than promising. Her realistic skepticism triggers laughter deep "within herself" at the notion that God himself could send her a child so unlikely late in life. When that good joke turns out to be on Sarah herself, we are as delighted as she is: "And Sarah

---

65. Zech 9:9.

66. Matt 21:2.

67. Isa 7:14.

68. Luke 1:27.

69. Gen 18:12.

70. Gen 18:11–12.

said, God hath made me to laugh, so that all that hear will laugh with me."[71] Much of the meaning of Sarah's laughter, as it transposes naturally from the cynically jocular to the profoundly joyous, revolves around the resonances of its frank realism.

Unlikely as it may seem, the Bible is capable of making us laugh as happily as the Lord made mournful Sarah laugh. We might want to give it the chance. The more so since, when we pay attention to the way the humor works, we are likely to find the laughter a large part not just of the experience but of the point. Both dimensions require our fullest attention. C. S. Lewis's poignant advice about needing to read psalms with our entire selves proves paradoxically "true of the recognition of humour in the Bible":[72] "No net less wide than a man's whole heart, nor less fine of mesh than love, will hold the sacred Fish."[73]

Humor "More Abundantly"

However hard to net, there's a lot of that humor floating in a lot of Bible currents. Once we train our eyes to it, humor can be seen flashing its slippery fins almost everywhere in the Good Book. We can even catch glimpses, in the unlikeliest biblical backwaters, of the God of Laughter himself. Take the earliest, and one of the gloomiest, of Bible scenes: the infamous Fall of Humanity. This sad scenario sets up about as unpromising a place to find anything funny as can be imagined, original sin not being noted for its inherent hilarity. Humanity's ineluctable degeneration, infected by our vicious carnality, diseased with our selfish miscreance, our tainted mortality fallen so far it has been spiraling evilly into the black hole of entropy ever since—not the cheeriest of prospects. Yet the essence of this bleak tragedy distills, as so often in the Bible, less into a frowning moral than into a rather whimsical question: *How did we get ourselves into this mess? Is life an absurd mistake?* And that underlying premise is not the only hint of humor here. Around the edges of this cosmic disaster, gleams of gentle amusement dance, the divine whimsy easing the anguish of the train wreck of mortal sin colliding with God's wrath.

Adam and Eve's response to God's ominous advance is as charmingly naïve as a three-year-old's: they hide. They're fully grown, but they're acting

71. Gen 21:6.
72. Medcalf, "Comedy," 129.
73. Lewis, *Reflections on the Psalms*, 119.

as childishly as Peewee Herman. The Lord, either too impatient to consult his omniscience or indulging in hide-and-seek with them, yells off the back porch of Eden "Where art thou?"[74] Instantly Adam, so hyped he forgets that the whole point of hiding is concealment, spills the beans, exposing in inadvertent confession not only where he is but why he's there, and, while he's at it, the guilt he feels about that: "I was afraid, because I was naked; and I hid myself."[75] Adam's letting the cat out of the bag cartoons the endearing silliness of trying to ditch an all-seeing and all-powerful God, belaboring as it does the obvious, its speaker cowering in a makeshift sanctuary that's turning out to be laughably inadequate as protection against the Landlord of all Sanctuaries. Humor warms and humanizes the blurted confession, the panicky vulnerability, the exposed nakedness. That humanizing humor makes it hard to miss the gleam in God's eye when his intriguingly whimsical omniscience resorts to another needling *gotcha* kind of question: "Who told thee that thou wast naked?"[76]

God could be a prosecuting attorney here, badgering the witness for a confession of guilt. But he sounds more like a father kidding his kid, more affectionate than sarcastic. Even if this clever question from the one who doesn't need to ask questions features (as so often with biblical multiple-choice options) both fatherly and legalistic functions, the ironic edge of that searching query continues to smile not only at Adam but at us. Why so disingenuous? How, if we're so wide-eyed innocent, did we come to understand so well these complicated machinations, to "be as gods, knowing good and evil"?[77] Despite all the dumb stuff they do, maybe mortals are smarter than they look.

Adam is. For somebody so fresh off the boat, he reacts with the savvy of a veteran. In the face of God's cross-examination, he quick-wittedly shifts the blame to Eve, with a sidelong glance at whoever it was that stuck him with this problematic female in the first place: "The woman whom thou gavest to be with me, she gave me of the tree."[78] Kids say the darndest things. Eve too, not so gullible as we expect, instantly figures out which way the wind of blame is blowing, passing the buck deftly to the serpent: "the

---

74. Gen 3:9.

75. Gen 3:2.

76. Gen 3:11.

77. Gen 3:5.

78. Gen 3:12.

serpent beguiled me."[79] The wily serpent, trapped at the end of this Three Stooges row with nobody left to poke, ends up without a leg to stand on in thin air over the precipice of blame, outsmarted as consummately as Wile E. Coyote. The poetic justice is priceless: the schemer, for the first time in the Bible but far from the last, ends up with egg on his face.

Sensitivity to the warm humor of the scene sensitizes us to its human significance. Theological theory of *original sin* is problematic not just because it's too serious, but because it's too abstract, distancing us from everyday concerns. This Bible version of our earliest human mistakes, by contrast, is as relevant and as warm as spilling morning coffee. From this more comic perspective we can catch more realistic and more promising visions of our nascent selves than sanctimonious Augustine and stern Calvin were able to see. We can glimpse a God who views us more positively than we guessed he might, who smiles tolerantly upon our foolishness, who can be entertained by our foibles, who looks at our mistakes, even when they are life-affecting sins, as we look at the stumblings of infants learning to walk. We see, in this humorous frame, God as a father, a father more focused on his family than on his work. Bill Cosby has considerable fun with God's inexperienced disciplining—"the first thing He said to them was 'Don't.'"[80] But even in his professional role as adjudicator the Lord seems more concerned with anticipating consequences than assessing blame, more disposed to motivate with honey than with vinegar. We might even glean from these genial interactions what precipitates so much of our own silly blundering, the very tendency that makes us reluctant to read smilingly in the first place: we take ourselves too seriously.

Crouching naked in the bushes with Adam and Eve we discover something more than the humiliation of exposure: we realize that what we took to be official proclamations of guilt are mostly a matter of our own shame. There is stunningly little condescension from this deity toward his creations. He doesn't Lord it over us. It's not just the obvious tender mercies, like his foraging clothes for his shivering children. It's the way he encourages us to see ourselves more generously, to consider the naked vulnerability of our situation, to contemplate how much courage and cleverness could be hiding in our infant fumblings, to notice the sharp upward learning curve in our clumsiest mistakes. Bible humor suggests God might like us better, maybe quite a bit better, than we like ourselves. Hard to imagine

79. Gen 3:13.
80. Cosby, *Fatherhood*, 64.

such a fatherly countenance in such a familiar situation under such friendly circumstances without at least a trace of a smile.

He may be smiling still, for all the tough-love sternness he manages to muster as he ushers us out of Eden, patiently out into life, "with wandering steps and slow."[81] The realizing humor of the Bible encourages us to feel better about ourselves, better still about God, "better and better and better."[82] Divinity looked at from the perspective of humor seems more down-to-earth than it usually looks, more realistically experienced. That can have unsettling consequences: "Even bein' Gawd ain't a bed of roses."[83] But the silver lining of that biblical humanizing of the divine is that there's more fun in it than we've guessed.

Humoring Our Reading

Those IED's of humor buried in the familiar scenes of the Bible explode into a compelling kind of paradox, a yin/yang commingling of the ideal and the real. Humor unearths a sanctified humanness, a kind of down-and-dirty holiness. Bible humor shows us, again and again, where earth meets heaven. At the most immediate level starry heaven mingles with dusty earth in biblical character—in, for instance, those earliest Genesis innocents, still wet behind the ears, deftly passing the buck of blame right under the nose of deity, slyly outfoxing in the process the wiliest serpent, aware already that it is easier to get forgiveness than ask permission.

Humor dramatizes where earth meets heaven at a deeper level—in Bible values. Traditional biblical morality is not only questioned but deliberately undercut by means of humor. One of the more fun-loving examples of that undermining of conventional values is the Bible's disrespect for gender correctness. This sacrosanct volume, honored for millennia as the bastion of patriarchal prerogative, does not hesitate to poke fun at venerable paternal privilege. Patriarchy is not simply outsmarted, not just outflanked, but thoroughly bossed around by its matriarchy. Women turn the tables on take-charge men all the way from Genesis through the Acts of the Apostles. The Bible, viewed by some as the apotheosis of all things hierarchical, actually seems less interested in keeping women in their place

---

81. Milton, *Paradise Lost*, 289.
82. Carroll, *Through the Looking Glass*, 231.
83. Connelly, *Green Pastures*, 569.

than in having fun with the foibles of men who think the women should be kept any place.

Humor highlights the commingling of earth and heaven, too, at the intersection of the real and the ideal in its most hallowed conventions. Take the supernal genre of the Prophets. At the heart of this textual holy of holies, the place where God most sublimely addresses man, a certified prophet is caricatured as so unimpressed he has to be upchucked on his errand by a whale right out of *Pinocchio* to persuade him to prophesy. More whimsical still, what the prophet ends up prophesying as a result of this unusually urgent inspiration turns out be the worst missionary pitch ever— *you're all going to die.* In a nice added touch, that callous death threat turns out to be the most persuasive call to repentance in history, converting the entire Ninevite nation. The parodic ironies are rich enough to make readers nod their heads Napoleon Dynamite-wise, savoring all three syllables of "sweet."

The Bible is full of that kind of laugh-out-loud surprises. Upsetting-of-the-nature-of-things, life-altering surprises, like barren women against all odds bearing, and not just bearing, but bearing "nations"[84]—and, incidentally, bearing the greatest heroes in history, no matter if those unlikely mothers be over ninety at the time[85] or manage their amazing motherhood without benefit of father.[86] The Bible is replete with life-altering surprises, like the lampooning of privilege in the persistent displacement of birthright heirs by younger siblings[87] in a topsy-turvy universe where we come to expect that "the last shall be first."[88] Surprises like the pillorying of power in the defeat of a horde of mighty Midianites by her wins Gideon's cohort of three hundred,[89] the destruction of the invincible Canaanite iron-wheeled chariots by Deborah's riffraff guerillas armed with nothing but wooden weapons,[90] the coup of the entire Persian Empire by its beauty queen.[91] Surprises like the parody of piety, when the foundation of Christ's church gets laid by the likes of bumbling Peter and bigmouth Paul. Surprises like

84. Gen 25:23.

85. Gen 18:11–14.

86. Luke 1:30–31.

87. Jacob, Isaac, Joseph, Pharez, Ephraim in Genesis alone.

88. Luke 13:30.

89. Judg 7:22.

90. Judg 4:15.

91. Esth 9:12.

the pricking of the bubble of pride, in the incredible and incredibly consistent success of underdog after underdog: David nailing Goliath, Jael nailing Sisera, Moses out-plaguing Pharaoh, dreamy Joseph besting his ten burly brothers, "plain man"[92] Jacob who, for all his mama's-boy tent-dwelling tendencies, wrestles blessings out of every awesome antagonist in sight, including angels.

And maybe the most compelling surprise of the Bible: people turning out to be who we and they and everybody, except maybe the Good Lord himself, didn't think they could ever be. Moses, a stutterer who calls himself "slow of speech, and of a slow tongue,"[93] manages quite adequately to spit out the six hundred thousand words of the Torah. Elijah, so nervous he flees fully two hundred miles in fear of Ahab's wife, proves in a directly adjacent chapter[94] fearlessly capable of confronting King Ahab, to say nothing of killing with his own hands eight hundred and fifty priests of Baal. Saul, who thinks so little of himself when we first meet him he "hid himself in the stuff,"[95] towers over all Israel as their first king, "higher than any of the people from his shoulders and upward."[96] Samson, who holds the record for self-serving self-indulgence in matters of Philistine women, sacrifices himself for his people.[97] David morphs dizzyingly from adolescent trickster to giant killer to cultural hero to daunting warrior to pretty-boy charmer of women to raving madman to shrewd politician to Robin Hood outlaw to beloved king to dastardly assassin, in just one dimension of those multiple transformations shifting identities from flagrantly neglectful fatherhood as far as heart-wrenching tenderness toward the son who betrayed him: "Would God that I had died for thee, O Absalom, my son, my son."[98]

Going for the Gideon Gusto

The light of such surprise shines everywhere in the Bible, as can be seen in the humorous halo that illuminates Judge Gideon. We come upon mighty Gideon, traditionally respected among Bible readers for his standout

92. Gen 25:27.

93. Exod 4:10.

94. 1 Kgs 18.

95. 1 Sam 10:22.

96. 1 Sam 10:23.

97. Judg 16:30.

98. 2 Sam 18:33.

standup courageousness, in markedly unheroic mode, "threshing wheat in a winepress to keep it from the Midianites."[99] The KJV's "by the winepress" suggests extreme carefulness; the NIV "*in* the winepress" version, closer to the Hebrew, ramps up those implications of caution to something closer to cowardice—readers would find it easier to admire Gideon's legendary courage if he dared to thresh outdoors. When under these compromising circumstances angelic proclamation declares "the Lord is with you, mighty warrior,"[100] it's tempting to picture a smile on the angel's face. The angel foresees heroic potential so at odds with Gideon's unpromising behavior that the over-optimistic assessment cannot help grinning with irony.

As with most biblical surprises, the humor of Gideon's situation is sparked by the friction between possibilities and contradictory realities. And as with almost all biblical surprises, the meaning of the humor is what is really meaningful. We are shown by this dramatically ambivalent introduction a Gideon who, rather than jumping into Judges as a full-blown war hero, grows into the role. We are shown by the humor not merely that he is a hero, but *why* he is, maybe even how we can be—how he matures into a master of military tactics from these laughably inauspicious beginnings as a hick farmer. And a cautious hayseed at that. Threshing was done then as it still sometimes is: the farmer (or his high-tech ox) stamps the barley loose from the stalks, then throws it in the air so the wind can blow off the chaff so the heavier grain stacks up at his feet. Anyone threshing grain indoors, in the contained area of a winepress where there is necessarily little of the necessary wind, is demonstrating more than normal nervousness about marauding Midianites. Gideon's overcareful behavior here is a facetiously far cry from prototypical Rambo activity, closer to the neighborhood of a Mike Myers version of Agent 007.

That caricature of a hero cautious to the point of timidity lights up with the strobe of its shifting pattern some realistic aspects not only of Gideon's demeanor but of his behavior. The caution may go so far as to explain his success, suggesting why he fights only at night, under cover of darkness.[101] His carefulness may clarify, too, his reluctance to commit to the call in the first place. It could hint at why the Lord allows such wide latitude for him to work up his nerve, encouraging him with sign after frivolous sign.[102]

99. Judg 6:11, NIV.
100. Judg 6:12, NIV.
101. Judg 6:27; 7:9.
102. Judg 6:36–40.

Our hero's characteristic cautiousness may even shed ironic light on why Gideon and his God are so bent on that extraordinary measure of reducing the number of volunteers from 30,000 down to 300.[103] That strange expedient may not serve so much to show off the Lord's power, as the text explicitly proposes. Rather it could provide guarantee that Gideon will be backed by the most able and reliable sort of warrior, the kind that instead of sticking face in the river to drink raises hand to mouth so as to "lappeth of the water with his tongue, as a dog lappeth"[104]—head up, eyes alert, spear at the ready.

The comedy here comes down to the reality of good tactics. What first seems funny—so funny *strange* it's funny *haha*—turns out to be militarily effective. Had Gideon attempted his Chinese-fire-drill lamp-flashing horn-blaring foray among Midianites at any time other than the carefully chosen midnight changing of the guard, with any more than the carefully selected high-efficiency three hundred, there might have been less success—there couldn't have been greater triumph than the total rout the three hundred managed—and there almost certainly would have been more casualties. Turns out Gideon's preposterous caution works. Partly the underlying humor here smiles at how God works with some mighty unlikely servants, folks a lot like us. Mostly the implications of the humor indicate God makes the most of whatever strengths we can scrape up, however idiosyncratic or even idiotic, and uses those peculiar assets to surprisingly efficacious ends—in Gideon's case capitalizing on carefulness so extreme it can look in a military context like cowardice.

The humor seems to be proposing such surprising insights as part of the Bible's wisdom. The foibles of biblical characters, remarkably and very humanly in these humorous contexts, generate epiphany. Maybe that capacity for making silk purses of insight out of sow's ears of characterization is the reason for the shocking honesty of biblical characterizing, for the wartiness of its most revered heroes. King David himself, the Hebrew Bible's fair-haired boy, is paradoxically a deceiver and a mercenary and an opportunist and an outlaw and a demagogue, a man not above exposing himself in crude proximity to the sacred Ark of the Covenant,[105] a man capable of the kind of ruthlessness that can murder a trusting friend to

103. Judg 7:3–7.
104. Judg 7:5.
105. 2 Sam 6:16, 20.

cover an affair with his wife.[106] And, all things considered from the Bible's perspective, an amazing man—an adulterer and a murderer and a fine human being.[107]

My father's clever sons occasionally accused him of failing to do the things he taught us we should do, as when he felt free to swear like a trooper while denying us an occasional *damn*. Dad's maddeningly reasonable response was that he expected his sons to be smart enough to learn not only from positive examples, but from negative. We learn something in the Bible from laughing at the human condition. We learn, from those incessant biblical surprises, that things might turn out differently than we expect. We learn, from not being able to see the end from the beginning (even with benefit of explicit prophecy), that anything can happen. We learn, from experiencing the significant unexpectednesses along the way, that the way may matter more than we thought, the path may be less regular and less constrained and more interesting than it appears from the oversimplified slant of our orthodoxy.

Reverential Inertia

The Bible has to be funnier than we thought, if only because we haven't thought it was funny at all. We have missed the humor so completely that some of our best readers are convinced it's not there. The superlatively intelligent Alfred North Whitehead shakes his learned white locks in obliviousness at the mystery of the missing humor: "The total absence of humour from the Bible is one of the most singular things in all literature."[108] W. W. Phelps regretted, over a century ago, the dearth of anything approximating anything like funny business in the Bible, a book he looked upon as a universally encyclopedic compendium including "all sorts of literature except humor."[109]

Bible experts get downright definitive in their exclusions of humor from the canon. "One thing the biblical writers cannot be accused of is levity. Jokes are not their forte."[110] There's striking critical consensus— particularly for a book where there's so little agreement on anything—that

---

106. 2 Sam 11:2–17.

107. In Acts 13:22 God calls him "a man after mine own heart."

108. Whitehead, *Dialogues*, 163.

109. Phelps, *Bible*, 16.

110. Jacobson, *Story of the Stories*, 169.

the Bible comprises a complete panorama of the entire range of literature, "with the single exception of humorous literature, for which the Hebrew temperament has little fitness."[111] That negative consensus is not only emphatic but longstanding. "For the last 1500 years the majority of biblical scholars, in the seriousness of their research, have not detected the slightest touch of humour in the Bible."[112]

There are advantages to noticing the humor that go beyond an occasional chuckle. In addition to being a whole lot more lively, the humor pathway into Bible study has the further advantage of uniqueness in a field where there is "nothing new under the sun."[113] It's a road less traveled among the constraining strait and narrow paths of traditional biblical criticism. Much as the Bible has been read in past epochs and is read even now, it has seldom at any time been read from the horizon of its humor—publications on humor in the Bible are so few and far between they can be referenced in their totality in the bibliography of this brief book. Moreover, a high proportion of these studies seem determined to compound their inconsequence by relegating humor to the periphery of biblical significance. Studies of biblical humor are not just few and far between; they're seldom serious. Scriptural commentary has mattered so much for so long from such various cultural perspectives that the Bible can be contemplated through a vast array of critical approaches. Of that smorgasbord of ruminations on Scripture, humor is among the most appealing, one of the most satisfying. It's definitely the freshest.

That happier reading from humor suggests the possibility we are being lulled to sleep less by the biblical text than by our own reading. We may be reading the Bible in a bad translation: ours. Humor might at the least prove a livelier way to read it, less faded by our jaded dispositions, more in synch with its own compelling tone. "When one first reads the Old Testament in the Hebrew, he is astonished at its roughness, its saltiness, and its Rabelaisian humor."[114] Seems a shame that liveliness gets "so successfully concealed, for the most part, in the English version," and concealed still more in many of our personal versions. We miss much when we read the

---

111. Moulton, *Bible as Literature*, 25.

112. Radday, *Comic in the Hebrew Bible*, 32.

113. Eccl 1:9.

114. Potter, *Is That in the Bible?*, viii.

Bible as a mirror of the staid limitations of our orthodox lives. The book itself "throbs with life, bizarre and beautiful, sublime and ridiculous."[115]

That untapped vitality may be why the rabbis insist Torah "discloses her innermost secrets only to them who love her."[116] "For the Jewish tradition, reading is more than reading, it is a love affair with the text."[117] Bertolt Brecht, of all people, admitted in a moment of sentimental weakness, "My favorite book? You're going to laugh—it's the Bible."[118] Brecht's enthusiastic atheism may read the Bible better than the proper piety of many of us, even the most devoted of us, our eyes closed reverently as we read. "The Bible is read, it is known. But I don't think it's *enjoyed*."[119]

What we are attempting here is not just a new dimension of biblical reading. It's a new way to read. Reading ourselves as deep as the humor between biblical lines requires more personal investment than we're used to. It's as much a matter of relationship as of intellectual intensity. This kind of reading demands not just that we think more about the text, but that we care more. The Bible, any way you look at it—let alone through the subtly nuanced and infinitely ramifying kaleidoscope of humor—is a challenging prospect, an unnervingly open-ended invitation to read ourselves as deeply into the tale of tales as we dare.

That may make the most productive Bible reading more interested in exploration than in closure, like Noah's dove finding "no rest for the sole of her foot."[120] Our tunnel-vision excavations in the Bible for definitive answers myopically miss how freely it proffers wide-open questions. It responds to our most nagging expectations of comfortable resolution with an almost infinite regress of provocative enigmas of the *Who created the Creator?* sort: *Who's the father of God?* The best Bible reading refuses to settle for reassurance, won't content itself with what it knows already. Bible reading at its best reaches into radically new possibilities. "Even when resolutions come, as in places they must, they do not let the text yield its prerogatives of mystery making and complication." That is why the most alert Bible readers realize that to read the Scripture well is to read it differently

---

115. Ibid.

116. *The Zohar*, 2.99a.

117. Holtz, *Back to the Sources*, 29.

118. Baxandall, "Brecht's 'J.B.,'" 114.

119. Van Doren, *In the Beginning, Love*, 223.

120. Gen 8:9.

than we have before—"to read biblical narrative is to submit oneself to a lesson in *how* to read."[121]

Humor Matters

There is humor in the Bible. There's so much humor, and it's so meaningful, I'm beginning to suspect it might be there on purpose. If we were to notice that humor, we might enjoy Scripture more. If we were to read the humor aright, we might be able to relate Scripture more helpfully to ourselves. We might even learn from biblical humor to extend our intellectual horizons, to plumb our emotional depths, to push the parameters of our personalities, to, heaven help us, stretch our souls. "A profound book on laughter might be almost a final theology."[122] Despite our double-millennial failure to notice it, the Bible still might be for us that book. Given the inherent significance of this revered text, maybe the best reason for reading the humor in the Bible is Sir Edmund Hillary's reason for climbing Mount Everest: because it's there.

So even though no one wants it done, and there is a long-standing tradition that it can't be done, I propose we look closely at the humor in the Bible. Maybe the challenge of the project and our natural resistances to it are the very reasons it needs doing. And because it's there. Humor is at the very minimum a dimension of the Bible's incomparably inclusive range— part of its being fully human. There are "more than 250 biblical references" to laughter, "heavily concentrated in wisdom literature" and, intriguingly enough, in the "gospel writers."[123] Amid that profusion of laughter and discussions about laughter, the Bible's written guarantee on laughter is encouraging: God's good Word, in the worst Job-like circumstances, can "fill thy mouth with laughing, and thy lips with rejoicing."[124]

Biblical laughter might even lift us from rejoicing to understanding, as when "the disciples were filled with joy, and with the Holy Ghost."[125] Most of us have noticed that God is speaking to us through this good book. What we haven't noticed is how good the book is, how positively disposed, how much of God's speaking comes to us through the happy medium of its

121. Holtz, *Back to the Sources*, 32.
122. Buttrick, *Sermons in a University Church*, 89.
123. Webster, *Laughter in the Bible*, 9.
124. Job 8:21.
125. Acts 13:52.

humor. Blessed are we if we hear: "Therefore speak I to them in parables: because they seeing see not; and hearing they hear not, neither do they understand. But blessed are your eyes, for they see: and your ears, for they hear."[126]

I admit right up front that Bible humor ain't for the fainthearted. It's risky business. Its scariness may be the main reason so many readers so assiduously avoid it. Reading the humorless Bible we're used to is like cheering the New York Yankees, playing it safe, investing yet again in the same old same old pin-striped sure thing. Reading the Bible with humor in it is like rooting for the Red Sox. It's scarier, more thrilling because you take your chances, but more rewarding when the higher risk pays off. Yankee fans, for all the reassurance of thirty-two world championships, will never know the life-shifting joys of a baseball year like 2004.

But, biblically speaking, you can. If you need reassurance, read the way you've always read. If you want unprecedented possibility, try reading the Bible by the light of its humor. Whether you are an earnest scholar whose unremitting high seriousness tends to rule out humor on principle, a dedicated devotional reader whose transcendent moral tone makes laughter irreverent or at best irrelevant to her Scripture project, or a plain old Bible reader who doesn't want to be bothered, awareness of the humor in the Bible can enrich your reading. Seriously. As well as we know the Bible, we have for too long overlooked the impact and the significance of its humor. It's not just that we've failed to appreciate the wisdom of biblical wit. We haven't even noticed it.

We may be missing the best part.

126. Matt 13:13, 16.

2

Jonah as Joke

Lightening Up the Orthodox

MODERN READERS TEND TO miss the point of biblical humor. In fact, we mostly miss the humor. The Bible may be the last place most twenty-first-century readers would find a laugh, but the main reason we fail to find it there is that the Bible is the last place we'd look. Humor informs biblical texts so thoroughly that to miss the humor of the Bible is to miss not merely much of its essence, much of its joy, but much of its meaning. Bible readers dedicated to revering this literary text rather than enjoying it have afflicted our culture with a blind spot toward biblical humor. We just don't see it. The problem may be our stilted reading approach. Our myopia might be a problem of perspective, of viewing the Bible through sanctimonious glasses. Consider what a difference it would make, for example, if in place of a distinguished Brad Pitt type in our David-and-Bathsheba Hollywood spectacle we cast instead someone as silly as Mike Myers.

Yet the Myers version may better illuminate the actual biblical context. God directs the disappointed prophet Samuel to "look not on his countenance . . . for man looketh on the outward appearance, but the Lord looketh on the heart."[1] Myers's goofy grin, astonished eyes, and dopey demeanor portray better than Pitt's perfect features the Lord's point that David may not be type cast for the hero role. And certainly Myers would be more misfit-appropriate as the teenage David trying on the armor of that mighty

---

1. 1 Sam 16:7.

Saul who "from his shoulders and upward . . . was higher than any of the people."[2] The Mike Myers David is not just easier to envision but truer to the text, overwhelmed by that oversize mail dragging on the ground, helmet down over his eyes, huge sword clutched desperately in adolescent hands struggling to heft it.

Maybe we would be wiser not to entrust so much of our Bible reading to the church, with its narrowly constrained point of view. That ecclesiastical perspective can get so restrictive it squeezes the juice out of the Bible. Pastors and priests and presbyters are disposed to insist upon Scripture as theological theory, to view it as ethereal abstraction distanced as far as possible from human experience. In direct resistance to that otherworldly reading, lay readers have taken a more natural approach, and that down-to-earth literary reading has resulted from earliest times in more humorous appreciation of the holy text. The popular mystery plays of the Middle Ages, for instance, thrived on that urge to realism. Dramatic enactment tends away from the moralizing of sermon and toward earthier embodiment of details of Bible passages that focus on the realization of how scriptural events could have actually happened.

That blossoming of realism in popular biblical adaptations finds its fruition in humor. Humor is so persistent in those good-hearted mystery plays, which are essentially paraphrases of Scripture, that viewers eventually made the logical connection—"ironies are everywhere"[3] in Bible texts themselves. The same texts that liturgy reads tragically take on in dramatic form a "black-comic quality."[4] In fact (these lay readings deal in facts rather than the theories of theology) flickerings of humor in the mystery plays can be seen to illuminate the darkest biblical disaster. Noah's wife, for example, a vague apparition in the biblical narrative, in the dramatic venue vividly vents her frustrations over her husband's silly apocalyptic notions that the sky is falling, the sky is falling, by giving him a solid whack on his patriarchal head.

The funniness is not just for fun. Anyone who has seen *The Second Shepherd's Play*, where Mak the rustic redneck shepherd in down-to-earth reverence wraps a newborn lamb in swaddling clothes—or anyone who has read Mark Twain's *Extracts from Adam's Diary*, or seen Richard Pryor in *Holy Moses*, or heard Bill Cosby's rendition of "Noah, Noah . . . can you

2. 1 Sam 9:2.

3. Fowler, *English Literature*, 19.

4. Ibid.

tread water?"[5]—will recognize that surprising insight goes hand in hand with the laughter in lifelike interpretations of biblical scenes.

Even something so traditionally and majestically serious as the Ten Commandments can be illuminated by the light of humor, because humor is everywhere germane to the text if not to our usual readings of it. Arthur Hugh Clough's "The Latest Decalogue" wittily updates a Victorian version of the Ten Commandments to make it more amenable to industrial-age moral sensibilities: "Thou shalt have one God only; who / Would be at the expense of two? / No graven images may be / Worshiped, except the currency." Holding up concurrent Victorian attitudes against Hebrew law makes a joke—a remarkably thoughtful joke—of ecclesiastical rationalizations of the most serious Mosaic "thou shalt nots": "Thou shalt not covet, but tradition / Approves all forms of competition."[6]

Clough's clever revelation of how readily we rationalize biblical directives to serve selfish purposes points to the bottom line of Bible humor: it is more concerned with informing us than with entertaining us. That versatile capacity of humor to illuminate biblical meaning is easiest to see in the funniest biblical character—not the quintessential trickster David nor Cosby's Noah nor Pryor's Moses, not (to mention but a few of the most nominated prime suspects) Peter nor Paul nor Eve nor Esther nor Samson nor Saul nor Miriam nor Aaron nor Herod nor Haman nor even wily Jacob. The funniest biblical character is Jonah.

Jokester Jonah

And the book of *Jonah*, in spite of its severe literary handicap—there's so little of it—may be the funniest book of the Bible. Whatever ancient redactor canonized *Jonah* between woeful Obadiah and mournful Micah choreographed cleverly. And *Jonah* is amusing in wittier ways than its grinning incongruity among scriptural companions that sound like they just bit into a bad pickle. Prophetic books are almost unanimously first person. Books like Isaiah and Jeremiah and Ezekiel feature august prophets addressing us directly, their own somber point of view, their sober words in their solemn voices. It is virtually unheard of for a prophetic book to be structured like *Jonah*—instead of being *by* a prophet, like Zechariah or Habakkuk or Malachi, *Jonah* is *about* a prophet. There's probably good literary strategy

5. Bill Cosby, *Very Funny Fellow*.
6. Clough, *Poems of Arthur Hugh Clough*, 407.

behind that. If we had Jonah's personal version of his adventures, stilted autobiography rather than honest biography, Jonah's antics might be less frankly displayed, and his book a lot less funny.

Prophecy is serious business. The biblical genre is long on doom and gloom and apocalyptic disaster. The circumstances of prophetic books are invariably cataclysmic, just as they are in *Jonah*, where the very survival, let alone the spiritual survival, of the capitol and urban wonder of the world, that sophisticated city, Nineveh—"that great city, wherein are more than sixscore thousand persons"[7]—hangs on a thread of the words of a single hero: Jonah. And that unlikely—nay, callow—hero, the would-be reformer of Assyria who hasn't bothered to learn any Assyrian, is expected to convert not only the most powerful but the most ruthless population in the world. Assyrian warriors routinely wracked captured enemies on sharpened poles so their own weight would impale them in agonizingly protracted torture. Assyria is the merciless nation that will sweep over Israel in 734 B.C.E. and deport Hebrew slaves so ruthlessly that the Lost Tribes are still lost. The prophetic prospect always specializes in woe and worry, yet *Jonah* stands out in that dismal company for the desolation of its situation.

Yet Jonah is funny. The very structure of this prophetic book is upbeat, deliberately comic. On Michael Tueth's list of the five key comic elements in Scripture,[8] *Jonah* scores high in every category. The book features "the downfall of the serious"—it's harder to get much more serious than Jonah, with his endless suicidal moanings of "it is better for me to die than to live."[9] *Jonah* features, too, the comic "element of surprise" in such central narrative actions as the prophet's burlesque flight from the God who is everywhere, shocking divine overreaction in that out-of-the-blue tempest, the unprecedented whale rescue, the implausible Ninevite conversion, the whimsical withering of Jonah's pet gourd, and the central narrative question: what in the world motivates Jonah's reluctance to heed God's call? "Readers are left to wonder, even as late as chap. 3."[10]

Jonah, to fill out the Tueth scorecard, "emphasizes the value of innocence and childlikeness" not only in the prophet's childish tantrums but in the book's concern for those morally untutored Ninevites who "cannot

---

7. Jonah 4:11.

8. Tueth, "Comedy and the Christian Vision."

9. Jonah 4:3, 4:8, 4:9.

10. Hauser, "Jonah: In Pursuit of the Dove," 21.

discern between their right hand and their left hand."[11] The story "reverses previously held assumptions and values," its whole point being that God's love extends beyond the limits that Hebrew prophets had imagined until *Jonah*. And, to complete its perfect alignment with Tueth's catalog of the scripturally comic, *Jonah* "thrives" on "physical danger": "Harold Lloyd hanging from the clock, Abbot and Costello meeting Frankenstein, or even the fat man slipping on the banana peel"[12] have nothing on Jonah plunging petulantly overboard or disappearing into the whale's gullet or stalking sulky and smelly into the hostile environs of his Nineveh nemesis.

And that's just the comedic premises. There's much more to the *Jonah* humor than farcical structure. Humor is key to the meaning of the book. Almost everything about *Jonah* is debated by experts, from its context to its literary mode to its implications. The book of *Jonah*, bristling with "literary difficulties," has been "a battleground among scholars for centuries."[13] Its very form is a source of deep disagreement; a voluminous number of genres has been proposed for this tiny volume. "Some see the book as prophet's biography," others as a legend or "ironic allegory";[14] some describe it as midrash,[15] others again as a "satire"[16] or "a parable."[17] That's not the half of it. Other perceptive experts read it as novella, as parody, even as burlesque, as in Rauber's delightful reaction, "The Prophet as Schlemiel."[18]

What all these astutely diverse critical readings have in common is humor. Whatever else Jonah is, it is "humorous story."[19] The humor of *Jonah* is so obvious few manage to miss it; it's so broad it would work in vaudeville, maybe even a circus. It plays with "the clearest stereotypes in Scripture. The characters in the narrative—the prophet himself, the summoning deity, the wicked king in his wicked city—are stock characters . . . stock scenes."[20] There is something almost of literary miracle in the richly nuanced manner that the *Jonah* writer deploys those broad brush strokes of humor into such

11. Jonah 4:1.

12. Hauser, "Jonah: In Pursuit of the Dove," 21.

13. Zimmerman, "Problems in Jonah," 580.

14. Good, *Irony in the Old Testament*, 40.

15. Crenshaw, "Jonah," 300.

16. Miles, "Jonah as Parody," 179.

17. Lacocque, *Jonah Complex*, 4.

18. Rauber, "Prophet as Schlemiel," 32.

19. Wolff, *Obadiah and Jonah*, 12.

20. Miles, "Jonah as Parody," 170.

"widely varied types of comedy" capable of provoking such telling implications. "Grotesque irony and satire, in their most subtle nuances, are pressed into the service of the writer's restrained proclamation."[21]

In fact, the humor of the book of *Jonah* may surpass parody, transcend satire, reach beyond even burlesque. *Jonah*, in direct defiance of its decorous placement in the venerable canon among the melancholy minor prophets, presents itself as something very close to joke. It's a variation of the classic fish story, the one about the prophet that didn't get away. If that seems a stretch, notice that I'm not the only one who thinks so. J. William Whedbee published a fine chapter serendipitously entitled "Jonah as Joke" in his book on the comic vision of the Bible at the same time I was publishing an article on a similar subject with the same title.[22] That "joke" description is so inimitably precise I'm sharing the title with him. Professor Whedbee sees Jonah as "the unwilling butt of God's joke,"[23] but we're both convinced that the "profound and provocative" humor[24] illuminates the text.

Lest I seem from locking arms here with Professor Whedbee or through other scholarly concurrences to have marshaled definitive evidence for humor in the Bible, I should admit at the outset that Whedbee and I are odd men out. A strong consensus of critical readers holds *Jonah*, like every other book of the Bible, to be a thoroughly serious text. Craig's careful analysis, one of the most careful and probably the most serious study to date of *Jonah*, concludes that "the story is too earnest for laughter."[25]

Preposterous Paradox

There is little question about the serious significance of the narrative, but there is no question that *Jonah*'s jocularity contributes richly to that significance. The book introduces itself humorously, getting off to a lighthearted start by setting up its cast of characters in such a "there was a prophet and some sailors and some heathens" sort of way that its hero can be compared to Charlie Chaplin.[26] From the first word of the narrative Jonah is cast as a figure of fun. Hebrew *Jonah* means "dove," that traditional symbol of peace.

21. Wolff, *Obadiah and Jonah*, 12.

22. Walker, "Jonah as Joke."

23. Whedbee, *Bible and the Comic Vision*, 218.

24. Ibid., 219.

25. Craig, *Poetics of Jonah*, 143.

26. Wilcox, "Staging Jonah," 22.

Jonah, fleeing from God's inescapable call, seems flighty enough to qualify for that dove image, yet his incongruously hawkish prophetic approach, anything but peaceful, turns the gentle metaphor on its head. Jonah accosts the Ninevites with such rancor that the very thought of him as an ambassador of peace urges a smile.

That kind of paradox is the tip of the iceberg of the volume's wry wit. The entire design of the book of *Jonah* chuckles under its breath. From the initial caricature of the prophet as an object of ridicule, this brief narrative's deliberately humorous structure works a slapstick technique that seems almost like "vaudeville"[27] to set up the book's shaggy-dog punch line. With the prophet playing straight man, the Lord delivers his whimsical climactic put-down of the prophet through a typically Jewish comedic question: If Jonah can't dredge up any compassion for naïve Ninevites, maybe he could manage it for their cattle? The very form indicates joke. The open-ended narrative ends "abruptly, without any resolution or moralizing, in fact very much as a humorous anecdote ends suddenly with the punch line."[28] As with any good joke that depends upon the hearer to catch the point, "the narrator confronts the reader with an ending-beyond-the-ending"[29] that thwarts expectations of closure so completely that the ultimate meaning is "left up to the whims of the reader."[30]

Jonah is funny in format, funny in content, funny even in its rapid-fire delivery. Narrative momentum approaches the manic. The casual little volume hurls scene after high-tempo comic scene, compressed skits volleyed at the pace of one-liners. Virtually every event in this story invites a smile of the kind provoked by the snapshot of the recalcitrant prophet spewed from the belly of the whale, reeking of whale vomit, trailing seaweed and barnacles and old fish heads, bleached of all his color by gastric juices, his robe shrunk up to his knees and elbows by that clammy humidity, disheveled and disgruntled, trudging into Nineveh muttering his message of doom in the theological jargon of a foreign language so bewildering that the Ninevites can only scratch their heads.

The ironies run deeper than that cartoon surface. Jonah's missionary success stretches beyond the unlikely to the absurd. Yet even the most improbable events in the story, like that perplexing conversion of the entire

27. Ibid.

28. Hyers, *God Created Laughter*, 107.

29. Crouch, "Closure of the Book of Jonah," 110.

30. Ibid., 101.

Ninevite nation, remain grounded in humorous realism—in this case, Jonah's ridiculous arrival in Nineveh looking, and likely smelling, like a disheveled version of Assyrian divinity. The preposterous apparition the prophet presents could have inspired heathen Ninevites to see him as an incarnation of their fish god Dagan, who was half man, half fish and—even handier for these humorous purposes—half god, half human.[31] Dagan in his alternate appellative *Oannes* sounds still more like a twin to Jonah. In that seafood-reverencing culture, Jonah's fish miracle could have facilitated heathen conversion when rumors of his coming forth from the mighty leviathan got around fish-worshiping Nineveh. All that ironic pagan implication incarnated in a Hebrew prophet could provide readers, if not the Good Lord himself, "a good laugh at Jonah's expense," while "accomplishing [God's] purposes despite Jonah's ill will towards the task."[32]

If that premise of implicit jocularity seems outlandish, consider how insistently such outlandish scenes dominate the book. The first chapter alone proposes enough amusing situations for a Marx Brothers movie. Surprising sitcom setups again and again revolve around blatant paradox, rife with comic irony. The central narrative situation is absurd. God calls Jonah to the Ninevite mission at a time when foreign missions hadn't been thought of. If they had, they would have been thought of as a bad idea. And the Ninevite mission, catering to the most vicious people in the universe, qualifies readily in a Hebrew mind as the worst of religious ideas. Almighty God commands "go east, young man"; his prophet heads due west.

Every scenario in this book is as risibly unexpected as a man in an Armani suit slipping on a banana peel. God pulls out all stops to get the prophet's attention, threatening Jonah with a "mighty tempest in the sea, so that the ship was like to be broken";[33] Jonah remains "fast asleep."[34] Sailors, a profession not particularly noted for religious conscientiousness, spontaneously break into prayer right in the middle of their frantic struggle to lighten the ship. The heathen shipmaster presumes to correct the Lord's anointed, urging God's prophet, apparently with a straight face, to "call upon thy God."[35] God himself demands Jonah be thrown into a watery grave so he can dramatically rescue him. And the means of that show-

31. Hooke, "Fish Symbolism," 536.
32. Ibid., 535.
33. Jonah 1:4.
34. Jonah 1:5.
35. Jonah 1:6.

boat rescue that the Lord devises—more outrageously still, has previously "prepared"?[36] Instead of exalted angels swooping down in divine glory from heaven, the discomfiting "belly of the fish,"[37] followed in delayed slapstick sequence by—wait for it, wait for it—the pointed indignity of whale puke.

The humor here is deliberate, signaled by more intentionally funny aspects than we might think could be crammed into such a tiny text. The book is overrun, for example, with that staple of the comic, exaggeration. The term *great* appears no less than fourteen times in these four slight chapters. And the exaggeration isn't simply rhetorical. Narrative events reflect that tendency to comic inflation; every action is "deliberately overdrawn."[38] The prophet dramatically overdoes the expected polite prophetic reticence about God's call; Whedbee sees "parodied comparisons" with the less extreme hesitations of "Moses, Elijah, Jeremiah, and Joel."[39] Jonah is so intensely focused and so utterly self-centered in his urgency to get away from God that he apparently charters the entire ship to himself. The city of Nineveh, not satisfied with its reputation as the place of utmost evil in the world, is stretched to such extent—"three days' journey"[40]—as to appear more extensive than modern-day Los Angeles. The instantaneous repentance of 120,000 stiff-necked Ninevites is not enough for this over-the-top narrator: even the livestock get in on the comedy act. "We cannot understand why the Ninevite cattle fast and don sackcloth (Jonah 3:8) without appealing to the notion of satire."[41]

Cartoon Caricature

Characters, too, tend to extremes in the book of Jonah. The actors in this narrative don't act so much as overreact. Our hero himself takes his drama-queen act so far as to melodramatically threaten suicide no less than three times in four chapters. After volunteering to get thrown overboard during the storm at sea, in what appears to be a rather extreme measure for avoiding God's Nineveh plans, Jonah petulantly wishes for death again in

---

36. Jonah 1:17.

37. Jonah 1:17.

38. Freitheim, "Jonah," 729.

39. Whedbee, *Bible and the Comic Vision*, 218.

40. Jonah 3:3.

41. Noegel, "Anti-Prophetic Satire," 103.

reaction to God's saving the Ninevites,⁴² and for the final astonishing time gets suicidal out of childish pique over the passing of his favorite plant.⁴³

The Ninevites' conversion is similarly overdrawn to the point of comedy. What may be the shortest and certainly reigns as the crankiest sermon on religious record (and that's going some) results in the most amazing missionary success in history, and this among people about as likely to humble themselves as modern New Yorkers. For his part, Jonah is so self-absorbed he's completely unable to empathize, "a selfish, sanctimonious Israelite, who begrudges God's mercy to everyone else."⁴⁴ His total lack of sympathy makes him win all awards for "unlikeliest to succeed as an ambassador of God's love." Hence readerly "amazement" and amusement when "Jonah's truncated message of imminent doom" so effectively "functions as a divine call to repentance." "Nineveh's intensely religious response is startling in the present narrative context to the point of being absurd."⁴⁵ The Ninevites respond to Jonah's abrupt and bluntly unsympathetic preachment with such over-the-top enthusiasm that their conversion may be "a more astounding miracle than the miracle of the fish."⁴⁶

There's a lot of that overreaction in this succinct narrative. One astute reader of *Jonah* thinks "perhaps the grotesque and fantastic achieve their pinnacle in the attribution of thoughts to the endangered ship."⁴⁷ God's storm gets so fierce that the ship itself, in terrified anthropomorphic tremors, "threatened to break up."⁴⁸ But my vote for the most laughable extreme is that delightful focal episode with the great fish: instead of a trained porpoise or a rescue submarine or a passing raft or scuba gear or an angelic miracle or a long rope for Jonah's vehicle of deliverance, let alone the kind of fiery chariot he vouchsafed Elijah, God, apparently for the fun of it, provides for Jonah's salvation a *Pinnochio* ride inside a whale. Then the Lord adds to the injury—the injury of fetid marine odor and caustic gastric juices and the clammy claustrophobia of those disgustingly close fish-entrails quarters—the insult of that slapstick touch of fishy regurgitation. In well-timed response to Jonah's long-winded and exorbitantly pious

42. Jonah 4:3.

43. Jonah 4:8.

44. Wolff, *Obadiah and Jonah*, 11.

45. Dozeman, "Yahweh's Gracious and Compassionate Character," 214.

46. Bewer, *Literature of the Old Testament*, 423.

47. Crenshaw, "Book of Jonah," 381.

48. Jonah 1:4, NIV.

whale-belly psalm, the fish, at the behest of an obviously unimpressed God, expresses its good taste with visceral disgust: "it vomited out Jonah upon the dry land."[49] Those implicit touches of humor are deft: "dry land," for instance—comfortably dry except where fish regurgitation makes things disgustingly sticky. That simple tactile description rubs our noses in the revolting experience still more emphatically in the Hebrew, where "dry land" is understatedly stressed as "the dry."

All that overflowing overreaction sets up the masterful understatement that underlines the book's humor. The author of Jonah is proficient with pregnant pauses, as when, in the climactic chapter, Jonah does not deign to reply to the Lord's gentle ribbing: "Doest thou well to be angry?"[50] It's a deft question of the "Have you stopped beating your wife?" variety, skewering Jonah however he responds. Either Jonah is unjustified in presuming to judge God's actions, or—or *and*—God is quite right to think his children the Ninevites, in whom he has so much invested, may matter more than Jonah's fly-by-night pet plant.

That momentary silence of Jonah, highlighting as it does his sulkiness, works the better because of a context contrasting Jonah's cantankerousness with God's amused patience. "It is through the modulations of the comedy itself that [the narrator] not only delights his readers but also makes it easier for them to perceive God's loving laughter over narrow-minded piety."[51] The writer takes great pains to juxtapose the Lord's restraint against Jonah's sassy eagerness to confront the Almighty. Jonah is mouthy, speaking three times as much as God. Yet God gets first and final word. His final statement is emphasized by the shift in the conversation from the pattern of three words to one in favor of Jonah to (in that climactic exchange) four words to one for God.[52] Those carefully stacked verbal odds seem to be saying that however talkative Jonah may be, in the end God's word counts for more.

That precise orchestration of the conversation between God and his prophet facilitates a confrontation ripe with laughable possibilities, "with sullen fury on Jonah's part and with keen enjoyment over Jonah's predicament on the part of God."[53] We imagine the Yahweh of this Old Testament

---

49. Jonah 2:10.

50. Jonah 4:4, 4:9.

51. Wolff, *Obadiah and Jonah*, 12.

52. Wesling, *Calling of Jonah*, 110.

53. Chase, *Bible and the Common Reader*, 197.

book "less as hurling thunderbolts than as rolling His eyes"[54] at his over-reactionary prophet. These contrapuntal rantings and pregnant pauses create a tone richly ambivalent, "a touch both of the miraculous and of the ludicrous,"[55] a tone enhanced by such delightful incidental touches as the portrait of the prophet who doesn't prophesy. Whereas prophetic books are typically all prophecy, "The Book of Jonah contains no prophecies."[56] In fact, only "a single brief prophetic saying"[57]—and that one doesn't come to pass. Insult gets added, yet again, to the prophetic injury. Much to his personal discomfiture, Jonah's sole prediction proclaiming the destruction of Nineveh fails to come to pass. That tonal ambivalence makes reader enjoyment of Jonah's comeuppance feel like giggling at a funeral, tickling all the more in light of concerns that this may not be appropriate atmosphere for laughter.

Character contrasts heighten the humor of that dissonance of tone. Jonah comes off second best not just in comparison with God, where we expect it. The prophet's character is found wanting in his interactions with every other character, some of those characters downright unsavory. We don't expect sailors to provide models of moral uprightness, yet these heathens prove demonstrably more moral than the Hebrew prophet. They work while Jonah is sleeping during the storm, importune him to pray as they have been praying, and even after clearly establishing his responsibility for the terrible storm, attempt patiently to understand his personal problems under threat of their lives in the hurly-burly of a crisis he's causing by his failure to care about the lives of others.

Most dramatic, in a situation where most of us would have chucked him overboard long since, is their tenacious concern for this ominously ill-omened passenger. He's so Joe Bltzfk a bad luck charm, so Ancient-Mariner-who-shot-the-albatross a monkey on their backs that all ill-luck magnets who have sailed ever since have been known as "Jonahs." Yet concern for his welfare rather than their own inspires these hardened mariners to row "hard"[58] to bring him to land. "One can imagine Jonah's chagrin as the pagan sailors try to save his wretched life while he screams so mightily to give it up," chagrin so pointed that "the total obedience of the sailors is

54. Wilcox, "Staging Jonah," 23.

55. Good, *Irony in the Old Testament*, 46.

56. Miles, "Jonah as Parody," 170.

57. Wolff, *Obadiah and Jonah*, 75.

58. Jonah 1:13.

now vividly etched against the total disobedience of the prophet Jonah."[59] In a complementary paradox of people who don't know any better yet do better than an ostensibly inspired prophet who should know better, the heathen captain demonstrates considerably more spiritual urgency than apathetic Jonah. "What meanest thou, O sleeper? arise, call upon thy God, if so be that God will think upon us."[60]

Even those reprobates the Ninevites, archvillains of the ancient world, "appear to understand more about the divine grace than Jonah does."[61] Jonah in pronouncing their destruction—the whole purpose of which should be to provoke repentance—doesn't even invite them to repent, does not in fact so much as hint at an escape clause. Yet, with preposterous alacrity for recalcitrant sinners, they do repent, immediately and humbly. For all their religious inexperience and their secular sophistication, they obey the Lord more readily and far more enthusiastically than his prophet: "So the people of Nineveh believed God, and proclaimed a fast, and put on sackcloth, from the greatest of them even to the least of them."[62] That overwhelming conversion includes, at the king's behest, even their cattle. "The wind, water, fish, Ninevites—virtually everything and everybody except Jonah—simply do what they are instructed to do."[63] That leaves our hero Jonah, outspoken spokesman for repentance, very much low man on the totem pole of righteousness, exposed conspicuously as "the only figure in the book (including the cows) who is at the end unrepentant."[64]

The Joke is on Jonah, and Jonah is Us

The joke is on Jonah. Jonah is shown as a paragon of self-righteousness, like the prodigal son's ungenerous elder brother or the over-orthodox Ezras and Nehemiahs against whose exclusionary views this book seems to have been written. Jonah, pouting under the searing sun in his petulant sit-in to demand fireworks be rained upon the Ninevites, is condemned by his own self-righteous certainty that he is worth saving whereas Assyrian sinners are not. The seer of the unfathomable Lord's will is unable to see the

59. Holbert, "Satire in Jonah," 68–69.

60. Jonah 1:6.

61. Good, *Irony in the Old Testament*, 50.

62. Jonah 3:4.

63. Craig, *Poetics of Jonah*, 146.

64. Holbert, "Satire in Jonah," 75.

elephant in the room, the simple fact that the compassion of God for these heathens is the same compassion that rescued him more dramatically and less deservedly from the bottom of the sea. Jonah's chronicle becomes "a devastating mockery of Israelite piety as it is exemplified by the dubious prophet whose sole concern was his reputation for accuracy of prediction or a restriction of divine compassion to Israel."[65]

Jonah has doubts about the sincerity of Nineveh's repentance, doubts historically justified by the unnerving fact that these diehard enemies of Israel are destined to overwhelm his nation in a few decades. But we readers have some similar questions about the sincerity of Jonah's own repentance. However profound his change of heart sounded when he was choking it up from the innards of the great fish, we still can't help speculating that whale gullets must be at least as efficacious in encouraging conversion as foxholes. The satire of Jonah's well-timed repentance is cutting. The only modicum of movement toward repentance that the preeminent representative of God's chosen people can muster is when he is forced to repent by the same kind of death threat he himself imposes upon the weak moral backs of untaught Ninevites. That raises edgy concerns: What, bottom line, differentiates chosen Jonah from the despised Ninevites? They're repentant. He's not.

Somewhere amid those moral qualms we begin to see that the joke on Jonah reflects on us. The humor of Jonah leads in the direction of the Okeefenookee Swamp in the old Walt Kelly comic strip where Pogo with his eye-opening wit realized "We have met the enemy, and he is us."[66] Much as we might resist the thought, "ultimately Jonah is all of us."[67] We, too, have a ridiculous tendency to flee from our divine duty. We, too, catch ourselves foolishly assuming that God favors us, our nation, our church, our way of thinking. We, too, have laughably small-souled inclination toward justice for all and mercy for ourselves. "When we look at the figure of Jonah, his self-centeredness and narrow-mindedness," it is small wonder that "we laugh at him and, as we laugh, realize that we are laughing at ourselves." "Our laughter at Jonah becomes a judgment on ourselves"[68]

The self-assessment sneaks up on us through humor. The moral of the story comes across with a kind of evanescent Cheshire-cat grin: the God of the Old Testament, more feared than loved, overwhelming in his

65. Crenshaw, "Book of Jonah," 381.

66. Kelly, *Pogo*.

67. Hyers, *God Created Laughter*, 108.

68. Ibid., 96.

imposing commands to Moses and his august challenges to Job and the awful destruction he brings down around the head of understandably nervous Noah, turns out to be a soft touch, a softer touch than those prophets we assumed he was bullying. The moral of the Lord's *Jonah* story is most clearly encapsulated in his own genial terms in the climactic verse of the narrative: "And should not I spare Nineveh?"[69] "This is, one hopes, how God feels about Man—unlike Man, who is less tolerant of himself."[70] Though the joke is ultimately on us, the moral of that amusing story turns out to be one we can relish: God likes us better than we do. "If even Nineveh can be spared, who cannot be forgiven?"[71] Maybe even Jonah. Maybe even us.

Looked at smilingly, as it seems to be inviting us to look, the theology of this slight scroll deepens. *Jonah's* "weighty message does not exclude humor."[72] It invites it. *Jonah* as joke is about repentance, about potential for change, about second chances. Nineveh, most evil of nations, repents. Jonah, most recalcitrant of prophets, repents, then whimsically repents of his repentance. Most amazingly, the Lord Almighty repents, changes his unchangeable mind. "God repented of the evil, that he had said that he would do unto them; and he did it not."[73]

However carefree those humorous implications may appear, God's grinding of orthodox gears here is theologically momentous. Jonah's God appears to Jonah "to be obliterating the distinction between Good and Evil: How can *ex post facto* repentance alter the significance of a deed, or God's appropriate response to that deed? The failure or even postponement of divine retribution is itself the cause of evil in the world."[74] That stone thrown into these deep theological waters ripples ramifications everywhere. If God himself can change, even change in response to human change, surely humans can change. Even the set-in-cement self-righteous among us, even the Jonahs, can change. We are led lightfootedly by this fanciful moral farce to profound spiritual depths, a place almost Zen-like, where we hear Hebrew anticipations of Yogi Berra inviting us into a transcendent sphere where it's never over til it's over because it's always *deja vu* all over again.

69. Jonah 4:11.

70. Mankowitz, "It Could Happen to a Dog," 110.

71. Hyers, *God Created Laughter*, 109.

72. Crenshaw, "Book of Jonah," 381.

73. Jonah 3:10.

74. Levine, "'Jonah' vs. 'God,'" 176.

Read as parable, the book speaks to us about obedience, about heeding the call of the Lord, hunkering down and doing our duty, even when that's in Nineveh. Read as satire, Jonah gently condemns cultural self-righteousness, urges us out of the ruts of our religious chauvinism into wider awareness of the goodness in others. Read as a kind of cosmic joke, the book of Jonah may be an even more profound theological book. Its perspective helps us see that repentance is always possible, that there is always something better in life, better in us, than we have seen. If recalcitrant Ninevites can change for the better, and even God can change, and even the cattle can repent, for heaven's sake, then maybe even Jonah, maybe even we are not too old to learn new tricks.

More than a Spoonful of Sugar

That insight is predicated in and argued through and illuminated by humor. From its initial parody of the prophetic call to its concluding portrait of those "much cattle"[75] penitently attired in sackcloth and ashes, *Jonah's* funniness matters. As its pervasiveness suggests, the humor in *Jonah* is not incidental, not decorative, not frothy frosting on the theological cake. The humor in *Jonah* is not merely fun; it's functional.

Jonah's psalm in the second chapter gets questioned as much as the book's genre. Most scholars are convinced, in part because the solemn poem seems contrary to the general humorous tone of the book, that the pious psalm is an interpolation, stuck in by a later editor to offset the book's irreverent humor.[76] Others of us feel that the psalm fits right in. Read humorously, Jonah's whale-belly repentance is a parody of conversion by coercion—like the Ninevites' lightning transmogrification under duress. And it seems delightfully put on, a "pastiche of psalmodic cliches, self-conscious parody."[77] Even if the humor of the psalm is unintended, "the joke may be on the redactor, for whoever wrote the passage has furnished an insertion" that in the context of the general joking of Jonah "can be read as one of the story's most audacious parodies."[78] This is "a hollow song sung

---

75. Jonah 4:11.
76. Southwell, "Jonah," 594.
77. Whedbee, *Bible and the Comic Vision*, 203.
78. Mather, "Comic Art of Jonah," 284.

in a hollow place."[79] "From Jonah expect the unexpected—why not sing a song of thanks when in the belly of a fish?"[80]

Thus there is, bottom line, an important moral to the Jonah joke. In the first place, the whole idea is outlandish. To a Hebrew of the fifth century B.C.E., the very premise of the story is absurd. Jonah is a midrashic tale in the usual manner of that genre's "imagine if."[81] But Jonah's case study makes the "imagine if" proposition unimaginable. The story's narrative situation is impossible for Jonah's Hebrew audience. The tale is for the Israelite of the time an invitation to think about the unthinkable. Yahweh just does not go around inviting brutal heathens like the Al Qaida to join his team, and for good reason: heathens are hopeless, incapable of repentance. "The audience is asked to ponder a theological riddle: what would have happened if no less a den of foreign devils than Nineveh had repented?"[82]

That tone of toying with biblical convention is set in the opening scene of the book with its parody of the prophetic call. Prophetic convention dictated a certain shy reluctance in responding to the Lord's summons; humble hesitance typifies responses to the call by such model prophets as Isaiah,[83] Jeremiah,[84] and even Moses. God's greatest spokesman responds with self-effacing eloquence to the burning bush: "I am not eloquent . . . I am slow of speech, and of a slow tongue."[85] Jonah carries that traditional reluctance to extremes that suggest parody. "Given Jonah's inclination to flee the task, one would expect Jonah to raise serious objections with God, as do Moses,[86] Gideon,[87] and Jeremiah[88] when confronted with similarly demanding tasks."[89] But when the Lord calls Jonah, he refuses to answer at all. "Jonah's silence has the parodic impact of silence after the question 'Do you take this woman to be your lawfully wedded wife?'"[90]

79. Ackerman, "Satire in Jonah," 235.
80. Ibid., 214.
81. Crenshaw, "Book of Jonah," 380.
82. Allen, *Joel, Obadiah, Jonah, and Micah*, 191.
83. Isa 6:5.
84. Jer 1:6.
85. Exod 4:10.
86. Exod 3–4.
87. Judg 6.
88. Jer 1.
89. Hauser, "Pursuit of the Dove," 25.
90. Miles, "Jonah as Parody," 172.

Funny as that introduction is, the conclusion of the book is funnier. Strong indication that the humor of *Jonah* is significant is that it is climactic; it gets funnier as it goes along. The book's closing statement is not so much a statement as a punch line, its whimsicality underlined by its form as a question. And that concluding question is deftly humorous: God wonders out loud to Jonah, with tongue firmly in cheek, "And should not I spare Nineveh, that great city, wherein are more than sixscore thousand persons that cannot discern between their right hand and their left hand; and also much cattle?"[91]

At the risk of analyzing the fun out of it, that great exit line is funny in at least five ways. The quantification is an insult to Jonah's accountant mentality, an early Hebrew equivalent of, "You want justice, I'll give you justice times one hundred twenty thousand"—the quality of mercy is not strained, Jonah is being reminded, let alone the quantity. The reference to Jonah's relative sophistication, the implication that the prophet of the Lord ought to know better than "persons that cannot discern between their right hand and their left hand," suggests Jonah might be wiser to worry more about God's living, breathing children, Ninevites included, than a dead gourd. In a clever reversal of Jonah's earlier "I told you so," the prophet's insistent "was not this my saying, when I was yet in my country,"[92] the Lord turns the tables on Jonah with that "he who laughs last laughs best" twist.

The most obvious source of humor in the closing line is the animal reference. That deliberately anticlimactic apparent afterthought, "and also much cattle,"[93] is carefully set up by earlier practical jokes involving unlikely creatures in unconventional roles, from the most overwhelming whales to the lowliest worms. God as Trickster doesn't miss a trick here. In this compassionate context where the Lord's concern clearly extends to all his creatures, with not so much as one sparrow falling "on the ground without your Father,"[94] that "also much cattle" jibe suggests something genially close to "Jonah, despite your petulance, I'd save the city for the sake of its camels or even its cats, let alone its people. Especially," the text smiles between its understated lines, "when those camels are so penitently dressed in sackcloth and ashes." The humor of the bestial imagery may burrow

---

91. Jonah 4:11.
92. Jonah 4:2.
93. Jonah 4:11.
94. Matt 10:29.

deeper still; the "worm" that wriggles into the short-lived gourd[95] could be a simile for Jonah himself, the unlikely instrument the Lord introduced into Nineveh to enact his life-affecting will.

The funniest thing about that divine last word at the conclusion of *Jonah* is the direct moral that it gives to the story, like David Letterman heightening the intensity of a joke by patiently explaining the punch line to a dim-witted audience. There is strong indication here, particularly in this context of ironic repartee, of a divine nudge in the ribs: "The reason you have too little compassion, Jonah, is that you have no sense of humor." There is also strong implication that God would have us have more of that, more of both the sense of humor and the compassion to which this book so warmly relates it. That anticlimactic closure focuses us back upon the second verse of this final chapter, where Jonah in his small-souled condemnation of God ironically declares the bottom-line moral of the story in his whiney "I told you so": "I knew that thou art a gracious God, and merciful, slow to anger, and of great kindness, and repentest thee of the evil."[96] Come on now, Jonah—Isn't God's mercy pretty much the point here?

That turning of the tables upon self-righteousness is the central joke in *Jonah*. What feels like condemnation to Jonah is for Jonah's God, and for us, commendation. Jonah reprimands God for his unreliability. The omniscient and omnipotent Ruler of the Universe responds to Jonah's impertinent attempt to put him in his divine place by deftly putting Jonah in his very human place, through that smiling question about being humane: "Doest thou well to be angry?"[97] Jonah rashly presumes to tell God how to be God; God's patient response shows Jonah what it ought to mean to be human. "In short, Jonah is unloving; Yahweh is love."[98] God invites Jonah outside his narrow theological parameters into broader perspectives, out of his religious certitude into the uncertain realities of life where things get risky and unpredictable and mind-boggling and as a result meaningfully funny.

---

95. Jonah 4:7.
96. Jonah 4:2.
97. Jonah 4.4.
98. Trible, "Book of Jonah," 75.

Life More Abundantly

The message of the book of *Jonah* is delivered with a divine smile that contrasts vividly with Jonah's sullen message of doom to the Ninevites. That message at its core is: live. Maybe Whedbee's finest insight in his thoroughly fine reading of *Jonah* is that it is fundamentally "symbolic of the comic vision that no one dies in Jonah."[99] The comedic intent of that happy ending is emphatic. Though every character in the book suffers under imminent threat of death, "no one perishes."[100] There's so much gloom and doom hanging like the Sword of Damocles over the head of this happy little book it's a relief to realize how G-rated *Jonah* is for violence, and that in stark contrast to the rest of the Bible. "Apart from the Song of Songs, it is the only book in the Hebrew Bible where no one dies."[101]

The God of Jonah, much to his prophet's chagrin, loves a surprise, delights in upsetting expectations, savors showing up anticipations as mirages. Jonah, from his glass-half-full perspective, feels God is pulling the rug out from under his relied-upon promises—he reads the moral of that divine unreliability as "damned if you do and damned if you don't." We are likelier to read it as God does—"blessed even if you don't, *way* blessed if you do." Life with the God of Jonah is not far from the proverbial view of heaven: better than we could ever imagine, and full of wonderful surprises. Those surprises are chancy business, like casting lots on a deck pitching in a storm so wildly the dice don't have to be thrown.[102] Such uncertainty is an understandable threat to Jonah. But to us the chanciness simultaneously holds promise of fuller life, of God holding out unprecedented opportunities to his children, "that they might have life, and that they might have it more abundantly."[103]

The humor of the book of *Jonah* urges us in the direction of that abundance. The laughter encourages us to find a way to laugh at ourselves, laugh off our restrictive expectations, laugh away our confining certitudes about our just deserts. The humor informs us that the most cherished orthodoxies may not be as bound by our expectations as we'd expect, that the "first

---

99. Whedbee, *Bible and the Comic Vision,* 219.

100. Ibid., 217.

101. Ibid.

102. Jonah 1:7.

103. John 10:10.

[could] be last; and the last . . . first."[104] "Among David's ancestors there may be a Ruth the Moabite, among the righteous a Job the Edomite; among the penitents a city of Nineveh."[105] "History would be more intelligible if God's word were the last word, final and unambiguous like a dogma or an unconditional decree." But human life wouldn't be as riskily rich or as improbably happy or as implausibly meaningful. If we dare venture outside the firelight of our certainties, "beyond justice and anger lies the mystery of compassion."[106] That elusive compassion reveals itself happily in the warm-heartedness of humor.

And intimately. The God of Jonah may be closer to us than we've thought, closer maybe even than some of us Jonahs want. The juncture of God's up-close-and-personal intersection with our lives is marked by laughter. Being "vomited out" by a great fish[107] is for Jonah trauma tinged with insult, a kind of Laurel and Hardy "another fine mess you've gotten me into." For the fish it must have been a relief, as the old joke goes—Jonah the worst case of indigestion he ever had. For God the vomiting out is, like all of his acts in the book, an act of compassion. For us, standing precariously between divine love and human selfishness, that incongruous juxtaposition of sublime possibilities and ludicrous actualities centers in the funny bone of the soul, close to the core of our lives.

Robert Alter reminds us that the Hebrew Bible's view "repeatedly had to make sense of the intersection of incompatibles—the relative and the absolute, human imperfection and divine perfection, the brawling chaos of historical experience and God's promise to fulfill a design in history." Alter feels, as I feel, that the biblical perspective, in *Jonah* and everywhere else, is informed "by a sense of stubborn contradiction, of a profound and ineradicable untidiness in the nature of things."[108] Theological certitude can stand in the way of what may be the Bible's richest treasure: the possibilities inherent in its open-ended uncertainties. *Jonah* is an open invitation to that provocatively untidy and inherently humorous biblical outlook.

Jonah may be the funniest, but it is far from the only funny book in the Bible. For a volume stereotyped into such decorous sobriety, the Bible exhibits some remarkably laughable moments. Like virtually every other

---

104. Matt 19:30.

105. Lacocque, *Jonah Complex*, 94.

106. Heschel, *Prophets*, 67.

107. Ibid.

108. Alter, *Art of Biblical Narrative*, 154.

book of the Bible, books where we even more routinely manage to over-look the humor, *Jonah* is a bighearted open invitation to life. And to the liveliness in us. Maybe there is more promise in us than we've dared dream. Maybe we are capable of living more abundantly, in a kind of comic Lake Wobegon world, where "all of the women are strong, and all the men are good looking, and all of our children are above average." *Jonah* invites us to live a fuller life.

Not that it's an easy invitation to read. The Bible's comedic come-on has proved anything but invitational to most readers—it can be daunt-ing. Theodore Roethke, a poet who knows a rhetorical challenge when he sees one, thinks that which is "really funny before the eye of God" may be "harder to achieve than the lyric: more anguishing, more exacting, more exhausting to its writer."[109] And, we might add, to its reader. So why go to the trouble? Why pursue the complexities and subtleties and ramifying significances of humor in the Bible? Maybe the biblical invitation to life de-pends upon laughter because life does, and maybe that God who invented life loves the laughter. Maybe that's why we miss so much of the vitality, so much of the possibility, so much of the joy, when we miss the Bible's humor. Certainly that's where we miss much of the point.

109. Roethke, *Straw for the Fire*, 258.

3

"Turned to the Contrary"

Comic Reversal in Esther

BIBLE READING IS BEDEVILED by a bewildering paradox. The Bible may be the most revolutionary book ever written, yet the reading of it tends to be reactionary. Readers typically go to Scripture to refocus faith, to reaffirm theology, to retrench traditional values. Most Bible readers are more concerned with reassuring themselves than with stretching emotional envelopes or pushing mental parameters, let alone with expanding souls. Most biblical reading is conservative even when readers themselves may not be.

That preoccupation with always reading the same old comfortable way makes the good news of the gospel never really *news*, never actually *new*. The miracles are mundane, the prophecies predictable. The parables, which depend for their rhetorical impact and for their conceptual import upon narrative surprise, are rendered routine. The incarnation itself downsizes from cosmos-shifting shock—*God is right here "with us"*[1]—into something closer to anticlimax—*apparently he came around in the past.* Our habit of rereading rather than reading is natural enough; we are used to thinking of the Bible as the ultimate bastion of religious reliability. It's our comfort, our defense, our rock, rather than our road to Damascus or Emmaus or the promised land. We prefer safe if uninspired spinoffs rather than the unnerving surprise of the original. Problem is, the Bible is actually the most

1. Matt 1:23.

48

revolutionary book ever written. Comfortable as our old-slippers habit of repetitive exegesis can make us, treating biblical text as tired rerun rather than fresh experience makes us miss much of what the Bible is about.

We might see more if we were more urgently motivated to go beyond what we already know of the Bible. We might be better off reading more like the aging grandma poring over her worn Bible "cramming for finals." Or like W. C. Fields's unique approach to Scripture, "looking for loopholes."² We might read better if we were to read more anxiously—the best biblical reading may be more about discovery, maybe even desperation, than reassurance. We are likely to read more richly not by comfortably confirming what we already know, but by struggling for innovative insight, stretching more yearningly toward "newness of life,"³ reaching for new bottles rather than refilling, yet again, our same old theological plastic containers. The New Testament is a declaration of independence from old ways of reading. Its express purpose is "new doctrine,"⁴ the "new commandment,"⁵ a whole new scriptural approach that "agreeth not with the old."⁶ And the Old Testament is no less innovative than the New in endorsing radical reading. The entire Bible looks to freshly inspired ways of reading, to reading with new eyes, with "a new heart and a new spirit."⁷

The Good Book, in contrast to our usual readings of it, stresses new possibilities over old certitudes. Disposed not to pacify but to provoke, the Bible is bent less on reiterating our received notions than on stretching our horizons wide as "new heavens and new earth."⁸ If we were to read it more openly, more alertly, we would find the Bible surprising, sometimes mind-blowing. We might even find it funny. Bible humor, like all the better brands of humor, has unimagined capacity to revitalize our notions, stand our old expectations on their heads. It can perform Lasik surgery on our perspectives, enabling us to see the familiar world from a fresh frame of reference. The unexpectedness of Bible laughter can jerk us out of our religious lethargy, churn up our cultural complacency, jostle us into unfamiliar

2. Anobile, *Flask of Fields*, 74.

3. Rom 6:4.

4. Mark 1:27.

5. John 13:34.

6. Luke 5:36.

7. Ezek 18:31.

8. Isa 65:17, and at least seven other places in Scripture.

stances, unsettle our settled notions, twist our habitual viewpoints toward new insights.

Telltale Twists

Looked at through the lens of its surprising humor, the Bible manifests itself as a veritable compendium of the unexpected. The book is trip-wired with surprises: diminutive David triumphs over colossal Goliath,[9] tongue-tied Moses stutters into his celebrated status as God's greatest spokesman,[10] outsider Ruth the Moabite establishes herself as ancestor of Israel's greatest king.[11] Self-serving heroes like Samson and Esther shock us by self-sacrificially saving their people,[12] candidates unlikely as greedy Jacob[13] and spoiled Joseph[14] and callous Judah[15] morph into God's good servants. Impulsive Peter, catch-as-catch-can fisherman, against all odds becomes the anchor of the church.[16] Reluctant Jonah converts every single one of those impervious Ninevites so convincingly they dress their cattle and camels and cats in sackcloth and ashes to certify the thoroughness of their repentance.[17]

A snapshot of that kind of reversal of the expected, so compelling it can serve as a paradigm for the Bible's persistent passion for surprise, can be glimpsed in David's cart-before-the-horse reaction to the death of his first child by Bathsheba: David fasts and prays intensely, almost melodramatically, for the life of his sick son. Yet as soon as the child dies, the king, rather than mourning, returns matter-of-factly to his normal life.[18] David turns the "ancient mourning rites upside down," behaving "*before* the death of the small boy as a normal man would have behaved *after*."[19]

---

9. 1 Sam 17.

10. Exod 4:10.

11. Ruth 4:13–22.

12. Judg 16:30, Esth 8–11.

13. Gen 30, for instance.

14. Gen 37:1–4, for instance.

15. Gen 38.

16. Matt 16:18.

17. Jonah 3:7–8.

18. 2 Sam 12:15–23.

19. Hvidberg, *Weeping and Laughter in the Old Testament*, 138.

Mourning rites aren't the only things in the Bible that get turned upside down or, even more illuminatingly (and more amusingly), inside out. Reversals are so prevalent in biblical narrative that the pervasive flip-flops add up to a paradoxically reliable pattern of unpredictability. Genesis, for example, begins with neophytes Adam and Eve turning the tables on the venerable serpent[20] and ends with baby Joseph repaying his big brothers' treachery with compassion.[21] Between those bookend reversals Rebekah tricks Isaac,[22] Jacob tricks Esau,[23] cheated Esau flabbergasts his little brother by his now-you-see-it-now-you-don't switch from murderous rival to empathetic twin.[24] Leah tricks Jacob,[25] Jacob tricks Laban,[26] Laban tricks Jacob,[27] Rachel tricks Laban with the household icons,[28] Simeon and Levi trick the Shechemites with their circumcision ruse,[29] Joseph's brothers trick Jacob with the coat of many colors,[30] Joseph befuddles his brothers with his Egyptian disguise and his sleight-of-hand planting of the chalice in Benjamin's grain sack.[31] The expected gets so consistently turned on its ear in the book that sets the trends for the Bible that the steady countercurrent of reversal looks more and more like the biblical mainstream. Bible narrative, when we look at what it actually says instead of what we thought it said last time we read it, upends expectations and overturns anticipations as frequently—and as humorously—as life does.

The insistence of that pattern of reversal is dramatized by the most fundamental motifs in Genesis—primogeniture, for example, the ancient tradition of double inheritance for the eldest. Cases contradicting that cultural norm multiply like rabbits. Younger sons in Genesis supplant their preferred brothers so commonly that even such a dramatic pea-under-the-walnut sleight-of-hand shift of inheritance as the one between

20. Gen 3:13–15.
21. Gen 45:5–8.
22. Gen 27.
23. Gen 25:29–34.
24. Gen 33.
25. Gen 29:21–25.
26. Gen 30:31–43.
27. Gen 29:26.
28. Gen 31:34–35.
29. Gen 34.
30. Gen 37:31–35.
31. Gen 44:1–13.

brothers Manasseh and Ephraim is not exceptional but typical. Over Joseph's emphatic objections, Grandpa "Israel stretched out his right hand, and laid it upon Ephraim's head, who was the younger, and his left hand upon Manasseh's head, guiding his hands wittingly; for Manasseh was the firstborn."[32] Thus Jacob, a younger son who himself finagled the birthright from his older brother, bequeaths the primogeniture blessing to his younger grandson—the son of his son Joseph, who is himself a younger son who managed to acquire his older brothers' birthright.

This intriguing reversal of the blessing is anything but a fluke: every single oldest son mentioned in Genesis—Ishmael,[33] Esau,[34] Reuben,[35] Manasseh,[36] Zarah[37]—gets bereft of both familial blessing and the anticipated double portion of birthright wealth. Even Leah, eldest daughter, is shunted out of line for the cultural right of marriage before her little sister.[38] That consistently surprising pattern of reversed primogeniture reflects a comprehensive paradox of biblical surprise, a pattern so widespread it becomes a biblical bottom-line moral: the Creator of the Universe cuts against the cosmic grain, the Ancient of Days disdains tradition, the Master of Everything roots for the lowliest underdog.

The New Testament is as inveterately inverting as the Old: "Comic reversals are to be found throughout Jesus' relationships."[39] Jesus's interaction with publicans and sinners and winebibbers[40] seemed so surprising to his culture that his anti-conventional behavior tipped the social order "topsy-turvy."[41] There's such persistent surprise in the Incarnation itself, with its kaleidoscopic permutations of human and divine, that the transcendent sometimes seems commonplace. Having met the Master of the Universe "among the animals, in a bed of straw, midst the scent of manure,"[42] we are not as surprised as his disciples must have been at his final Passover feast

32. Gen 48:14.

33. Gen 21:9–10.

34. Gen 27:34.

35. Gen 49:3–4.

36. Gen 48:9–14.

37. Gen 38:28–30.

38. Gen 29:23–26.

39. Hyers, *God Created Laughter*, 48.

40. Matt 9:11; Mark 2:16; Luke 7:34; Matt 11:10.

41. Ibid., 49.

42. Ibid., 56.

when he assumed the menial task traditionally assigned to servants, often slaves: washing none-too-fragrant feet, sweaty and grimy from dragging sandals through the dusty roads of Palestine.[43]

No wonder that "a major theme of the proclamation of Jesus was reversal."[44] No wonder we see again and again in his parables traditional expectations "turned upside down and radically questioned."[45] The Lord's teachings dramatize the unexpected as consistently as his life, so much so that Crossan sees these Jesus reversals as a summary of widespread Bible process. "If the last becomes first, we have the story of Joseph. If the first becomes last, we have the story of Job." But if "the last becomes first *and* the first becomes last we have a polar reversal,"[46] a reversal of everything—we have, ultimately and definitively, the story of Jesus. The New Testament as emphatically as the Old is grounded in "reversal of expectation and situation, of value and judgment."[47]

Esther, Queen of Reversals

The gyroscope of all that surprising narrative reversal revolves in a surprising place in the Bible: the book of *Esther*. *Esther*, dancing lightfootedly through its minuet of graceful comic turns and counterturns, competes with *Jonah* as funniest of biblical books. I second Adele Berlin's ranking of *Esther* high among "the most humorous of the books in the Bible, amusing throughout and at certain points uproariously funny."[48] People who have looked closely find the book so funny "Esther emerges as perhaps the clearest embodiment of the comic vision among all the biblical narratives."[49]

That humor is all the more witty for its subtle understatement. "The humor of the Bible is deadpan."[50] It sneaks up on you. In *Esther* the fun is muted so artfully as to amp up both the sneakiness and the funniness. The pomp and circumstance of this narrative disguises its comic dimensions: we are "lulled into dignity by the gravity of the style, awed into respect by

43. John 13:5–9.

44. Perrin, *New Testament Introduction*, 419.

45. Crossan, *Challenge of the Historical Jesus*, 65.

46. Ibid., 55.

47. Ibid., 68.

48. Berlin, *Esther*, xvii.

49. Whedbee, *Bible and the Comic Vision*, 171.

50. Samuel, "The Comic as Fool," 291.

the splendor of the setting."[51] But as we begin to catch the scent of court rhetoric, ripe with sound and fury and oratorical overkill, we are alerted to something rhetorically rotten in Denmark that taints these overblown statements, especially statements as officiously formal as "to destroy, to kill, and to cause to perish."[52]

That kind of exaggeration exceeds plausibility to the point of comedy. Seventy-five thousand enemies get knocked off without a single Jewish loss[53]—so much poetic justice we "discern in the casualty reports a continuation of the kind of hyperbole and macabre humor that run through the whole book."[54] Haman's inflated bribe amounts to an incredible ten thousand talents[55]—"two thirds the annual budget" of the opulent empire[56]—enough at current exchange rates to buy most of Central America. Incidental narrative details are stretched ludicrously: the six-month royal drinking binge,[57] the year-long beauty treatment of the queen contestants,[58] that gigantic impaling stake looming nearly eighty feet high[59]—gallows humor overkill by a factor of ten.

"It is difficult not to recognize the satire implied in this deliberately overblown enumeration."[60] All the more difficult when the endless lists of courtiers and ostentatious royal appurtenances seem to be poking fun not just at cumbersome state machinery but pompous language, "officialese" that can't help but "sound comical" in a narrative that "seeks to lampoon the pretensions of the Persian government."[61] Thus behind the "majestic facade" of Esther's setting lurks "invitation to mirth: a progressive mirth, developing from a startled and timid grin into a joyous chuckle to explode at last into a convulsion of the diaphragm."[62] Samuel is right that *Esther* humor grows on a reader; it may be an acquired taste. But even those of us

51. Samuel, "Comic as Fool," 292.

52. Esth 3:13.

53. Esth 9:16.

54. Whedbee, *Bible and the Comic Vision*, 184.

55. Esth 3:9.

56. Clines, "Esther," 391.

57. Esth 1:3–4.

58. Esth 2:12.

59. Esth 5:14.

60. Radday, "Esther with Humour," 312.

61. Levenson, *Esther: A Commentary*, 12.

62. Samuel, "Comic as Fool," 291.

who don't get to the laughing-out-loud point find it hard to read *Esther*—and almost impossible to read the book insightfully—without that grin.

The very situation of this romantic comedy plot sets us up for the humor of surprise: Who will win the First Annual Miss Persia Beauty Pageant? Will unassuming Esther, minion of bossy Uncle Mordecai, too unassertive to adorn herself with anything except what the king's chamberlain "appointed,"[63] so self-effacing as to disguise her own identity[64]—will this shy outsider somehow manage to catch the high society brass ring? Is there the slightest hope for readers on the edge of their seats that demure Esther might somehow inspire love at first sight in the roving royal eye of tall, dark, and has-some Ahasuerus?

Against all expectation—expectation piqued by Esther's tryout against the overwhelming odds of the well-oiled one-night stands of 256 other "fair young virgins"[65]—the king, astonishingly, "loved Esther above all the women."[66] Just how true and lasting that royal love is likely to prove for this prolifically promiscuous king we are not informed. But it's clear Esther has bested the competition. The humor of the situation is equally clear, notably in the wry irony of the king's selection of a royal partner (to say nothing of his intimate ultimate dream of true love) through the improbable means of a beauty contest in which the judge sleeps with the contestants.[67]

The context in which that plot is situated is similarly humor prone. *Misteh*, the term for feast in Hebrew, appears almost as many times in this brief book as in all the rest of the Hebrew Bible.[68] Revelry abounds everywhere we look in the narrative, revelry lubricated by remarkably heavy drinking. "Royal wine in abundance"[69] flows throughout the story; the king and his drinking buddies are "merry with wine"[70] more often than not. "And the drinking was according to the law,"[71] custom about as dignified as chugalug games at a frat party. Apparently each guest is expected to consume a minimum of wine, a ration so copious that rabbinical lore

63. Esth 2:15.

64. Esth 2:10.

65. Esth 2:3.

66. Esth 2:17.

67. Esth 2:13–14.

68. Meyers, "Esther," 326.

69. Esth 1:7.

70. Esth 1:10.

71. Esth 1:8.

claims "the guests used to tip the waiters not to denounce them if they cheated and drank a little less."[72]

Drunk Enough for Purim

It is in that emphasis on riotous celebration, with drunkenness as the key-note of the celebrating, that the relationship of the book of *Esther* to the Purim holiday becomes most apparent: this handbook for the celebration of Purim[73] is as dedicated to hilarity as the festival itself. Informed by a rabbi at my first Purim that I was "not drunk enough" to celebrate properly, I—a puritanic teetotaler whose unfortunate lips have never touched liquor—was bemused. But I understood the Purim spirit better after imbibing it directly from *Esther*. Craig nails precisely the tone of this guidebook to revelry: "carnivalesque."[74] The text—like the disorienting feast where it is read in its entirety to raucous accompaniment of cheers and jeers—revels in Mardi Gras topsy-turviness, the greatest political figure of the age dead drunk, the most sophisticated administration in the world partying so heartily for six full months that we've cause to wonder if anybody is left sober enough to run the realm.

"And watch those plot twists": Jewish "Esther wins Miss Persia contest" in erotic coup displacing the Persian first lady. "Sexy Jewess announces, 'If I perish, I perish,' and reveals secret of birth. Beauty queen becomes savior of her people. Evil scheme foiled, wicked Haman impaled on his own scaffold."[75] In an unprecedented reversal of fortunes, the entire exiled Jewish populace, in hundred-eighty-degree contrast to their long-standing historical role as victims, morph into vanquishers who triumph exultantly over brutal enemies. "The low social status of the Jewish protagonists is radically altered by the story's conclusion," altered so dramatically that "the initially powerless Jews attain great power with the denouement of the tale."[76] The bottom line of this comedic triumph is that everything can turn "to the contrary"[77]—the most grandiose villain could get his due, the lowliest worm turn.

72. Radday, "Esther with Humour," 296.

73. Esth 9:28.

74. Craig, *Case for the Literary Carnivalesque*, 30.

75. Ostriker, "World Turned Upside Down," 18.

76. Berg, *Esther: Motifs*, 105.

77. Esth 9:1.

Esther's author has an acute sense of irony of situation. The melodramatic villain of the book generates Rube Goldberg plans with the myopic single-mindedness of Wile E. Coyote, and those best-laid plans backfire as routinely as *beep-beeps* from the Roadrunner. Again and again archvillain Haman hatches extreme schemes that cut off the limb he's standing on—he erects the very gallows that will be the death of him,[78] proposes the precise means of honoring his detested enemy Mordecai,[79] boasts unabashedly and unabatedly to friends who are bound to *schadenfreude* savor his shame as soon as the page is turned.[80] He indulges triumphant pride in the invitation to Esther's dinner party that is to prove his downfall.[81] He manipulates—even goes so incomprehensibly far as to finance—a hoped-for holocaust of the Jews that results in the destruction of his own people.[82] He condemns himself to death by conniving to persuade the king to sign the death warrant of an enemy already condemned to impending genocide.[83] And, in his last desperate moments, Haman kneels before his Jewish nemesis Esther in dramatic counterpoint to the Jew Mordecai's refusal to kneel before him, his pathetic plea for his life misconstrued as, irony of ironies, a rape attempt.[84] Haman earns nomination as the all-time foiled villain. He comes close to qualifying for a *Darwin Award*.

The plot's central tension revolves around a whole series of reversals featuring that wonderfully wishy-washy sovereign Ahasuerus, whose written-in-stone decrees ("writing which is written in the king's name . . . may no man reverse")[85] bounce back and forth between Jewish and anti-Jewish fortunes like a ping-pong ball, first favoring Haman,[86] then backing Mordecai's faction,[87] approving Haman's decree,[88] then canceling it with Mordecai's memo.[89] For the most responsible man in the known world, the

78. Esth 7:9–10.

79. Esth 6:8–10.

80. Esth 5:10–11.

81. Esth 5:12.

82. Esth 3:8–9.

83. Esth 3:12–15.

84. Esth 7:8.

85. Esth 8:8.

86. Esth 3:10.

87. Esth 8:2.

88. Esth 3:12.

89. Esth 8:9.

Persian monarch is laughably impulsive. "The saying pleased the king"[90] is repeated so often it forms a litany of his vulnerability to any suggestion, no matter how outrageous, whether a royal plan for drunken revel or an empire-wide beauty contest to find a new wife or a plot to destroy an entire people. Considerable suspense accrues from the emperor's suggestibility, suspense revolving around the crucial narrative question: Which of those avid teams, Haman's or Mordecai's, will score the final royal ping-pong point?

This pinwheel king is a frank "caricature."[91] His name in Hebrew is *Ahashwerosh*, chief of rulers, but simultaneously and sidelong-glance onomatopoeically "something like King Headache in English."[92] The parodic impact of that jeering title and of his emperor's-new-clothes behavior is heightened by the glowering presence of historical Xerxes in all his colossal dignity looming behind these *National Lampoon* high jinks. The king as he appears in *Esther* is a masterpiece of indulgent impetuosity in his undisciplined appetite for immediate gratification, the opposite of authoritative in his willingness to do whatever he's told, the antithesis of regal in his eagerness to party.

His unkingly demeanor is epitomized by his reaction when Haman crosses his royal palm with no less than ten thousand talents for permission to destroy every Jew in the kingdom, a proposal justified on the outrageous grounds that the Jews refuse to assimilate[93]—the ludicrous insistence that immigrants to Persia should speak Persian, on pain of death. The blasé king doesn't check Haman's information, doesn't ask specifically what's been going down with these allegedly unlawful citizens, doesn't look into his minister's motivations for this drastic move, doesn't wonder why his officer offers so stupendous a bribe, doesn't deliberate on the moral implications of destroying an entire people, doesn't even consider the economic impact of the extermination. Ahasuerus doesn't so much as inquire what people is to be destroyed. On the spot, in the moment, sucked in by one of those deals that's only good for today, he does the last thing we would expect a competent monarch to do. He hands over to Haman his royal seal, a blank check to kill all Jews and, by the way, enable whatever other mayhem Haman's whim wishes to wreak upon the kingdom.

---

90. Esth 1:21; 2:4; 2:9.
91. Radday, "Esther with Humour," 295.
92. Ibid., 296.
93. Esth 3:8.

Turn, Turn, Turn, Turn

There are so many plot reversals that readers debate just where the story reaches its climax. Sandra Berg sees the major turning point as the crucial reversal at 4:13–14, when Mordecai calls Esther away from self-interest to her social responsibility.[94] Michael Fox thinks "the plot takes *its* sharpest turn in 6:10"[95] when Haman is ordered to shift his elaborate plans for honoring himself to Mordecai instead. Others consider the most meaningful plot turnabout 6:1, the rewarding-of-Mordecai scene that Levenson finds "the funniest of the book,"[96] when the king tries to cure his insomnia by reading the most boring thing he can think of, the history of Persia—which happens to be, come to think of it, exactly what we're reading. Yet others see the sea-change shift in the book where I think it is, at 4:16, where Esther throws caution to the winds with her life-threatening life-changing "if I perish, I perish." That definitive decision cartwheels the narrative and metamorphoses heroine Esther miraculously from a woman so diffident she conceals her identity to the proactive champion of her people.

Those insistent turnabouts in *Esther*'s overall narrative direction accumulate from incessant reversals of the fortunes of its individual characters. Haman is the most obvious sufferer of severe narrative setback, and the most ironic, hoist on his own petard as he so often is. Time and again "his wicked device, which he devised against the Jews" returns "upon his own head."[97] The king's savviest counselor consistently outsmarts himself, and the funniest thing about that is that he thinks he's so darn clever—"he would be mortified to be revealed as an impulsive bungler."[98] Yet in direct contradiction of his officially certified court smarts, after his triumphant promotion in chapter 3 Haman's whole life is a humiliation. "Everything Haman does is manifestly foolish."[99]

We love to see him get his comeuppance not just because he's nasty but because he's so proud of himself. Like an obnoxiously boastful brother-in-law, he enumerates *ad infinitum* his accomplishments to those who already know them only too well: "Haman told them of the glory of his

94. Berg, *Esther: Motifs* ,81.

95. Fox, *Character in Esther*, 162.

96. Levenson, *Esther Commentary*, 3.

97. Esth 9:25.

98. Fox, *Character in Esther*, 183.

99. Ibid.

riches, and the multitude of his children, and all the things wherein the king had promoted him"[100] and on and on and on. We relish observing how that fierce egotism about his accomplishments blinds him to his own limitations, setting up the inexorable poetic justice of his disappointment: "Now Haman thought in his heart, To whom would the king delight to do honour more than to myself?"[101]

This farsighted counselor's self-absorbed inability to see beyond his own nose is another jibe at the emperor's judgment; Haman's rampant egotism may rank him with Joseph Goebbels and Rasputin among history's most disastrous political ministers. We might feel some sympathy for some of the disaster if his obsessive self-serving didn't make it apparent he deserves whatever he gets. We relish the realization that he would have been wiser to make his proclamations sweeter in anticipation of having to eat his words. His unmitigated arrogance tempts us to chuckle with satisfaction even when he is unfairly blamed, after all his culpability in so many other matters, for a rape he didn't commit, didn't attempt, didn't plot, didn't even aspire to. There's such priggish pride before the fall of this officious official we can't help but delight in Haman's tumble from the pinnacle of Persian success to "become the laughingstock of the whole world."[102]

Every character in the book of *Esther* gets her or his life upended as emphatically as Haman's. Queen Vashti is unqueened, unceremoniously kicked off her throne.[103] In an impressive reversal of the passive role of a Persian woman, she refuses to obey her husband's orders to strut her stuff "with the crown royal"[104] in front of his drunken friends—the implication may be she's to wear *only* that crown. If that regal striptease is not funny, the "pure farce" reversal of that tragic reversal of fortunes is: "We observe that her punishment, never to come again before the king (1:19), is conceivably her dearest wish."[105] There is delicious irony not only in the escape from the obtuse king, but in the *denouement* of the story: the king's hottest mistress turns out to be a proto-feminist.

100. Esth 5:11.

101. Esth 6:6.

102. Laniak, *Honor in the Book of Esther,* 102.

103. Esth 1:19.

104. Esth 1:1.

105. Clines, "Esther," 389.

Mordecai's world, too, gets turned upside down, from sackcloth to riches, from the shadow of the gallows to ultimate power in the kingdom.[106] His Horatio Alger story becomes an even more drastic reversal if we see him initially not as a minor official in the kingdom but "simply one of the crowd of loungers who gather outside the palace gate."[107] There may be some mischievous irony in Mordecai's heroism, an "excessiveness about Mordecai's behavior."[108] "Had it not been for his obstinacy" in refusing to bow before Haman, an obeisance no more onerous for Jews than Joseph's brothers bowing before Joseph, "the Jews would never have been threatened with a pogrom."[109] The inadvertence makes it worse—Mordecai should have known better. That makes it poetically just that Esther's uncle has to save his people, he being the one who got them into trouble in the first place. Mordecai's bossiness of Esther and his ready conscription of his countrymen could even be tongue-in-cheek indications that Persia may be falling out of the frying pan of Haman's self-serving governance into the fire of Mordecai's ineptness.

Esther's Turnabout Is Fair Play

It is in our heroine Esther herself that the worm in this book most thoroughly turns, and her metamorphosis is most dramatic in her transformation from Persian harem seductress to Jewish messiah. The Esther of the early narrative is easy to criticize. She is subservient to anything in pants, whether her uncle or the king· "Esther is putty."[110] She is at the same time opportunistic, promoted to queen because she takes advantage of the fallout of Vashti's noble refusal of the king's demands by seducing the king. She is disloyal, breaking faith with her Jewishness in her refusal to divulge her ethnicity. She is in this and more kosher matters impious, failing to stand up for her cultural heritage, shamelessly unconcerned with Jewish observance. Her very popularity speaks against her, a popularity impossible among the Persians without some assimilative "'compromises,' in the

---

106. Esth 9:3–4.
107. Clines, "Esther," 388.
108. Ibid., 389.
109. Radday, "Esther with Humour," 302.
110. Fox, *Character in Esther*, 197.

area of religion"; she must have "eaten, dressed and lived like a Persian"—"a Judith or a Daniel could never have won the good will of all."[111]

She is, moreover, ambitious and self-serving. If we were making the movie in current terms, we might cast her as a rising Hollywood starlet played by someone like Reese Witherspoon in her lawyer mode, shark teeth glinting within the winsome smile. She is superficial, too, to the point of dumb-blonde laughability; she responds to Mordecai's sackcloth-and-ashes grief over the threatened pogrom of his people with the gauche offer of new clothes.[112] Thus Esther is tormented, like so many Old Testament heroic figures, by a complicating humanity. We wonder about her. Shouldn't she have refused to sleep with the king? Why did she not, given her obvious influence with the chamberlain,[113] sidestep Persian orgy in favor of Jewish righteousness?

Yet this malleable girl, midway through her self-serving career, out of the blue, manages mature moral will. This opportunistic woman suddenly develops a social conscience. It may be significant that Esther "has two names,"[114] Jewish *Hadassah* as well as Persian *Esther*. Her shadowy Jewish side, brought into the light of Persian public view in the second half of her story, makes for a more richly faceted character. Spurred by Mordecai to consider her obligation to her people, she initiates a fast,[115] the only explicitly religious moment in the entire book. It may not seem a momentous decision, but it's one that requires personal sacrifice. A three-day fast, however likely to make her more appealing to God, is certain to make her "less attractive to the king."[116]

Esther heroically proclaims "so will I go in unto the king,"[117] though that means flouting a law whose flouters are impaled on stakes littered throughout this narrative, "whosoever, whether man or woman."[118] She dares to risk finding favor with the fickle king, for an unlikely second time, and at a point when his favor has obviously focused elsewhere: "I have not

---

111. Moore, *Esther*, 28.

112. Esth 4:4.

113. Esth 2:8–9.

114. Meyers, "Esther," 324.

115. Esth 4:16.

116. Moore, *Esther*, 51.

117. Esth 4:16.

118. Esth 4:11.

been called to come into the king these thirty days."[119] In tones that can only bespeak mature realism and courage, so fiercely understated it hurts to hear the implications, she declares, "If I perish, I perish."[120] Lest we miss the point that Esther's character has undergone fundamental reversal, we are informed explicitly in the following verse that no longer does officious Uncle Mordecai direct Esther; rather, "Esther . . . commanded him."[121]

It's a remarkable shift. As a counterweight to Haman's doing everything wrong after his promotion, Esther is shown as henceforward doing everything right. "She acts with great wisdom—in fact, she is the only person in the story to do so,"[122] including even Mordecai. The cleverest of manipulations are required of Esther to save her people. Her persuasive speech to the king is a particular masterpiece of rhetorical subtlety, from do-you-love-me appeal ("if I have found favor in thy sight") through gripping revelation (of the death threat) to an ingratiating cry for help (I wouldn't bother the king with these matters if it were a mere matter of slavery: only genocide warrants my troubling your all-important self).[123] This once-opportunistic woman is now so principled she passes up repeated offers of "half of the kingdom."[124] Her transformation from sycophant to sovereign is total: "Esther's personality has evolved into the near-opposite of what it was at the start. Once sweet and compliant, she is now steely."[125]

Esther's reversal of fortune at the heart of the narrative upheavals in her book highlight the central theme of *Esther*. The concealed is now revealed. But we can't see it—we are left tantalizingly in the dark about Mordecai's motivations for charging Esther not to reveal "her people nor her kindred."[126] Is this just good Persian political tactics, aimed at increasing her queenly chances? Is Mordecai anticipating Esther's future usefulness to her people? Are we being shown the tension between the young woman's loyalty to her culture and her personal ambition? Is it being suggested that deception is a necessary means to the best ends? Whatever those beguilingly undisclosed motivations for concealing and revealing, they clearly matter,

119. Esth 4:11.

120. Esth 4:16.

121. Esth 4:17.

122. Radday, "Esther with Humour," 305.

123. Esth 7:3–4.

124. Esth 5:3, 6; 7:2.

125. Fox, *Character in Esther*, 203.

126. Esth 2:10.

narratively and thematically. The bottom line of the story is ambiguously clear: in Hebrew *hester* means "concealment."[127]

Turned On, Tuned In

Esther's reversals, Vashti's upheavals, Mordecai's machinations, Haman's schemings, Ahasuerus's capricious mood swings accumulate such impetus they turn the Persian world upside down. Those narrative turnabouts are stressed by *Esther* imagery, where we see two dramatic fasts strategically placed amid the perpetual feastings of Persia.[128] They are dramatized in the story's milieu by the contrast of Jewish simplicity set against Persian sophistication. The reversals are underlined more deeply at structural levels, where "Haman's rise and fall in the first five chapters is neatly matched by Mordecai's fall and rise in the last five."[129] Radday takes that so far as to surmise that "the writer took great pleasure in this private kind of humour," setting Haman's triumph carefully in the center of the first half, then placing Mordecai's ascendancy in the "exact middle"—Radday counts the verses—of the second part. The book's overall structure is so symmetrical that this precise critic sees large-scale parallelism in the plot, a narrative seesaw where every rise in the story line predicts a downfall, every descent anticipates a resurgent upswing.

So at the end we have neatly come "full circle and are back at the beginning! Ahasuerus is at a banquet; he has been drinking; he has been affronted; he is angry."[130] Only the characters have changed: instead of Vashti under royal duress we have Haman, and with that shift the cosmos is inverted. This time the imposing imperial machinery that was earlier indulged to "round up virgins for the king" is marshaled disastrously to "slaughter the Jews. It is an ingenious contrast, which teaches us something about the diverse uses of power in the hands of a fool."[131]

There is a plethora of that monkeyshines mismanagement in the book of *Esther*. Perhaps the most humorously perceptive is the inanity of male insistences that they rule the roost. Persian princes wring their hands over the Vashti rebellion lest "this deed of the queen shall come abroad unto

---

127. Radday, "Esther with Humour," 300.

128. Larkin, *Ruth and Esther*, 97.

129. Radday, "Esther with Humour," 311.

130. Samuel, "Comic as Fool," 306.

131. Ibid., 299.

all women, so that they shall despise their husbands."[132] There is surely sly smiling in this misfired *Taming of the Shrew* at the precariousness of male dominance: "the personal has become the political, and both have become laughable."[133] The royal council called to deal with Queen Vashti's insubordination arrives after convoluted debate at an apparently straight-faced solution, ponderously proclaiming throughout the kingdom that "Every man should bear rule in his own house."[134]

The delightful thing about that cornball edict is the television-sitcom situation that necessitates it. No Persian male does in fact bear rule—not Ahasuerus, who is outmanned by Vashti and outmaneuvered by Esther; not Haman, who breaks his own law and ruins his life by listening to the advice of his wife; not even Mordecai, whose pontifical directives to his niece give way to directions from her. Only women in this story are maturely self-actualized. Vashti as she exits stage left declares her independence with dignity; Esther, so compliant as a girl, ends up schooling wise Mordecai, Machiavellian Haman, mighty Ahasuerus, in fact the entire Persian population, most impressively its most macho males.

Radday may overstate that "the author has nothing but contempt for males," but there is in the book of *Esther* a definite "pro-female bias."[135] *Esther*'s author is "very much aware that males, at least in the quirky gentile world, must use political power to enforce their position—and even so they do not really succeed."[136] It isn't enough that Persian males fail to win the gender race. They don't even get out of the starting chute. Things have come to a pretty pass, and a pretty funny one, when wifely nagging gets so bad it is "treated as a capital crime,"[137] and when one woman's refusal to bow down to male dominance "threatens to collapse the entire structure of patriarchy in the entire Persian empire. So much for indomitable patriarchy."[138]

That chortling reversal of gender power embeds at yet another level the underlying moral of this amusing story. As everywhere else in the Bible—David against Goliath, Moses confronting Pharaoh, Samson taking on the entire cohort of Philistines—underdogs succeed in *Esther*, and arrogance

---

132. Esth 1:17.

133. Levenson, *Esther Commentary*, 54.

134. Esth 1:22.

135. Radday, "Esther with Humour," 309.

136. Fox, *Character in Esther*, 209.

137. Samuel, "Comic as Fool," 298.

138. Fewell, "Feminist Reading of the Hebrew Bible," 84.

consistently gets its comeuppance: "Many that are first shall be last; and the last shall be first."[139] *Esther* ranks high among the most maligned books of the Bible, beats out even the too-sexy Song of Songs and the too-crabby Ecclesiastes as the Bible book whose canonical status is most consistently questioned. There is strong sentiment in a lot of religious camps—sentiment that casts a cold eye on anything approaching the humorous—that the book is too secular to be appropriate for the Bible.

Disapproving theological fingers have long been pointed at *Esther* as the only book in the Hebrew Bible that fails to mention God. "The king of Persia," on the gratuitously secular other hand, "is mentioned 190 times in 167 verses."[140] Rabbis have traditionally looked down their noses so critically at the book's blatant unbiblical refusal to discuss God that the additions to *Esther* in the Greek version go way out of their way to correct the omission, throwing in references to deity not just wherever it's possible, but sometimes where it isn't. Scathing indictment of the book comes from other directions as well—some readers find *Esther*'s moral failings as severe as its failure to properly reverence deity: "There is not one noble character in this book."[141] Some readers find it hard to find anything whatsoever worthwhile in the volume: "love, kindness, mercy, and forgiveness are also conspicuously missing."[142]

Almost everybody is critical of the frivolousness of the text, left as much as right, across the board. Feminists have found in *Esther*, surprisingly enough in the face of what looks like its persistent female dominance, "full compliance with patriarchy."[143] An even more amazing criticism of a tale this penetrating is that some see it as shallow to the point of being boring: "Characters are so superficially drawn that it is difficult to identify very long or intensively with either the book's villains or heroes."[144] Morally rabid readers go so far as to find it disgusting. Dozens of early commentators thought the book should never have been included in the canon, and Martin Luther declared himself so "hostile" to *Esther* that he not only wanted it kicked out of the Bible but wished "it did not exist."[145]

139. Matt 19:30.

140. Moore, *Esther*, xxxii.

141. Paton, *Commentary on the Book of Esther*, 96.

142. Moore, *Esther*, xxxii.

143. Laffey, *Old Testament: A Feminist Perspective*, 216.

144. Moore, *Esther*, liii.

145. Paton, *Commentary on the Book of Esther*, 96.

High Seriousness

Those are serious criticisms. They're so serious it makes one wonder whether the seriousness might be the problem. Perhaps we would see more in *Esther* if we read it more in terms of its own scintillating lights than on our duller traditional terms. Perhaps we need to recognize its humor. If we did, we might find surprises in this lively narrative, might discover more in it, maybe more insight, more perhaps about ourselves—possibly, even, more about God. If we were able to "enjoy the comedy,"[146] we might see more in such ironic moments as Haman's triggering the loss of his life by attempting to save it.[147] To Haman, of course, as with our own disasters to us, "it is anything but funny."[148] But our nervous laughter at his discomfiture may be a window into a better understanding of how egocentricism can undermine our own best interests.

That sort of introspectiveness runs deep in the book's humor. Though *Esther* has been criticized for its Jewish chauvinism—its "judaizing" was Luther's major objection to the book—some of the author's subtlest insights border on satire of Jews themselves. The portrait of Mordecai's obtuse pride suggests a less-than-reverent attitude toward pious Jews. At the same time, at the opposite pole, the readiness of Esther to assimilate seems to critique failure of loyalty to the culture. At the same time, on the other hand, the compromise between nationalism and ethnic loyalty is cast in question by the very names of Esther and Mordecai, suspiciously echoic of the Persian gods *Ishtar* and *Marduk*. The narrator seems at times so honestly self-analytical as to wonder whether being Jewish is an unmixed blessing; he is, for instance, "far from rejoicing in this increase of the number of Jews by proselytes."[149]

That humbling of the haughty—especially when that's us, the privileged, the orthodox—in reciprocal concert with the encouraging of the humble, informs the lighthearted thesis underwriting the serious implications of the laughter in the book of *Esther*: the story "hath put down the mighty from their seats, and exalted them of low degree."[150] Championing the underdog is clearly the bottom line of this good book, but the

---

146. Berlin, *Poetics and Biblical Narrative*, 54.

147. Esth 7:7–8.

148. Berlin, *Poetics and Biblical Narrative*, 54.

149. Radday, "Esther with Humour," 309.

150. Luke 1:52.

humorous resonances of that moral raise more questions than they resolve. Esther's climb from lowlife underdog to top of the high-society heap is so unconventional we cannot help but wonder how flawed—how ambitious and nonconforming—a savior can be and still save. The book "raises the question of whether a person of dubious character strength and (initially) unclear self-definition can carry the burden of national salvation."[151] Esther is clearly limited, as we are; she is just as clearly successful, as successful as we would like to be. Her unlikely triumph suggests there may be more than humor in the human reality of her narrative. There may be hope—even for the none-too-religious. If Esther can do it, we might. "Her very ordinariness suggests that ordinary people too can rise to the moment and take on unexpected strengths."[152]

The most telling turning "to the contrary" in *Esther* may be in its paradoxical theology. Despite adamant refusal to refer to God, the book faithfully reflects the most essential aspects of the most characteristic Jewish narratives. Larkin, who has her hesitations about *Esther*, nonetheless posits that the book may be modeled on Exodus because it "contains all its essential features":[153] the foreign court intrigues, the death threat to the Jews, the deliverance and the revenge, the establishing of a festival, the heroes' parallel adoptions, their shared secretiveness, their frequent intercessions with monarchs to save their people. The *Esther* text shares enough of those same essential elements with the Joseph saga and the Jacob epic and the David annals, too, to certify itself as a clear instance of Hebrew Bible underdog motif, with its recurrent assurance that God will champion his people, standing by them in their worst of times, succoring their most desperate needs.

Thus the lighthearted comic reversals of the volume may ultimately convey, as Fox suggests, "a particular worldview."[154] In Mieke Bal's antiestablishment terms, "obedience has been revealed as the wrong attitude."[155] That is why humor-inspired hope may be the essence of the smiling insights of the book of *Esther*. We are told here, not for the first but perhaps for the funniest time in the Old Testament, not to settle for things as they are. Conditions change, situations shift, stability doesn't last. Rocks, even rocks

151. Fox, *Character in Esther*, 205.

152. Ibid.

153. Larkin, *Ruth and Esther*, 89.

154. Fox, *Character in Esther*, 158.

155. Bal, "Lots of Writing," 238.

of ages, erode. We are never secure. But neither are we ever done for. There is at least as much room for hope in our ongoing lives as there is reason for fear. Character, and particularly that dimension of it that most matters to Hebrew culture—moral stature—is never an accomplished fact, but it is never ever wholly beyond human possibility.

That may answer the most persistent question about the book of *Esther*: Where is God here? A kind of never-say-die religious tenaciousness makes the God who is never mentioned in *Esther* very much present. He is present not merely peripherally, by implication in the fasting and religious feasting, in the sense of providence, in the miraculous salvation of the good guys. He is present centrally, at the core of the book's concerns. When we wonder where God is between the lines of Esther's narrative, we are doing precisely what the writer invites us to do, reading God into the text. This artful author is in the same breath inviting us to do the same reading-in of God in our own lives: "He is teaching a theology of possibility."[156] *Teaching* is too pompous a term. The writer of *Esther* is cajoling by gentle joke, suggesting by artful surprise that anything might be possible. The amused theology of *Esther* here reflects Yogi Berra's immortal mortal insight—it's not over til it's over. There is always, in the infinite economy of God, hope that things—all things, the worst things and even the best things—could change for the better.

It's obvious *Esther* can be read many ways, and not just because we just have. One ingenious reader sees it as "historical" narrative competing with "burlesque."[157] Another reads it as both "wisdom" and "heroic tale,"[158] another as "farce" and "satire,"[159] another as "travesty," "romance," and "fablioux,"[160] yet another as "folklore," "caricature," and "carnivalesque story."[161] Those competing readings are manifestly paradoxical. Seen as carnivalesque, the story of Esther "reifies power relationships" in society.[162] Seen as satire, it serves to undermine those very relationships. Read as wisdom literature, "the central protagonist—Esther—should provide

---

156. Fox, *Character in Esther*, 247.

157. Berlin, "Book of Esther and Ancient Storytelling," 7.

158. McGeough, "Esther the Hero," 53, 64.

159. Levenson, *Esther Commentary*, 12.

160. Sasson, "Esther," 339.

161. Craig, *Esther Carnivalesque*, 32, 40, 41.

162. Ibid., 40.

the model for emulation." Read as heroic tale, *Esther* "breaks the rules of behavior."[163]

The significance of that responsive flexibility of interpretation may be more important than the fact of it. Almost all of those competing eye-opening ways that *Esther* has been recently read revolve around humor. Whatever else this small masterpiece may be, "Esther is very comic."[164] "The comic potential of the story is richly exploited, and laughter at human vanity, gall, and blindness becomes the vehicle by which the writer gives his tale integrity and moral vision."[165] That moral vision, grounded as it is in humor, gives us readerly options. We can read this biblical text as we've always read it: dully, unimaginatively, narrowly, condescendingly, suspiciously. Or we can read it as it is written.

Comic reversal in *Esther* accumulates to something close to cosmic. In the overweening officiousness of its courtly Persian idiom—"thus it is written," irreversibly—things will and should be always as they are. But the lively and delightful humorous reversals of *Esther* reveal, as do the real ups and downs of our own lives, that there is always a chance for something better. That possibility encourages the taking of risks, even against the greatest odds. It is no accident that the narrative movement of the book of *Esther* pivots upon an axis of gambling, revolves around the casting of dice,[166] around whether the Jews or the Persians will prove unlucky on the thirteenth of Adar,[167] around those high-risk chances taken by its heroine when she hazards the rest of her life in servile exile in the king's harem against the outside chance of a queendom,[168] when she risks her lovely neck to try to save her people.[169]

Life's like that, *Esther* is saying: no guts, no glory. Just so with our Bible reading. This compelling little book insists in its every lively reversal that our reading, like *Esther*, is at its best not when it is seeking security but when it is taking chances. *Esther* trains us to explore possibilities. *Esther* urges us to look for opportunity in the direst circumstance, to wonder, when things look worst, "who knoweth whether thou art come to the kingdom for such

163. McGeough, "Esther the Hero," 53, 64.

164. Trible, "Esther," 7.

165. Sasson, "Esther," 339.

166. Esth 3:7.

167. Esth 9:17.

168. Esth 2:14.

169. Esth 4:16.

a time as this?"[170] Who knows whether our lives, too, given more risk, given more openness to the possibilities of surprise, given more Esther disposition to seize the day, may yet, in our most desperate straits, be turned like all comedy "to the contrary," be turned "from sorrow to joy, and from mourning into a good day."[171]

170. Esth 4:14.
171. Esth 9:22.

4

Eve's Initiative, Sarah's Sassiness, and Jael's Nail

Humor as Social Justice

"WHY CAN'T A WOMAN," wonders Professor Henry Higgins wistfully in *My Fair Lady*, "be more like a man?":

> She will beg you for advice,
> Your reply will be concise,
> And she'll listen very nicely,
> Then go out and do precisely
> What she wants.[1]

That upstart *Fair Lady* Eliza Doolittle is far from the first lady to upset masculine expectations. The tradition of the woman with a mind of her own, the woman who does what she wants in the face of the most formidable male bluster, stretches sturdily throughout the Western literary tradition—back as far as Lear's disrespectful daughter Cordelia, way back to the irascible Wife of Bath. It's a longstanding tradition: the woman with a mind of her own; the woman who does precisely what she wants.

---

1. Lerner, *My Fair Lady*, 1964.

Where Have All the Women Gone?

The Old Testament has been so frequently held up as a standard of patriarchal prerogative for browbeating uppity women into their expected place that it may come as something of a cultural shock to observe that the Hebrew Bible, that most venerable bastion of entrenched masculine authority, features what could be the earliest prototypes of the strong-willed woman. What's really shocking is we seem not to have noticed. We have somehow managed to miss these Bible women with minds of their own, not just prevalent but striking biblical examples of women insistently doing their own thing—being real, natural enough and earthy enough to be feisty and funny. We have underestimated the fierce independence of these fine Old Testament females so completely that we have overlooked the women themselves.

That blind spot toward Bible women looms large among even the best of readers—some feminists, of all people, have all but decided to throw out the entire Bible on grounds of non-participation of women. It's not hard to see their point: less than half as many women as men qualify for mention in the book, and even among those the Bible bothers to notice, many don't so much as merit their own names; they're relegated to dismissive patriarchal relationship tags like "the wife of Manoah"[2] or "the daughter of Jephthah."[3] And even among the elite who lay claim to a personal name, many biblical females display a brand of femininity that advertises the kind of woman who might, in a pinch, stoop to tricking a man into marrying her by pretending to be her prettier sister,[4] or claim she's menstruating in order to frustrate her father's search for the sacred idols she stole from him,[5] or covet children so desperately she'd order her husband into bed with her sultry young Egyptian handmaiden.[6]

And that's just the major matrons—Sarah, Rachel, Leah. When we read down as far as the supporting cast, the playlist of biblical women gets seriously compromised. Tamar sells her sexual services by the roadside to her own father-in-law.[7] The "serpentine . . . destroyer"[8] Rahab is

2. Judg 13:11.

3. Judg 11:40.

4. Gen 29:25.

5. Gen 31:34–35.

6. Gen 16:2.

7. Gen 38:14–18.

8. Miles, *Biography of God*, 45.

recommended to readers by two major skills: prostitution and prevarication.[9] Apocryphal Judith unceremoniously hacks off her host's head on a date because he's contemplating getting friendly with her.[10] It's so hard to see such biblical women as any way admirable that it may be hard to see them at all. Such dubious characters sink so low as feminine role models we can hardly blame anyone, let alone feminists, for overlooking them, or even deliberately ignoring them.

It's not difficult to comprehend how political concerns could fashion gender blinders thick enough to obscure the most obvious biblical examples of dynamic females. Given the constraining ideological lenses some readers have to look through, misreading of biblical women is understandable. It's harder to understand how a religious perspective, let alone a Christian one, could fail to notice how crucial women are to biblical narrative—how pivotal, how proactive, how creatively productive women are in the Bible, their presence every way significant. Hard to imagine how Christians manage to miss the many women who grace this faithful text, harder to fathom how they fail to appreciate how much women contribute to the biblical story, how much they matter.

There are more women in the Bible than we have realized. All of us, Christians and feminists included, might see more of them and more in them if we looked closer. We might at least notice they're there. We might, as a bonus for keeping our eyes halfway open as we're reading women in the Bible, come to appreciate how significantly they impact Scripture. We might be more alert to who it is that initiates the crucial action in the Bible, and more particularly pick up on who is shaping the key events in such pivotal historical books as Genesis and Judges. This ancient text has been crying in the wilderness of gender misconception for millennia, insisting that women matter. It may be time we listened. Awareness of the ways women in reality appear in the Bible might shake up our habitual readings enough to help us see biblical women not in terms of the roles we think they should be playing, but as they actually are. Attention to those realistic aspects, the earthily human and hence potentially humorous dimensions of biblical narrative, can help us appreciate how significantly women shape what happens in the Bible.

9. Josh 2.
10. Jdt 12–13.

Selective Seeing

A direct look at Old Testament women, not slanted through the lens of our usual biases—Christianity or feminism or whatever other predispositions we bring to this traditional text—might reveal a lot more than we're used to seeing. I asked my local Sunday school group, readers who know the Bible well, to list as many Old Testament women as they could remember. They averaged seven. The actual count of named women in the Bible approaches two hundred, and more than twice that many are referred to.[11] That dismal level of attentiveness may account for our skeptical reaction to news of women in the Bible—to say nothing of women who display any indications of life, to say nothing of any intimations any females might be presented realistically, to say nothing of any hint that any woman could show any sign of any capacity for humor. We respond to reports of women in the Bible as we would to rumors of leprechauns at Walmart—not so much from surprise at what they're doing as from shock that there are any.

The unlikely rumors nevertheless turn out to be true. There *are* women in the Old Testament. There are, in fact, so many vital women that given how long some of us have been reading the Bible, the wonder is how thoroughly we've failed to notice them, to credit them, to see them as real women who actually matter in the biblical narrative. Maybe that's the problem with our reading of Bible women. Maybe we've known them too long. Maybe our very familiarity with Bible characters has bred contempt, or at least a sense we no longer need to notice because we've been there, seen that. Maybe the reason we can look right at the Bible and fail to see the women who are right before us in its very pages is we already know too assuredly what is in it, or what we assume to be there, what we thought was there last time we looked.

Maybe the Bible is so much a part of our culture that we don't even have to read it to be convinced we've read enough of it. Some of us know the book intimately without actually knowing what it says. The Bible is so significant a source of cultural values that it's possible to be convinced it speaks our theology before we even read it. It's not only possible but common to read it as proof text for what is already known, to read biblical text not to discover but to confirm belief. It's even possible for determined readers to train themselves through that kind of knee-jerk reading to react to the Bible the way Pavlov's dog was trained to salivate when the bell

11. Achtemeier, "Women," 807.

rang—to respond automatically with habitual personal theology no matter what the Bible is saying.

That tendency to overlook actual biblical content is compounded by the fact that many well-trained readers of the Bible learn not only their version of its theological implications but its textual details before actually reading them, sometimes without ever reading them. Most Bible readers, in fact, know before they are old enough to read who Eve is, and probably Sarah, possibly even Rachel and Leah. People of the book, dedicated Bible-reading cultures, know not only who Moses is, but his sister Miriam, maybe his wife Zipporah, maybe even his mother, Jochebed. We get so much of the Bible by cultural osmosis that when we get around to reading it we some-times see not what is actually on its pages, but what we've already absorbed about it. Commendable as our familiarity may be, what we already know of the Bible may make us miss some of what it really says, may make us miss most of what it says about women. Next to the women themselves, what we most readily miss about Bible women is their earthy realism. And what we most miss about their realistic actuality is their humor.

If it seems improbable anyone could look at a page of Scripture and fail to see the women who are in it, let's take a direct look at the phenom-enon of the phantom Bible female as witnessed by certified first-class Bible readers. When I was writing Bible lessons for a Christian women's group, our committee proposed a lesson on patriarchal government in the fam-ily, using the relationship of Abraham and Sarah as example of the best of all possible marriages. I was enthusiastic. I like Abraham a lot, and Sarah rather better, and I think the Bible describes a working relationship in their marriage worthy in every way of emulation. But it soon became apparent that though we were looking at the same Bible passage, we weren't seeing the same marriage. The essential point our committee wanted stressed was that the biblical husband is in charge in the family. The model of marriage they planned to present in the lesson was a relationship where husbands decree, wives obey: like Sarah.

Sarah's Sassiness

When I laughed because I thought that not at all like Sarah in the Bible, my fellow writers were dumbstruck by my reading of Sarah as anything but domestically submissive. They made it painfully clear that what I was seeing in Genesis wasn't there, was never there, could never be there—"If

Abraham, the greatest of patriarchs, won't do as a model of patriarchy, who will?" I've deep respect for those lesson writers as readers. They are faithful readers, dedicated readers, informed readers, textually expert readers. They have read the Sarah passages multiple times, read them painstakingly, read carefully and thoroughly. Yet these superb readers were failing, from my perspective, to see what was right there in Genesis about women. It seemed to me from looking at the Bible itself that if we were to insist upon Sarah and Abraham's marriage as a model for our idea of patriarchy, we needed to reexamine just what patriarchy is, what it looks like in actual biblical practice.

Some Bible readers are doing that. We're starting to notice that "Christianity has a long history of sex bias," beginning to realize that slanted reading of the Bible looms large "at the center of this cultural bias."[12] The central problem in that general misreading of biblical women seems to be a "Give Me That Old Time Religion" disposition to read the Bible as we have always read it, which lures us into thinking that's the way it has always been read, however inconsistent that reading may be with what it actually says. "Research on religion and sexism increasingly points to fundamentalism," with its rigidly traditionalist reading, "as an important religious source of prejudice toward women."[13]

The implication shouting from such unfortunate data is that readers who aren't reading at all well—in a surprising number of cases not reading at all—may be hijacking the Old Testament to support profound prejudice against women. That's doubly ironic in light of the inconvenient fact that gender hierarchies don't come into serious play in the Bible until late in the New Testament. It wasn't until then that "political power struggles for control of ecclesiastical districts (cf. 3 John) led to the formation of a male hierarchy in the church that often continues to this day."[14] It's triply ironic that those conventional hierarchies continue "in opposition to the witness of much of the Bible."[15]

It takes some determined misreading, requires reading with a severe lack of a sense of humor, to read the Hebrew Bible as repressive toward women. Not that there isn't a depressingly long list of brutalizing mistreatments of women in the Bible, including such horrific examples as Lot's

12. Peek, "Fundamentalism and Sexism," 1207.

13. Ibid., 1205.

14. Achtemeier, "Women," 807.

15. Ibid.

reprehensible offering of his daughters to the lusts of the Sodomites,[16] or Jephthah's stony-hearted sacrifice of his daughter to his rash vow,[17] or the Levite's callously allowing the murderous gang rape of his concubine.[18] But even "those pre-exilic stories in the Bible that exhibit cruelty toward women and treat them as objects of degradation reflect the environment in which Israel lived and are intended as protests against it."[19] It should be obvious to the most hardhearted and hardheaded reader that scenarios this pointedly vicious can hardly be recommending such specious behavior.

The Hebrew Bible is clearly less misogynistic than some of its readers. When read as it is, rather than as some readers think it ought to be read, the Bible never demeans women. Nor does it subordinate women nearly so much as certain readers might like. It's quite clear that "if marriage had been a repressive relationship for the woman" in Hebrew culture, there could hardly have developed a social situation where the "marital relationship was so prized that it could serve as a metaphor of the love between God and his covenant people."[20] Bartowski's studies of the debate among conservative Protestants about "traditional patriarchy" indicate that several of the writers who argue against a patriarchal model for modern marriage cite examples of women like Sarah. "Many of these authors seek to buttress this criticism of 'husband-headship' in the home by pointing to women in the Bible who exercised leadership and authority"[21]—from Sarah's centering of the Old Testament family to Phoebe's CEO work in the early church, plus a sturdy cohort of matriarchs that includes some of our most senior and respected elders, revered women like Rebecca and Rachel and Miriam and Deborah and Esther and Ruth and Mary and Mary Magdalene and the redoubtable Eve.

To reconsider our view of women in the Bible—even to notice them— will require reading realistically, reading more responsively, seeing what is actually present on the biblical page. Nowhere is reader responsiveness more crucial nor more challenging than in discerning the humor that backlights the significance of women in the text. It's not just that modern readers assiduously avoid anything in the Bible tending in the direction of

16. Gen 19.
17. Judg 11.
18. Judg 19.
19. Achtemeier, "Women," 806.
20. Ibid.
21. Bartowski, "Debating Patriarchy," 406.

the humorous with a paranoid closing of the eyes to the slightest possibility of any hint of levity that might taint our ingrained and well-trained pious respect for what is perceived as the volume's severity. It's not only that we approach Bible humor in general with the nervous reluctance of three-year-olds checking for monsters under the bed. Chronic aversion to Bible humor becomes acute when it comes to women. That is a serious readerly handicap. In many biblical scenarios—dramatically, for instance, in the case of the relationship of Abraham and Sarah—humor can be key not only to subtle shadings of tone, but to the essential meaning of the narrative.

Henpecked Patriarchy

When we attend to what is really in the Bible, when we listen to what Genesis actually says, Abraham doesn't sound much like the macho master of Sarah. Disposed as we are to read the marriage narratives of the Old Testament as if they were the formal notes of a church committee, we tend to be tone deaf to the wry gender humor they persistently display. When Genesis 16 is read aloud as it speaks itself, in as female a voice as we're up to, a female voice with a sense of humor, as sassy a Sarah sort of voice as we can manage, the text itself manages very well to convey the peremptory tone of Sarah's audacious and assured orders: "And Sarai said unto Abram, Behold now, the Lord hath restrained me from bearing: I pray thee, go in unto my maid; it may be that I may obtain children by her."[22] She makes it clear who is in charge in the childlessness crisis. She makes it clear who will have custody of the child. The determination that filters through Sarah's tight-throated "that I may obtain children" makes pretty clear who's directing this scene.

And how does prime patriarch Abraham, master of his male-centered household, lord of the Israelite manor, respond? "And Abram hearkened to the voice of Sarai."[23] Abraham in this representative Bible passage doesn't come off like the stereotypical dominating Middle-Eastern male, doesn't sound at all like the insensitive representative of repressive patriarchy. He sounds more like Mr. Rogers. He responds to his wife, however subordinate her social position, with a ready deference more suggestive of a butler than of a baron. Any domestic partners of the female persuasion inclined to scoff at the possibility of any sort of male yielding his authority under any

22. Gen 16:2.
23. Gen 16:2.

circumstances should notice that the patriarch actually minds his wife—his deference here is not mere verbal assent, the kind of "yes dear" avoidance of conflict that characteristically terminates most masculine action at this sort of gender juncture. Abraham does exactly what his wife asks, even though what Sarah asks is shocking for us and may well have been a stretch for an aged patriarch: "And he went in unto Hagar, and she conceived."[24]

It doesn't get in the way of either Abraham's readiness for the project or the inherent humor of the situation that Hagar is young and quite likely exotically Egyptian good-looking. And it certainly complicates the comic-opera conflict that Sarah may be playing that traditional wifely "don't do what I say, do what I want" card. Sarah might well be miffed, having hoped her hubby would reject her gracious offer of cohabitation with a younger woman, especially since the entire project aims at progeny for him. Still and all, Abraham, we're told quite clearly here, does what Sarah directs—if not nags—if not orders—him to do. That's made clear by the unequivocal fact that her unworkable family strategy, whatever its unintended conse-quences, works: Hagar gets undeniably pregnant. The wife demands, the husband complies. Female initiative blooms into full fruition.

And then, despite those best-laid plans, everything goes south. Suddenly no one, particularly the prime proposer of the plan, is so sure that it's altogether a good idea that Hagar is pregnant, particularly by Abraham. Things go directly to hell in a domestic handbasket, just as we longsuffer-ing husbands in the audience worried they would if marital well-enough weren't left alone: "And when [Hagar] saw that she had conceived, her mistress was despised in her eyes. And Sarai said unto Abram, My wrong be upon thee."[25]

We're thousands of years from the cultural context here, so have scant notion of whether the slave Hagar may be overstepping her subordinate role, talking back to a social superior—in the case of outspoken Sarah, a stern superior it is obviously not wise to sass. Or whether the servant is simply looking down with irksome self-satisfaction on a less successful competitor in a world where childbearing is such valuable social capital. Or whether the matron is seeing the pregnancy as inherent insult, both to her and to her tribal standing. What we do know is that Hagar the Egyptian sexpot somehow reminds aging Sarah of her relative fruitlessness, perhaps with no more than a smug glance or self-satisfied pat of her bulging belly.

24. Gen 16:4.
25. Gen 16:4.

Even though Sarah as matron of the clan has traditional claim to inherit the child for herself, surrogate motherhood doesn't change the frustrating fact that inconsequential Hagar can have a baby and her mistress, for all her social superiority, can't. Worse, the source of the childlessness so long afflicting the family is now clearly diagnosed—it's Sarah's fault, not Abraham's.

So the joke's on chortling Sarah, she who feels free to laugh at authorities, even when they're fertility experts, even when they're angels. The culture's extreme cure for matriarchal infertility—a surrogate concubine—proves for Sarah worse than the disease. It's probably cold comfort for the clan matriarch that it is not unprecedented for a childless wife, in order to forestall her replacement by another wife, to "give her own personal slave to her husband to bear the children"[26]—desperate measures, and humiliating measures for one who holds her head so high as noble Sarah. Meanwhile Abraham's hands, the very hands that just fooled around with the nubile maid, remain exasperatingly clean, at least legally. He conforms dutifully to his wife's directions, and still gets to father a child with a more fecund woman. The annoying fact that Abraham on top of everything else gets to be the good guy in these marital aberrations can't make Sarah's harrowing sacrifices of herself for her family any less frustrating for her, nor any less demeaning.

For all that complicating cultural distance, and for all our modern struggles with translating empathetically, Sarah's wifely voice here is as familiar as dinner conversation in twenty-first-century marriages. Reluctant though we may be to reduce this ancient text to the status of a television sitcom situation, Sarah's archaic "my wrong be upon thee"[27] accosts her husband in a tone that sounds disturbingly like a very up-to-date "it's all your fault." The edgy irony of that "*my* wrong be upon *thee*" raises Dr. Phil psychological issues intriguing as soap-opera scandal. Is it indeed Abraham's fault? Whose idea was it to have a child at all costs, even at the cost of the relationship? Would Abraham have been a better husband to have refused his wife's urgent request? Who in fact is responsible for this fine mess the first family of the Hebrew nation has gotten itself into?

26. Frymer-Kensky, "Patriarchal Family Relationships," 211.

27. Gen 16:5.

All Families Are Dysfunctional

Sarah assures us from her feminine point of view that it is, as usual, the man's fault—Abraham after all is in point of fact the dirty old man who got Hagar pregnant. From the diametrically opposed husband's viewpoint, the whole thing was Sarah's plan, Sarah's directive, Sarah's responsibility. From our more gender-objective perspective as readers, the family problem may be less invested in either husband or wife, and more a matter of the relationship—the predicament may be mostly a matter of prevailing cultural attitudes toward marriage. The quarrels among those gender perspectives make the situation as implicationally fascinating as it is sitcom-amusing. If society is seen as at fault here, Genesis may be taking a dimmer view of these traditional views of the family than we've been thinking. We're not so far away, even from our chronological and cultural distance, that we can't appreciate the pressure Sarah is under to come up with a baby. We can see how the social conditions conspire to make reproduction so much the meaning of the matriarch's existence that the birth of a son becomes her obsession.

What we have trouble seeing, probably because it is so close to our own personal experience that we lack objective perspective, is the degree to which Sarah colludes in her culture's conclusion that without a child her life must be meaningless. The humorous tensions in the text here make clear to alert readers that the child obsession may be more Sarah's fundamental value than it is Abraham's—more even than it is the Hebrew culture's. That suggests our disposition as readers to see this lust for progeny as a moral good if not an unmitigated blessing may say more about us than it says about what the Bible is saying about Sarah's difficult situation. We tend to read Genesis's fierce focus on reproduction as not just necessary, but inherently worthy. Could this unsettling melodrama of family *Über Alles* be not so much an endorsement as a warning against similar obsessions of our own?

Could this Sarah-Abraham confrontation, instead of reinforcing our family prejudices, be calling them in question? Might the marital conflict smile a little at familial bias that's as likely to exacerbate as to mitigate relationship problems? Without a second thought for the practical realities of economic conditions, the significance of the pressing social and psychological implications, let alone any consideration of crucial tonal indications of what the Bible is attempting to tell us, we tend to look on these halcyon times as the good old days of family values, when—and even *because*—everybody wanted more kids. We tend to downplay the most obvious and important factor in these consistent Bible texts, the salient fact about these families that we hold up to ourselves as models of what families should be: Every single Genesis family turns out be dysfunctional, dramatically dysfunctional. That less-than-enthusiastic view of the *Married with Children* family is not a Genesis aberration. If we're looking at family paradigms, at models of marriage, not just in Genesis but throughout the Bible, what we're looking at mostly is models of marriage that are working, when they're working at all, not idealistically but realistically.

Much of what we're missing in the Bible—the wild and woolly winsomeness of its women, the longsuffering deference of its patriarchs, the persistent problems of its families—we're missing mainly because we don't want to see it. Our unwillingness to look frankly at Sarah in the way the Bible presents her may explain how we've managed to miss so much about biblical women, sometimes to the point of missing the women altogether. Our supercilious idealizing makes realistic matters in the text, matters like its humor, feel irreverent to us, disrespectful. Our expectations of perfection, of models to be uncritically emulated, blinds us to their practical reality. We replace the earthily real portraits of women of the Bible with posters of Mary Poppins with her white parasol, "practically perfect in every way."[28] We seem fearful that "in criticizing the peccadilloes of Sarah, Rebecca and Rachel," we might "shadow the virtues of Deborah, Huldah and Vashti."[29]

The Bible, in direct contrast with our feeble modern idealizations, is quite willing to take the bad with the good in its women. We will have to, too, if we are to have *real* Bible women rather than the mirage of them with which we seem determined to displace actual biblical women. We're culturally afflicted with allergic reaction to anything real in our Bible women, and respond with something like anaphylactic shock to any reality that has any kind of humorous edge—to women who badger their husbands[30] or who want to wear the pants in the family[31] or who try to manipulate their male consorts in any degree of deceptiveness[32] or who tend toward the termagant[33] or who use their feminine wiles to outwit susceptible males,[34]

28. *Mary Poppins,* Buena Vista Pictures, 1964.
29. Stanton, *Women's Bible*, 13.
30. Gen 16:2.
31. Gen 27:8–10.
32. Gen 29:25.
33. Exod 4:25.
34. Gen 38:14–16.

let alone to women who take an "off with their heads" approach to their dates[35] or who are inclined to nail masculine brains to the ground with tent pegs.[36] In our readerly hesitations about seeing women as they are, we may be mostly missing the women in the Bible as they actually were. Worse, we may be missing realistic models of all that women can be.

That's a lot to miss. Maybe the best things about biblical women are the things we haven't wanted to see. Maybe Sarah's sassiness is the most admirable thing about her. Maybe that refusal to compromise, to back down from her impossible dreams, to bow to unfair social expectations, to kowtow to authority, is the most realistic, most illuminating, ultimately—even in its most cranky and naggy and amusing mode—the most *inspiring* thing about Sarah. She tickles me. She reminds me of my mother. She reminds me of my pioneer grandmothers. When I really see her, all frankly outspoken and honestly unadorned and so vigorously dynamic she's worked up a sweat, see her laughing so enthusiastically and inappropriately she looks downright silly, as the Bible sees her, she reminds me of the best women I know.

That realistic portrayal, with its earthy flashes of humor, doesn't simply illuminate the biblical text. It reaches so deep into the story it motivates the narrative. Sarah's concerns, however egocentric or even hysterical they may be, drive the action in Genesis. Sarah's planned parenthood scheme, for all its burlesque complications, makes things happen—family-altering things, the sort of things that have to happen, for better or for worse, if things are ever to get better. And Sarah manages that world-changing alteration with few recourses, few resources, forever battling her independent way out of tight cultural corners. Despite fairy-tale social status and a favored standing in her marriage befitting the noblest epic hero, she labors under duress beyond the anguish of infertility. "Though the spouse of the founder of the Jewish nation," her very "marital status is twice threatened,"[37] first by cultural privilege in the form of pharaoh's sexual predation,[38] then by reproductive competition from comely Hagar.[39] When the going gets tough, Sarah gets going. Sarah is anything but passively obedient.

35. Jdt 6.

36. Judg 5:26–27.

37. Neihoff, "Sarah in Philoci Midrash," 413.

38. Gen 12:14–16.

39. Gen 16:1–4.

A Real Live Girl

Looked at as it is in the Bible itself, as opposed to what we remember seeing when we last looked, the Abrahamic crisis of childlessness looms as more of a problem with the patriarchal culture than with Sarah. Yet, as the matriarch makes clear in her accusation that "my wrong be upon thee,"[40] the barrenness, paradoxically enough, is more of a problem with Sarah than with Abraham. That makes patriarchal Abraham's response to that patently unfair, "it's all your fault" allegation all the more remarkable. He, with all the cultural, all the marital power here, doesn't say "Get thee hence, wife. I'll do what I darn well please." He doesn't insist with male-dominating recourse to reason and denial of emotional reality, "No way, Sarah, it was actually your idea." He doesn't resort to "I'm the boss around here" rank pulling, as some of us would be tempted to pull even in modern circumstances—"I pay the bills and bear the burden of family responsibility, and I'll not concede your hysterical accusations." Instead "Abram said unto Sarai, behold, thy maid is in thy hand; do to her as it pleaseth thee. And when Sarai dealt hardly with her, she fled from her face."[41]

That peremptory banishment of his new wife can't have much pleased this aged new father, childless so long, his life so recently refreshed by new relationship and by the renewed possibility, at long last, of the much-desired child. Abraham can't have enjoyed seeing Sarah badger Hagar. He probably liked even less the threat of the yet-unborn Ishmael exiled from the camp, thrust out into the lethal desert. Sarah has rights here, of course: "Isaac, as the son of Sarah the prime wife, could be legally considered the first-born even though he was chronologically younger than Ishmael."[42] But the matriarch, not satisfied with preferential status for her boy, "does not want Ishmael to have any part in the inheritance." She carries her antipathy toward her rival's son so far as to have him "sent away."[43]

That's hard. Sarah is so hard here that our sympathies, resonant with the sympathies of the text, are all with Abraham and more especially with those vulnerable outcasts beloved by him but not by his beloved wife. As soon as the clan mother gains the upper hand, Genesis 16 turns its back on Sarah to focus on that perennial biblical concern, the underdog: Hagar, the

---

40. Gen 16:5.

41. Gen 16:6.

42. Frymer-Kensky, "Patriarchal Family Relationships," 213.

43. Ibid.

surely-much-missed-of-Abraham Hagar, so bereft in exile out in the desert she requires comfort from an angel. The angel's plangent questions sound as sympathetic as readers feel toward outcast Hagar, in the last stages of pregnancy, without water in the hostile desert: "Hagar, Sarai's maid, whence camest thou? and whither wilt thou go?" And the birth mother, now single mother, is poignantly explicit about the anguish of heartless rejection by her sponsor: "I flee from the face of my mistress Sarai."[44]

Quite clearly the locus of domestic power in this family, to say nothing of most of the narrative interest, resides where it mostly resides in families: with the women. The most remarkable thing about Genesis 16 is not its insistent proto-feminist stance but the fact that this progressive passage comes to us by way of the ultraconservative King James Version. No modern female agenda wrote it in, no up-to-date, right-thinking Christian edited it for political correctness vis-a-vis the modern view of the family. It's right there in the traditional text, big as life—Abraham is not dictatorially calling the familial shots. He's not calling them at all. That firm focus on the feminine in this patriarchal setting is anything but incidental. The female-centeredness prevails throughout Genesis. It's every bit as evident in Genesis 18 two decades later, when so much has changed with the patriarchal couple that their names are altered to reflect the extent of the shifts of character.

When ambassadorial angels arrive dramatically to announce the impending birth of Isaac, "Sarah heard it in the tent door."[45] There's a kind of "woman's place is in the tent" bias in that: "The tent is an overwhelmingly female space in Genesis."[46] Stereotypically in this environment of tent-dwelling nomads, "men are confined to the field, the outside, or the tent opening. Women, by contrast, frequently appear inside tents, especially in passages that emphasize their deep concern over uncertain or contested motherhood,"[47] as here. Sarah's tent setting makes her a lively paradigm of women in patriarchy. Confined to the traditional female place, she finds a way to surmount her cultural restrictions, venturing into patriarchal space.

"Sarah heard it in the tent door, which was behind him."[48] Not officially invited to the patriarchal proceedings, as usual, she with pragmatic

44. Gen 16:8.

45. Gen 18:10.

46. Seeman, "Where is Sarah?" 107.

47. Ibid.

48. Gen 18:10.

female ingenuity participates peripherally. Taking matters into her own enterprising hands, Sarah is eavesdropping. And that's not the only subversive initiative the woman takes. Even in the face of the official pronouncement of these awesome ambassadors, Sarah calls in question the powers that be. She dares to doubt. Sarah jerks these transcendent masculine idealizings right back down to earth: "Now Abraham and Sarah were old and well stricken in age; and it ceased to be with Sarah after the manner of women."[49] Since she's no longer menstruating, she's of the opinion, with her usual steely skepticism, that the likelihood of having a child is probably diminished. "Therefore Sarah laughed within herself, saying, After I am waxed old shall I have pleasure, my lord being old also?"[50] Since she and her husband are expressly no longer making love—Abraham may not even be up to it, Sarah hints here none too diplomatically—the chances of pregnancy are rendered further unlikely. Sarah's laughter here is far from girlish giggle, closer to contempt. Her scorn cuts to the quick of practical realities, needling unrealistic male obtuseness. Humor informs the entire scenario, and the cutting edge of that sharp irony opens up the implications of the passage.

I can't help but like the woman's tone—the honesty of it, the realistic practicality of it, the humor of it. Whether we like it or not, we certainly have to respect the *chutzpah* of this woman's irony. The passage would warrant a historical plaque honoring the inception of the stereotype of the Jewish mother-in-law if Eve hadn't gotten there first. Sarah's sassiness waxes flamboyant enough to invite rebuke from the Lord—oblique rebuke, intriguingly enough, through a warning to her husband. That "get your wife in line, Abraham" directive may suggest that God himself, in his sternest mentoring mode, would rather not cross swords directly with Sarah. With good reason. When the quarrel between Sarah and God waxes personal on the touchy issue of Sarah's disbelief, "Then Sarah denied, saying, I laughed not."[51] How about that Sarah, the woman my church writing committee wanted to pose as a model of feminine passivity, a domestic doormat who would not raise her eyes, let alone her voice, to her husband? She's arguing, arguing with at least an angel and maybe "the Lord"[52] himself, brazenly arguing on a point where it must be as clear to Sarah as to us and the Lord

49. Gen 18:11.

50. Gen 18:12.

51. Gen 18:15.

52. Gen 18:1.

that she's flat wrong. Sarah is so confidently confrontational here I'm surprised that God gets the last word. It says a lot about Sarah that Abraham, knowing her more intimately than the angel does, stays out of the quarrel altogether.

What Sarah actually does in the Bible is more troublesome for some readers, more ironic and unorthodox, more unsettling and unnerving, than what they think she should be doing. For a wide range of readers, from feminist to faithful, what Sarah actually does in this text is counterintuitive to accustomed readings, literally unthinkable. But it's also more realistic. It's also more interesting. It's also much more illuminating. What women actually do in the Bible, as opposed to assumptions about what they should be doing, reaches energetically from what's entertaining to what's exciting—sometimes unnerving and frequently intimidating and often funny and invariably significant.

Women Might Be People Too

We might see more if we were to look outside our orthodoxy boxes and past our bias blinders and beyond whatever other predispositions we bring to our Bible reading—better yet, through those wonderfully diverse if individually reductive views, as we would focus through binoculars. Looking with open eyes, we might see what the Bible actually says about women, how the Bible itself presents those of the female persuasion. It presents them a lot like people, real people. The Bible portrays women as it portrays all its characters—true to life. Far from cardboard stereotypes, Bible women are nothing like paragons of womanhood. These women are anything but poster representations of the ideal, far from pristine models of perfection. Women in the Bible are as whimsical and changeable as women we know personally—it is that realistic protean quality that enables them to serve so well as catalysts for change. And they're self-activating. The Bible presents women as individuals whose individuality makes a difference. The realism, the true-to-life dynamism of these dynamite women frequently features and even more frequently is sparked by humor.

One of the strongest recurrent patterns of Genesis, so strong as to become a motif not only in that foundational book but throughout the Bible, is that *women start things*—things like quarrels, certainly; definitely things like trouble; but also things like families. Also things like essential cultural change, things like universal expansion of human horizons. In Genesis the most notable narrative characteristic of women is that they initiate the narrative action. That reiterated dynamic stands out all the more dramatically in a text where men are so cocksure they are the essential movers and shakers. Every single Genesis woman—Eve, Sarah, Hagar, Rebekah, Rachel, Leah, Tamar, even Potiphar's wife—kicks off the narrative events.

And it's not just Genesis that features dynamic females. It's the entire Bible. "We can arguably find more major women characters in the narratives of Judges than in any other book in the Hebrew Bible"[53]—"Achsah, Deborah, Jael, Sisera's mother, the woman of Thebez, Jephthah's daughter, Samson's mother, Samson's Timnite wife, Delilah, Micah's mother, the Levite's concubine, and the daughters of Shiloh."[54] It's probably not insignificant that women work the water wheel of the liveliest biblical narratives, Genesis and Judges and the Samuel books, the narrative heart of the Hebrew Bible. That energizing pattern of female proactivity is straightforward and insistent; the bare outline will bring a dozen biblical examples to mind: [1] A man is presented. [2] He's stable, orthodox, static. [3] A woman enters the scene. [4] The plot thickens: she outflanks him, outmaneuvers him—gets downright tricky in fooling him or manipulating him or seducing him, often all three. [5] The relationship and, for good measure, the entire culture is altered fundamentally. [6] The change, however much it upsets traditional applecarts, is invariably for the better.

Men may have overlooked that persistent biblical pattern because it makes them feel less masterful than they like to feel, less in control. Women may have overlooked the motif because it makes them look more manipulative, more devious than they like to look. Whatever the gendered reasons for ignoring that leitmotif of dynamic females who proactively alter the world, the pattern is clearly not just present but persistent, the dominant female paradigm in the Hebrew Bible. The recurrent dynamic of women stirring things up is invariable: wherever women are, things get roisterously roiled. The churnings—disturbing, even distressing, for the men—in the long run almost always result in better butter. That may be why the divine disposition toward expansion of human experience, toward illumination and maturation of mankind, works so directly and so effectually through these willful females. It could also explain why readers have not noticed the pattern.

53. Ackerman, "Digging up Deborah," 175.
54. Ibid., 176.

Looked at in broad outline, the recurrent motif of women initiating action in the Bible suggests some surprising insights. In the Bible—as perhaps in life—"men in group procure change, but remain stagnant as individuals, whereas women in group are inert, but innovative as individuals."[55] Contrary to their placid group stereotype, biblical women in their individual individualistic manifestations are stunningly proactive. Even in the area most proscribed by patriarchal constraint, "A number of women help themselves to husbands they are not destined for."[56] More shockingly still in this conservative biblical context is the frequency with which "sex takes place prior to marriage, symbolic of the suggestion that the status of a wife has to be acquired by action."[57] Unconventional as it might seem, then as now, whatever men may like to think, it is women who propose.

The Bible intimates in the recurrence of that dynamic pattern that if we're going to insist on gender categorization, which it would rather we wouldn't, it is women who tend to be proactive; it is women who tend to be risk takers; it is women who tend to be imaginative and progressive; it is women who tend to stretch our human possibilities. Before we reject that unpopular and unorthodox but thoroughly biblical probability out of hand, we should consider whether the Bible could possibly be accurate in its revolutionary view of gender. Could it be women actually are less passive than our cultural stereotypes suggest, more like the Bible paints them? Some of my students who worked up a gender analysis, assessing comments in our Bible as literature class, rated the women's contributions on average slightly less than twice as innovative as the men's.[58]

Eve Started It

In Greek mythology, which we've bought into via modern psychology and its Oedipus complexes and Electra syndromes at deeper levels than we like to admit to ourselves, woman is self-indulgent Pandora. Woman as Pandora instigates troubles, compounds problems. In the biblical view, which may be truer to actual psychological experience, paradoxical woman creates complications, but she also provokes improvements. She initiates troubling upheaval that ushers in human progress. The Old Testament woman

55. Andriolo, "Myth and History," 275.

56. Ibid., 271.

57. Ibid.

58. Hickens, 2004.

is as annoyingly curious and as exasperatingly disruptive of the status quo as Pandora, but her results are more positive. In the Bible, woman is Eve.

Eve establishes that obvious biblical gender pattern we've so clearly overlooked. The cautiously obedient Adam is uncomplicatedly alone in the garden, comfortable and complacent. All's quiet on the edenic front. Then Eve leaps dramatically into the scene and jump-starts the action. Activity ramps up to confusion levels: life gets distressingly complicated, with frenetic worries about what to have for dinner and what style of leaf to wear and where to live. It is clearly Eve who does the complicating. It is she who debates with the serpent; it is she who is the logician, even the scriptorian. It is she who makes the decision to eat the fruit, to take the risk, to go for the gusto. Eve as seen in Genesis is inquisitive, imaginative, intellectual, ambitious, aggressive, daring, independent, aware. Most dramatically, Eve is, both before and after the eating of the fruit, responsible—and this in a patriarchal situation where the fiercest feminist and the most orthodox Christian would agree Adam is supposed to be in charge.

It's clear that without Eve this would be a very different story. It might not even be a story. Certainly it would be a far less lively story, because Eve initiates all the narrative action. The steadfast Adam, bless his dependable heart, doesn't do much. It's not that the Bible indulges in any way here in denigrating men, let alone male bashing. The Adam of Genesis is a great guy, in his orthodox and obedient and uncomplicated way, dedicated to the status quo, committed to stability and tradition, hoping in his loyal if unimaginative manner that the furniture can be left in the same familiar place. I relate with Adam; I know exactly how he feels in the face of these female hysterics, all these undue feminine complications. I hope for his sake that during these life-affecting deliberations he is, as he appears in Genesis to be, off somewhere in the garden taking a nap. The pivotal passage is Genesis 3:6: "And when the woman saw that the tree was good for food, and that it was pleasant to the eyes, and a tree to be desired to make one wise, she took of the fruit thereof, and did eat, and gave also unto her husband with her; and he did eat." Eve considers, deliberates, and then decides. It is she who determines the fruit to be nutritious, satisfying, edifying; she carefully, consciously, thoughtfully decides to eat it.

Here we see clearly, even dramatically, "woman as priestess"—"the vehicle for divine wisdom."[59] On the way to that wisdom she outmaneuvers the cleverest of masculine maneuverers. "All that the serpent was, said J

59. Eisler, *Chalice and the Blade*, 88.

[the Jahwist redactor], was crafty. But Eve was crafty too. Quite the serpent's match. In his best lawyerese, the serpent began by inquiring 'Is it true that God has forbidden you to eat from any tree in the garden?'"[60] Clever Eve debates better than the master debater. Official "regulations had never said anything about touching, only about eating. She made the other part up. J cannot have left this one to chance: already Eve was showing an independent wisdom separate from God's."[61]

"Eve was not irrational: J made her display the fullest and most acute of mental faculties. Eve was not bullied or bludgeoned or bamboozled into eating the fruit. Sure, the snake was smart, but that was all he was. And so was Eve. Eve, J showed us, made a deliberate, considered, rational choice."[62] The ironic text is so fraught with implication it can accommodate the opposite reading, not only triumph here but also disaster: "Some critics have plausibly imagined this whole large process of biblical literature as a divine experiment with the quirky and unpredictable stuff of human freedom, an experiment plagued by repeated failure . . . first Adam and Eve."[63] Whatever way it's read, from tragedy to triumph, the fulcrum of that encompassing swing of significance is the charming, human, and often charmingly humorous, portrayal of Eve.

The levity with which these matters are presented backlights their momentousness. "The negotiation between the snake and Eve, this dialogue among equals" of human imagination matched against the machinations of evil, becomes "the hinge in the development of Western moral thinking." "Both the snake and Eve possessed deeply human qualities, both had been jocularly provided by J with their own kind of *arum* [guile], and both were crafty,"[64] Eve craftier. How she got a reputation as a Pandora airhead on the basis of that passage eludes me. She is willful, certainly, but anything but witless. Adam, bless his easily satisfied male heart, follows along. He is her sidekick, "her husband with her."[65] In the Hebrew his non-deliberation is striking by contrast with Eve's complexly responsible agonizings: "And he"—without a word of questioning or even of acquiescence, with not so much as a "Yes, Dear"—"did eat" (3:6). Bill Moyers sees Adam as "a sort of

60. Dekker, "Eve and the Serpent," 576.

61. Ibid.

62. Ibid., 577.

63. Alter, *Genesis*, xliv.

64. Dekker, "Eve and the Serpent," 576.

65. Gen 3:6.

divine simpleton. Eve is the more interesting of the two. She's proactive, while he's passive."[66]

The results of that deliberate eating may be more debatable. If this forbidden picnic is a disaster, as many theologies would have it, a disaster from which the human race has never recovered, Eve is to blame, and Western culture is right to have blamed her and every other misguided member of her diabolical Satan-consorting sex through three long millennia of Judeo-Christian history. Eve is clearly responsible. If we read impulsive indulgence in her Genesis behavior, we do right to continue to castigate Mother Eve as "the symbolization of woman as the incarnation of moral evil, sin, devastation and death."[67] Maybe we even do right to persist in our universal stereotyping of women "as socially, culturally, and racially Other, as tropes for evil."[68]

If, on the other hand, these edenic events amount to what some theological minorities can call a *fortunate fall*, a flawed moving into larger experiential territory, an expansion of the possibilities of the human soul, Eve deserves more credit than we've accorded her. She deserves credit, as the Bible points out quite clearly, for life as we know it. If it's a bad life, shame on her. But if it's a good life, bless her intrepid heart. If we want life to move toward maturity and complexity, if we are glad to struggle in real life rather than some kind of preadolescent limbo, we have Eve to thank.

That's typical of those Genesis women; we have them to thank. An unexpected authority in the field, Woody Allen, puts the point tellingly:

> I have always preferred women to men. This goes back to the Old Testament where the ladies have it all over their cowering, pious counterparts. Eve knew the consequences when she ate the apple. Adam would have been content to just follow orders and live on like a mindless cybarite. I'm personally glad men and women run to cover up their nakedness. It makes undressing someone much more exciting.[69]

A slightly less flamboyant but far more respected authority in the field of biblical studies on gender, Harold Bloom, insists that the Hebrew Bible has "no heroes, only heroines."[70] Bloom is so impressed by Bible women he

66. Bill Moyers, *Genesis: A Living Conversation*, 47.

67. Yee, *Women as Evil*, 3.

68. Ibid., 3.

69. Allen, "Reflections of a Second-Rate Mind," 4.

70. Bloom, *Book of J*, 32.

wrote a long learned volume, *The Book of J*, proposing that the best parts of Genesis must have been written by a woman. According to Bloom, the Bible's "male personages," by pointed contrast with women, have a difficult time rising above "their childlike and also childish qualities. The only grownups in [the Hebrew Bible] are women: Sarai, Rebecca, Rachel, Tamar."[71]

We could wander all the way through Genesis, observing how Eve-like are the likes of Sarah and Hagar and Leah and Rachel and especially Rebekah and Tamar—Sarah putting patriarchal Abraham firmly in his place,[72] Hagar manipulating her servitude into motherhood of a great nation,[73] Leah managing the same trick by means of a ribald ruse on tricky Jacob,[74] Rebekah finagling shortsighted Isaac into the correct blessing,[75] Rachel indecorously fooling her father out of the household gods,[76] Tamar seducing Judah into doing his levirate duty.[77] The insights that bubble to the top of that piquant domestic stew are flavored with humor.

Those critical relationships formed by these dynamic women are fraught with understated but outlandish levity, perhaps most tellingly with that Genesis odd couple lethargic Isaac and ADHD Rebekah. Rebekah is so hyper that when God tells her that her beloved Jacob is to be the blessed boy, she jumps to the rather presumptuous conclusion that the Lord must need her help to manage that, and shamelessly manipulates all the males on the scene to make sure that he does. Meanwhile, laid-back Isaac folds his hands and waits patiently for God to do his thing. The parental pair proves impossibly contrary, hopeless opposites mismatched as comically as casual Dean Martin and frenetic Jerry Lewis. The comedic happy ending of this farcical episode revels in a mismatched miracle where two blundering parents manage between them to make one competent parent, the unequally-yoked couple somehow together in harness enough to get the right boy blessed. The moral of this Punch-and-Judy gender struggle is all the more illuminating for being backlit by humor: "Most like an arch" this

---

71. Bloom, *Book of J*, 32.

72. Gen 16:1–6.

73. Gen 16:10–12.

74. Gen 29:21–26.

75. Gen 27:5–29.

76. Gen 31:34–35.

77. Gen 38:14–26.

marriage—"two weaknesses that lean/ into a strength. Two fallings become firm."[78]

The pattern of female dynamism crossbred with male stability is so persistent that cataloguing all the proactive Genesis females would be monotonous. Every Genesis narrative that features a woman—and almost all do—is cut from the same cookie-cutter pattern of psychological realism: passive man plus dynamic woman equals excitement and expansion. Dull boy meets lively girl. Girl jolts old habits out of their ruts, into better places. The pattern is ubiquitous, so pervasive that even readers who are not consciously aware of it tend to emend any alteration from the paradigm, as when Noah's uncomplaining biblical wife is turned by the mystery plays into an overbearing nag. The smiling moral seems as win-win winsome as the old Coke commercial: from the earliest Eve to the most modern Mary, things go better with girls.

Judge Deborah

Women are understatedly but clearly central to the narrative in Genesis, invariably not simply active but proactive. A definitive place to determine whether that pattern of life-changing females is universal throughout the Bible is the book of Judges, the annals of the dark ages of the House of Israel when Hebrew civilization sank to its nadir, the misogynistic epoch "when men were men and women were glad of it." There can be found, even in the chronicles of this primitive patriarchal society, a surprising percentage of take-charge women. The women in fact look dramatically dynamic in contrast with their men. The wife of Manoah hobnobs with angels her husband can't even recognize.[79] Wily Delilah outwits indomitable Samson.[80] Jephthah's daughter is so responsible that she sacrifices her life to compensate for the irresponsible act of her father, the judge.[81] Text after Judges text says in its every line that if men are supposed to be superior to women it would certainly like to be shown just how they are. As one of my sharper-tongued students pinpointed the issue of gender superiority: "If men are God's gift to women, God must love gag gifts."[82]

78. Ciardi, *Poems of John Ciardi*, 196.

79. Judg 13:3–21.

80. Judg 16:4–20.

81. Judg 11:30–40.

82. This statement was made by Jane Fremore in *English 350: The Bible as Literature*

That inclusive pattern of proactive women features in Judges 4–5 a dynamic female duo that represents the social range of Hebrew womanhood from housewife Jael to Deborah the prophetess. That "prophetess"[83] title is difficult to explain away in terms of usual perceptions of patriarchal power. General Barak didn't even try. The macho master of the Israelite army pleads with Deborah like a five-year-old to his mother: "If thou wilt go with me, then I will go: but if thou wilt not go with me, then I will not go."[84] In direct contradiction of the weak, timid, passive role assumed for women, "mother in Israel"[85] Deborah proclaims: "I will surely go with thee: notwithstanding the journey that thou takest shall not be for thine honour; for the Lord shall sell Sisera into the hand of a woman"[86]—partly that is the ultimate insult to the misogynistic Canaanites. But it is also a demonstration of just how strong these women are.

With Deborah holding her general's nervous hand, the Israelites conquer the Canaanites so decisively that their indomitable champion Sisera runs and hides.[87] That is not his first tactical mistake, nor the first indication in the passage of male inadequacy. The climax of the poem reminds readers, with scathing sarcasm, that in light of how things turned out for him, Sisera might have been wiser to stay at home where his mother could protect her boy.[88] Shadowed by that fraught maternal context, the commander of the fearsome Assyrian army cowers in the tent of Jael. This unlikely woman, a common housewife—commoner than that: a tent wife[89]—enacts slavishly, as role-bound women will, proper social rites, the dutiful matron fulfilling her domestic duties. She welcomes the stranger, provides him food and a place to rest, even, in a fond maternal touch, tucks him in with a goodnight drink of milk before she nails him.[90]

"And he said unto her, Give me, I pray thee, a little water to drink; for I am thirsty. And she opened a bottle of milk, and gave him drink, and covered him. Again he said unto her, Stand in the door of the tent, and it

---

course. Brigham Young University: Winter Semester, 2007.

83. Judg 4:4.
84. Judg 4:9.
85. Judg 5:7.
86. Judg 4:9.
87. Judg 4:17–18.
88. Judg 5:28–30.
89. Judg 5:24.
90. Judg 4:18–20.

shall be, when any man doth come and inquire of thee, and say, Is there any man here? that thou shalt say, No."[91] No way. Because there is truly about to be no man left there. Macho masculinity is about to be called definitively in question. "For Sisera, the answer 'No, there is no man here' is intended to be a lie, but for the reader attentive to irony, the answer 'no' reflects the truth. The mighty man" no more.[92] "Then Jael Heber's wife took a nail of the tent, and took an hammer in her hand, and went softly unto him, and smote the nail into his temples, and fastened it into the ground: for he was fast asleep and weary. So he died."[93]

Good hand. Good woman, if we'll allow women to be strong, as the Bible emphatically does. Biblical women more often than twenty-first-century women are permitted to be strong as men, even men posturing in their most commanding roles. The ironies here are pounded into thick macho skulls as emphatically as that tent peg (wooden, so it requires even fiercer pounding than we were thinking) into Sisera's temples—plural, we note: she drove that tent peg with a single hammer blow (wooden hammer, wooden peg) all the way through that male head. It's not just that she overwhelms him; she overwhelms him with deft female grace: "Like a persuasive Leah coming out to 'hire' Jacob's sexual services Jael comes out to meet Sisera and to invite him into her tent."[94] The alpha male is not just putty in her hands; he's a babe in her arms. "Now, like a child in a womb, Sisera lies sleeping in Jael's tent," resting in infantile security, soporifically full of maternal milk, well tucked in. It would take a reader with a harder head than General Sisera's to fail to see "the mighty man has become a vulnerable child; the virile man lies impotent."[95]

In case there's any doubt in anyone's mind that this text is calling into question any assumed superiority of men, Barak, the Israelite general (his name means *Lightning* in Hebrew, and there's some joke in that) arrives on this grisly scene, as is the male wont, a day late and a dollar short: "And, behold, as Barak pursued Sisera, Jael came out to meet him, and said unto him, Come, and I will shew thee the man [interesting what gender freight the simplest terms take on in such ironic context] whom thou seekest. And when he came into her tent, behold, Sisera lay dead, and the nail was in his

91. Judg 4:19–20.
92. Fewell, "Authority of Violence," 393.
93. Judg 4:21.
94. Fewell, "Authority of Violence," 392.
95. Ibid., 393.

temples."[96] In this ironic rhetoric it may even be significant that the hero of the Canaanite host, mighty Sisera, requires three tries to die: "At her feet, he bowed, he fell, he lay down: at her feet he bowed, he fell: where he bowed, there he fell down dead."[97] Hard man to kill, but female Jael managed it handily, single-handedly. Some feminists hype that triumph, with its ironic subtext of gender concerns, so far as to see images of sexual domination in this grisly scene, so that the great warrior, undone by a woman, is dying not only of head wounds but of humiliation.

What Is It Women Want?

There we have it: the good old Bible days when women were women, and men were glad of it. Evidence of the dynamism of biblical women is incontrovertible. "Judges 4–5 reverses many expectations that readers of the book may bring to the text, especially concerning the roles played by women."[98] It's hard to miss who is wearing the pants here. Thought to pre-date Judges 4 by at least a century and hence to be more historically reliable because it's closer to the events it recounts,[99] Judges 5 is also much more female oriented—"much more emphatically depicts Deborah as Israel's chief military commander, whereas Barak, the military hero of Judges 4, appears only as her second-in-command."[100] If anyone of either gender is wondering exactly who's in charge here, the climactic passage should be read as Hebrews would have read it: "Jael here is in turn seductress, ministering mother, and sexual assailant, whereas the sharp focus of the poem is simply on the powerful figure of Jael the hammerer, standing over the body of Sisera, whose death throes between her legs, kneeling, then prostrate, may be, perhaps, an ironic glance at the time-honored martial custom of rape."[101] That pushes the scenario further than some of us want to go, but it leaves little question as to who is ruling this roost.

Everywhere in the Old Testament we see women who dominate the action. This is hardly the delicate femininity Bible readers expect. But the Bible clearly commends it. In instance after instance throughout the Old

96. Judg 4:22.

97. Judg 5:27.

98. Fewell, "Authority of Violence," 390.

99. Niditch, "Judges," 181,

100. Ackerman, "Digging up Deborah," 176–77.

101. Alter, *Art of Biblical Poetry*, 49.

Testament these proactive women precipitate the crucial events, drive the narrative as emphatically as that tent peg through Sisera. Biblical women make things happen. You can call them vicious, you can call them manipulative, you can call them meddling, you can call them words we ought not say in the vicinity of the Bible. You can declare them downright ornery. But you can't pretend they're not there. And you can't call these women passive. You can't call them non-participants. This is the book, we should remember, that blessed us with the notion of the Jewish mother-in-law. These are tough ladies. For all the laughter associated with biblical women, the Bible seldom dares laugh *at* them—almost all the laughing is *with* them.

Biblical ladies are not required to be all that ladylike, as a brief summary of some of the remarkable accomplishments of a scant tithe of the women who are named in the Bible indicates. The sterling qualities of biblical women starring in stirring feats are not limited to Deborah's courageous assurance that empowered those mongrel tribes to defeat the invincible Canaanites, nor to Jael's fierce determination that drove that wooden tent peg clear through Sisera's skull. They are not even exhausted by Eve's enthusiastic appetite for wisdom, the foresight that ushered mankind into mature mortality. Women make energetic difference everywhere in the Bible.

Sarah's hearty integrity dares to laugh at angels.[102] Hagar's fierce concern for her child engenders a world-shaping religion.[103] Rebekah's intense vision of what is right for her sons dictates the nation-establishing blessing of Jacob.[104] Leah and Rachel's ravenousness for children outmaneuvers no less a manipulator than the wily Jacob to found the Israelite people.[105] Tamar's sense of social justice wrests dynastic children from Judah against his will.[106] Zipporah's dauntlessness stands up to the angel of death to save Moses.[107] Prophetesses Miriam[108] and Huldah's[109] administrative prowess pilots national affairs. Judith triumphs over Holofernes, the tyrant of the age, hauling his decapitated head home in her handbag as a grisly trophy

---

102. Gen 18.
103. Gen 21.
104. Gen 27.
105. Gen 29.
106. Gen 38.
107. Exod 4.
108. Exod 15.
109. 2 Kgs 22.

of war.[110] Esther, in a no-holds-barred contest with the best man in Persia, bests Machiavellian Haman hands down to rescue her entire people.[111] The Daughter of Jephthah's unflinching respect for her ignoble father sets a new standard of loyalty.[112] Hannah's drive to self-fulfillment inspires her to go over her husband's head directly to God to bargain for that miracle of a son, Samuel,[113] the same way the wife of Manoah's tenacity in appealing to the angel results in the hero Samson.[114] Abigail's political savvy leverages her into a queendom.[115] Bathsheba's canniness secures a kingdom for her son Solomon.[116] Ruth's fearless loyalty empowers her to abandon the safety of her familiar male-centered world to remain with her intrepid mother-in-law Naomi, rescuing their lives and the lives of the future generations that foster such cosmic heroes as King David and Jesus of Nazareth.[117]

By saying that women are strong, the Bible is not by any means implying that men are weak. The Bible is saying just the opposite: the stronger the women, the stronger the men. For all the ironic overtones of strong women in relationships, making women outspoken doesn't make men voiceless; making women strong doesn't make men henpecked. There is real strength in people—all people, the Bible suggests—strength that tends to dissipate or even erode completely when undermined by the role playing of gender stereotypes. Strength in women, the Bible demonstrates in scenarios from Genesis to Revelation, is cause for celebration, even for the most nervous of male sensibilities.

Looking at Bible women through the lens of humor, there is real cause for celebration. Looked at as they actually are in the Bible these Old Testament women are vigorous, energetic, enterprising, intrepid. When we really see them, we cannot help but be impressed by the determination of the Rebekahs, the tenacity of the Naomis, the fearlessness of the Esthers, the gutsy triumphs of the Jaels and Judiths and Jephthah's daughters. These are heroic women. That intrepid giant-killer David himself could relate—*The Terminator* could relate—to a champion capable of driving a tent peg through an

110. Jdt 13.

111. Esther.

112. Judg 11.

113. 1 Sam 1.

114. Judg 13.

115. 1 Sam 25.

116. 1 Kgs 1.

117. Ruth.

enemy head, as Jael dramatically does, or to a warrior who with her own refined hands and his own sword beheads the enemy general, as Judith does,
or to a hero who cool-headedly risks her life—"If I perish, I perish"[118]—and
succeeds in saving her entire nation, as Esther does. Against the fiercest
odds, Bible women are movers and shakers, dynamic doers.

Modern readers might not like the way Rachel and Ruth manipulate
or Rebekah and Sarah dominate or Esther and Tamar seduce or Judith and
Jael kill with their own hands. But to label these women as role-model stereotypes or to see them as Mary Poppins dressed in a pressed pinafore,
"practically perfect in every way,"[119] is simply not to see what is in the Bible.
The women of this idealistic text are real people. However unsettling it
might seem to modern sensibilities, women are represented in biblical narrative as emphatically realistic. Humor is a significant aspect of that realism. To view these women as humorless is to fail utterly to see what the
Bible says, let alone what it means. To make that mirage of ancient women
a model of virtue for modern women is a bad joke.

The Bible does a notably poor job of putting women in their place if
their place is hiding in a corner. Biblical women are consistently characterized as having minds of their own, narratively represented as making things
happen. We remember the psychologist Freud—some of us remember him
none too kindly—for his plaintive question: "What does a woman want?"[120]
The Hebrew Bible's answer to that question is straightforward: women want
a piece of the action. Women want to get in on the act, to be a real part of
things. In the Old Testament they are.

The moral of that story for the way we see women is simple. These Old
Testament women are good old girls, just plain folks—real people, neither
paragons put on a pedestal nor disempowered doormats. They are not ide-
alized but actual models of what women might be. I think we do well to
look to them. I'm delighted to have a daughter named Rebecca, and almost
wish we'd named her Jael. The functional moral of that admiring Old Testament view of dynamic women is even more apparent: Say what you want
about a woman's work never being done—but when you really want to get
something done, get a woman to do it.

118. Esth 4:16.

119. *Mary Poppins*, Buena Vista Pictures, 1964.

120. Jones, *Sigmund Freud*, 377.

5

"Peter Stood at the Door Knocking"

Slapstick in Acts

THE BIBLE IS THE perennial and all-time bestselling book not only in the United States but throughout the world—six billion sold as of 2005 in the English-speaking world alone, nearly one for every living soul on earth.[1] One study indicates that American families own a prodigiously re-dundant average of nine copies each of the Bible.[2] But there's a flip side to our obsession with the Bible. Our infatuation with the Good Book may be less fervent than it appears—relatively few of those multitudinous copies, so enthusiastically acquired, are ever opened. Apparently the last time a lot of Bible owners saw the actual inside of the book was in Sunday school a long time ago, long enough that some couldn't yet read it. At the same time it is far and away the most bought book, the Bible may also compete for singular honors among bought books as the book least read.

Gallup surveys indicate "about six in ten Americans (59 percent) say they read the Bible at least on occasion."[3] But the occasions appear to be few and far between. Most Americans aren't picking up the Bible often enough to pick up on much of what's in it. A follow-up survey, one that didn't sim-ply take the word of Bible readers for how much they are reading, showed that fewer than half of Americans can name the first book of the Bible,

1. Ash, *Top Ten of Everything: 2006*, 101.
2. Marty, *Bible Mania*, Oct. 27, 2007.
3. Gallup, "Americans Read the Bible," Oct. 20, 2000.

even though *Genesis* means "beginning." Only a third can say who delivered the Sermon on the Mount—almost as many opted for Billy Graham as for Jesus. The most familiar Bible narratives come as a surprise to many who claim to be Bible readers, and not only among Christmas-and-Easter Christians. Fully a quarter of well-meaning Bible owners do not know what it is that Easter celebrates, despite the fact that Christ's resurrection stands out dramatically as the foundational event of Christianity.[4]

The Bible's capacity for gathering dust on bookshelves is legendary. Even among those who earnestly attempt to read it, actual eyes-on-the-page readers, the Bible tends to be more of a physical sedative than a spiritual stimulant. It has been cynically observed that if all the readers of the Bible were laid end to end, they'd be asleep. Scripture, however felicitous its potential, can't be of much practical use to readers who don't read it. The infrequency with which the Bible is read redlines the distressingly limited extent of our enthusiasm for the book as actual good reading.

The Problem: Preachers and Pedants

That Bible reading crisis is more critical than it sounds. You'd think Christians would at least read the *New* Testament. You'd be wrong. Limited as Old Testament reading is, New Testament reading appears to be worse. Worse still, even those who are actually reading, even the best of readers in this crucial Christian venue, don't seem to be reading at all well. Those who read the New Testament and stay awake may read it even more blurrily than those of us who routinely drift off to sleep. The foremost Bible readers in modern America, the most focused and intense, fall into two essential categories. First and most emphatic are the pulpit thumpers, who read the Good Book with fervent dedication as the literal word of God worded the way he worded it, spelled the way he spelled it, with every last comma placed precisely where he put it. Last time I tried to suggest to a fundamentalist Christian friend that there *were* no commas in ancient Hebrew—in fact no punctuation at all—she made known to me in no uncertain terms that such overintellectual textual considerations have nothing whatsoever to do with her biblical concerns because (whatever the problems with my Bible, even if it is the identical King James Version) the Bible she held in her hand was, commas and all, every jot and tittle, the literal word of God.

4. "Bible in the Hand Still May Not Be Read," Dec. 4, 2000.

When I inquired, perhaps a little impatiently, whether the typographical errors were also God's, she hit me with a withering Church Lady look of pity for my ignorance that insisted there were not only not any typographical errors in God's book, but *could* not be. If there *were* errors, she explained in a disturbingly caustic tone, they would not *be* errors, since this is *God's* book, inerrant. On the theological level, it struck both my Church Lady friend and me as incredibly fortunate that God's inflexible word turned out to be a point-by-point elaboration of her fundamentalist doctrine. Her King James Version spoke with a clear conservative Protestant accent, serendipitously akin to her own secular—I'm not so sure for her it *was* secular—Deep South dialect.

That *inerrant* reading isn't as obtuse as it sounds. The belief of a third of Americans that the Bible is to be taken "'literally word for word' isn't even that rigid."[5] However counterproductive—downright inspiration-killing—the inerrant approach can be when it means to say "the way I read the Bible is the only way it can be read," in usual practice it's less arrogant, sometimes even self-corrective. Fundamentalists who have thought about it, of whom there seem to be increasing numbers, realize that the term *inerrant* could accurately characterize *God's* part in the Bible process, the writing part, but not so much *their* part, the reading part. Most fundamentalists aren't claiming they're perfect, only God.

That cuts some interpretive slack within the tight confines of inerrancy, allows a little room for interpretation. That room to read is a fortunate find for fundamentalists, since differences in reading God's inerrant word are everywhere evident among them. Sometimes those variations are bitterly evident, not only *among* the different faith conclaves of the ultraconservative Protestant camp, but *within* each of those groups. Often interpretive differences are apparent between a given congregation of a particular faith and its neighboring congregations, more often than not split-off factions, the splintering a direct result of readers at some juncture having read God's good word in a dissimilar way. However many fundamentalists think the Bible can only be read one way, all of them read it differently.

The opposing camp of dedicated New Testament readers, of people who actually pore over its pages with their eyes open, are scholars. If that makes you all wide-eyed with anticipation that we might get to see, through this objective scholarly lens, more of what's actually going on in the New Testament, you might want to think more about it. Hard though it may

5. Newport, "Americans Believe the Bible," May 25, 2007.

be to believe, scholars are capable of an even more restricted, more limiting view of the text than fundamentalist theologians. Biblical scholars, like scholars generally, are disposed, in Wordsworth's bitter phrase, to "murder to dissect."[6] I think I can fairly say as one of their auspicious number that New Testament scholars, committed as we are to incisively critical analysis, tend to end up distressingly often with a dead-ended or even thoroughly dead text, a Bible with little literary vitality and almost no morally relevant value of its own. The New Testament serves scholars all too often as a kind of "this is really about something else" Rosetta stone, a skeleton key to other linguistic or historical or anthropological ends rather than a text meaningful in its own right.

I have nothing against the reading of the Bible by either pedants or preachers. I myself am something of both, and appreciate that both perspectives can illuminate important dimensions of the text. But I do believe that theological tunnel vision and intellectual reductiveness tend to cause readers of the Bible who see only from those angles to miss much of what is going on. Maybe we Bible readers, even the best readers, even theological and textual experts, would do better to read our New Testaments as unblindered as possible by prior expectations. Maybe we could go so far in that revolutionary reading direction as to read the New Testament as it invites itself to be read. Maybe we could read the New Testament as literature.

Can't You Take a Joke?

Maybe we could even manage, on a really good reading day, to look at the New Testament's literary quality in terms of its humor. I propose such a radical approach to this conservative text because, frankly, I like the humor. But like it or not, the humor is drastically underappreciated. Like so many aspects of the New Testament, the humor is underappreciated to the point of being ignored altogether.

There may be hope in that. Because humor in the New Testament is among the least of its concerns, it may in its very peripheralness provide telling evidence that the intent of the New Testament is literary. If this book is intentionally amusing—deliberately, definitely, significantly funny—the presence of that humor strongly implies that the concern of the book is not solely, if indeed at all, to preach to us. The presence of humor in the New Testament would suggest that the book is something more than a Sunday

6. Wordsworth, *Lyrical Ballads*.

school manual or a historical artifact, more than a Jerry Falwell theological laundry list, let alone a Rudolph Bultmann case study. The New Testament, if there's laughter in it, is a definitely *literary* book. That makes it a book not just for religious reactionaries and academic reductivists, but a book for *us*—readers who actually like the Bible for itself rather than for extra-biblical purposes—to laugh with and to cry with and to live with.

We are at this point exactly half way through the painstakingly thorough and scintillatingly insightful argument of *Illuminating Humor of the Bible*. So far in this groundbreaking study our reading of Bible humor has leaned heavily toward the Hebrew Bible. Partly that bias toward the volume we Christians slightly insult as the *Old Testament* is because there's more of it—twice as much as the New Testament. Partly the strategy of this study is chronological, and climactic—"last the best of all the game." But mostly the reason for our heavy emphasis on the Old Testament up to now is that, based on surprising indications that we Bible readers know it better, we seem to be reading it more. If that is true, we're not reading the New Testament nearly enough, because we're not reading the Old Testament enough. Given how much we Christians have riding on this consummate Christian text, we read it disturbingly little. Maybe attention to the humor might make us like it better, and that might help us read it more.

That's potent motivation for pursuing intimations and implications of humor in the New Testament. We hunt humor here not so much for the fun of the chase as to track how much the humor matters—the ultimate quarry is biblical understanding. We want to find, in the New Testament as we have in the Old, the ways humor contributes to meaning. So as not to poach game in the park, we'll look for humor where it will least probably be found in the New Testament. A serious competitor for unlikeliest location of anything funny is the book of Acts, that august volume that chronicles the momentous march of ancient Christianity across the world under the austere stewardship of stoic Peter and stern Paul. Acts provides a telling sample: if anything ironic or witty or any way amusing can be ferreted out from the venerable Acts of the Apostles, humor is widespread in the New Testament.

It should be conceded up front that there are not, in fact, many belly laughs anywhere in the Bible, let alone in the New Testament, least of all in Acts. Biblical humor is more quiet and intimate than that, more integrated and innate. It tends to be so subtly understated that modern readers cannot be expected to pick up readily on New Testament jokes. About the only things we laugh at in Acts are situations or symbols that were probably not meant to be funny from a first-century Palestinian perspective, descriptions or images unnaturally skewed by our modern mindset into scenarios not originally intended for amusement.

That sort of unintentional humor can be seen when the trial judge at Jerusalem, perhaps showing off a little for "the chief priests and all their council,"[7] proclaims with all the pomposity of his high priestly position and proud disposition that Paul should be slapped on the mouth. Paul reacts to this highhanded indignity indignantly: "God shall smite thee, thou whited wall."[8] His quick-witted comeback might make us smile if we're fans of the scatological and recognize that Paul is likening the proud priest to an outhouse—the kind of wall Jewish males, in that vivid biblical term, "pisseth against."[9] A present-day perspective might grin some at the readiness of Paul's retort, the modern funny bone tickled by the extravagant insults of trash talk. But Paul wasn't chuckling, and neither was the high priest.

Our twenty-first-century acculturation, our entire training in the complex conventions of humor, disposes us in the direction of a modern-minded tendency to laugh loudest at humor in the New Testament when it isn't actually there. My wife's Sunday school students tittered gleefully with the young man in the class whose brow furrowed at the thought of "Jesus standing on the right hand of God"[10]—"Wouldn't that be uncomfortable?" But the martyr Stephen surely viewed that scene from a vastly different perspective, in the throes of being cut to shreds by the sharp stones of Paul's friends,[11] as he struggled to look "steadfastly into heaven"[12] at a shining vision of Jesus with the Father. If the New Testament can reverence what modern readers see as ludicrous, clearly our cultural perspective makes us prone to missteps in the complicated and well-camouflaged minefield of New Testament humor.

7. Acts 22:31.
8. Acts 23:3.
9. 1 Kgs 21:21.
10. Acts 7:55.
11. Acts 7:58–59.
12. Acts 7:56.

From Subtlety to Slapstick

As inside-out compensation for that tendency to read unintended amusement into the New Testament, moderns tend to miss the intended humor. We rarely notice biblical jokes, seldom get the punch lines when we do notice. That same chapter in Acts where Paul calls the high priest a whited wall makes understated ironic play upon the "more than forty Jews"[13] who "bound themselves together under a curse, saying that they would neither eat nor drink till they had killed Paul."[14] Even if that sort of fast-to-the-death conspiracy were common cultural practice, and no matter how religiously it would have been carried to its morbid extreme, amusing *Darwin Award* implications lurk in this situation—the forty cursers curse themselves. If they actually keep their wrongheaded oath, the conspirators have not in the least increased the likelihood they'll do away with their intended victim, but vastly increased the likelihood they will starve to death. That's something short of hilarious. But the irony of that self-obsessed self-defeating behavior is significant, and its topsy-turvy implications meaningful: doing unto others is to have it done unto you.

The most significant humor in the New Testament tends to be that subtle, a humor of irony and implication and innuendo. For instance, "God wrought special miracles by the hands of Paul."[15] Intriguing implications percolate from the irony in this pious rhetoric. Paul, however miraculous his hands, is presented here not as a "religious superman"[16] so much as a hard-sell snake-oil provider, maybe something of a minor-league con man. Intimations between these lines suggest that the apostle might even need legal defense. Those "special miracles," examined more closely, turn out to be more unusual in their earthy means than in their miraculous effects: "from his body were brought unto the sick handkerchiefs or aprons, and the diseases departed from them, and the evil spirits went out of them."[17] The NIV translates "special" as "extraordinary," hinting that those dubious miracles might be less numinous than commercial.

The disciples have apparently hit upon a convenient way to transport the Spirit, a sort of canned Holy Ghost. They "conserve Paul's miraculous power and take it home to the sufferers, using *sudaria*, i.e., sweat-cloths

13. Acts 23:13.

14. Acts 23:12.

15. Acts 19:11.

16. Klauck, *Magic in Early Christianity*, 98.

17. Acts 19:12.

that Paul wore on his head, and *simicinctia*, loin-cloths or aprons or even handkerchiefs that had come into contact with Paul's skin."[18] That healing practice, efficacious though it may be, raises eyebrows. Bad enough that it's magical. It's materialistically magical, profitably occult. The humor at the heart of this sweat-relic situation revolves around the passage's delicate spin of the occult dubiousness and the entrepreneurial embarrassment shadowing Paul's spiritual powers. Miraculousness is being stressed in an attempt to disguise the seaminess of the used underwear, to make it appear less magical and, more especially, less mercenary. Their public relations defense is deliberately understated. Luke "plays down the possible association with magic" and in its place substitutes the disciples' overzealous charity and Paul's astonishing miraculousness, so extraordinary it overflows in ways he just can't control. Facts are being twisted toward "charges that can [more] easily be refuted."[19]

But typical as that subtlety is, some of the humor, even in the dignified Acts of the Apostles, is hard to miss. Some New Testament humor is so obvious it approaches slapstick. When the entrepreneurial sons of Sceva launch into the apparently profitable business of casting out spirits "by Jesus whom Paul preacheth,"[20] one unimpressed spirit responds: "Jesus I know, and Paul I know; but who are ye?"[21] The derisive demon, showing "signs of sense of humour,"[22] sarcastically demands to see their official sorcerer I.D. cards, "dismissing every claim they make to authority as exorcists."[23] Then in a scene of poetic justice so slapstick it's fit for a Keystone Cops comedy, the possessed guy, who's turning out to be the sanest guy around, chases the impostors out of town: "the man in whom the evil spirit was leaped on them, and overcame them and prevailed against them, so that they fled out of that house naked and wounded."[24]

Admittedly you have to be a little sadistic to find that funny, a little fatuous to enjoy the multiple moon shot of those robeless retreating charlatans. Usually in the New Testament to notice the humor you need only be sensitive, alert not just to theological implication or scholarly ramification

18. Klauck, *Magic in Early Christianity,* 98.

19. DeVos, "Accusation against Paul and Silas at Philippi," 62.

20. Acts 19:13.

21. Acts 19:15.

22. Klauck, *Magic in Early Christianity,* 100.

23. Ibid.

24. Acts 19:16.

but to literary tone. You definitely have to be awake. In this understated context, where there is little "sounding brass" and "tinkling cymbal,"[25] but rather a stillness that runs deep, there's an almost inverse relation between obviousness and importance—the subtler the humor, the more significant. Take the way, for example, humor in Acts characterizes Peter, humanizing him, endearing him to us as it wryly reveals his personality.

Disrespecting Peter

The Peter of Acts, as perhaps befits the neophyte prophet of the fledgling Christian church, is presented as a Rodney Dangerfield "I don't get no respect" sort of guy. The parody of Peter is playful to the point of being satiric, though never Juvenalian sarcastic; it's endearing rather than insulting. The satire is in fact so tongue-in-cheek subtle that it's almost evanescent, a will-o'-the-wisp floating in and out of the somber seriousness of early church piety. That portrait of pontifical obtuseness is all the more fun for being anything but obvious. Way between the austere biblical lines, Peter is portrayed as lacking in dignity. It's a psychologically precise portrait that on close inspection comports well with the realistic probabilities of a prophet-proto-pontiff with no prior role models, who is drafted, after all, off a fishing boat—and a *Galilean* at that, at a time when the term was synonymous with *hick*. Galileans were seen as "country-folk," rednecks "regarded with a certain amount of patronizing contempt by the pure blooded and more strictly theologically minded Jews of Jerusalem."[26]

The undercutting characterization is at the same time a clever inversion of Peter's secular powerfulness. The brash leader of tough fishermen finds himself suddenly awkward in the more sensitive role among God's "fishers of men."[27] Fishermen are by default in this New Testament context manly men—have to be, to survive the lethally sudden storms of the Sea of Galilee in their vulnerable vessels. Peter is clearly the man among those men. His brusque professional competence makes all the more dissonant—and the more amusing—his bumbling, stumbling struggle to come to terms with his new call. We feel for Peter, empathize so completely we relate. That makes the best literary effect of Acts' portrait of a put-upon Peter its hopefulness, the way the apostle's awkward struggle for spiritual

25. 1 Cor 13:1.
26. Thatcher, "Galilee," 634.
27. Matt 4:19.

mastery provides for all New Testament readers prototypical experience of the-strong-man-become-meek-in-Christ. The greatest disciple—like the rest of us not-so-great disciples—clearly has a great deal to learn. But if Peter can do it, hard as the spiritual learning curve obviously was for him, we might do it.

That wide range of compelling literary effects in the characterization of the primary disciple's character gets generated mostly by the simple—sometimes simply delightful—recurrent insistence in Acts of Peter's un-readiness for his challenging role. He has trouble getting the proper feel for the dignity of his position, constantly going out on an overconfident limb and cutting it off behind himself. As enthusiastically as Yosemite Sam rushing out into thin air above disaster, Peter walks fearlessly on the water until the inertia of his waning enthusiasm lets him disappointingly down.[28] He's downright compulsive about those anticlimaxes. When his mentor Jesus heals the man by the pool at Bethesda, he sends him off with a fitting flourish: "Rise, take up thy bed, and walk."[29] Peter under precisely parallel circumstances, appalled by the fact that his subject has lain eight years in the same bed, says in dramatic contrast: "Arise, and make thy bed"[30]—we can almost hear the unspoken Jack Benny "O for *heaven's* sake."

That's not just incidental joke. Such scenes work to subvert readers' expectations, even change readers' outlooks. These improbably realistic scenarios push us beyond our comfort levels. They rub our noses in situa-tions less decorous than we normally face in order to stir up through that humbling if not humiliating experience a great deal more of God's grace than we are able to find in most Sunday school lessons. "The ancient world . . . treated the disabled and especially the lame as objects of ridicule and derision."[31] It speaks to the generously democratic and graciously compas-sionate tone of the New Testament that in this scenario featuring "a cripple who walks into a bar," the joke's all on Peter, the Lord's apostle. And the bed-making faux pas is so gentle a joke it's less of an insult to Peter than a quiet reminder of the human awkwardness of all of us.

Even so, Peter's oratorical awkwardness contrasts lamely with the Master's deft defenses of the faith. In amusing contrast with Jesus's astute skewering of learned lawyers and sharp-tongued Pharisees, Peter has

28. Matt 14:25–31.
29. John 5:8.
30. Acts 9:34.
31. Parsons, *Body and Character*, 114.

problems dealing with common hecklers. During that glorious outpouring of the Spirit at Pentecost,[32] all nationalities present hear the untutored Galileans proclaiming the "wonderful works of God" in their native tongues, a Babel-like cacophony of gifts of tongues, every man of "the multitude" hearing them "speak in his own language"[33] everything from Parthian to Arabian—seventeen languages are specified.[34] Amidst that linguistic uproar, hecklers jeer that it sounds to them as if "these men are full of new wine."[35] New wine is famously "very intoxicating,"[36] so we have here something like the street-insult equivalent of "wasting away in Margaritaville."

Peter takes the bait like the country bumpkin that he is, ponderously prefacing his preaching with "these are not drunken . . . seeing it is but the third hour of the day"[37]—*nobody could be drunk at nine in the morning,* literal Peter carefully explains, *let alone denizens of such unstinting moral rectitude as you see before you. We don't drink at all, let alone before noon— except, of course, for high holy days.* The naiveté of perspective is exceeded only by the ponderousness of the rhetoric. Even in his most prophetic moments—for a prophet, he doesn't do much prophesying—Peter shows signs of uncouth or at least uncultured background. His major vision, the one that universalizes the gospel for the gentiles, occurs under similarly unseemly circumstances: "He became very hungry, and would have eaten: but while they made ready, he fell into a trance"[38] and dreamed of (what else, in his famished fisherman condition?) seafood buffet.

Straight Man for Angels

And Peter gets no respect. Even from angels, Peter gets no respect. The prime apostle's dramatic rescue from Herod's jail has to be the most nail-bitingly glorious prison break in the history of angelic rescues—for everybody but Peter, who pretty much sleeps through it. No matter how bright the divine light shines in the gloomy prison, the heavenly spotlight fails to rouse a Peter slumbering so profoundly he snores away the jail break, undisturbed

32. Acts 2:1–4.
33. Acts 2:6.
34. Acts 2:9–11.
35. Acts 2:13.
36. Ripley, *Acts of the Apostles,* 73.
37. Acts 2:15.
38. Acts 10:10.

by imminent threat of death—even though that peril is made more imminent by the recent execution of another high church leader, James, lately imprisoned and liquidated in circumstances ominously parallel to Peter's. The SWAT angel, despite his celestial imperviousness, is animated by the desperation of the situation far more than the apostle. Forced to resort to less subtle measures than turning up the klieg lights, "he smote Peter on the side."[39] Still only half awake, virtually sleepwalking, the prophet requires instruction in some detail, the kind a child would need—first to put on his sandals,[40] then to rearrange his sleep-disheveled garment, even to don his robe.[41]

All of this anxious action is carried off while the apostle enjoys a dream-like serenity, apparently undisturbed by hissed instructions and frenetic signals and vigorous body blows, blithely unconcerned that such violent gestures might at any moment arouse hostile guards. The narrator is panicky because "Peter was sleeping between two soldiers,"[42] but the prisoner himself seems oblivious to the precariousness of the situation. The passage's patient "now here's what we'll do" pace is so far from the hectic quality of other escapes in the Bible the comparison has to be satirical. Joseph's unhesitating "got him out"[43] to escape Potiphar's wife—so hastily "he left his garment in her hand"[44]—lampoons vividly Peter's unhurried donning of his robe with no sense whatsoever of any urgency whatever.

Much of the narrative emphasis and most of the stressed-out angel's anxiety gets conveyed through the angelic thwack on Peter's backside, "sufficient in force to bring Peter out of sound sleep to his senses though dazed."[45] That "dazed" aspect plays delightfully through the passage—even the Greek grammar makes immoderate fun of it. Careful modulations of tense emphasize Peter's slowness to wake with an exaggerated gradualness that comes close to conjuring up cartoon stars circling irreverently around the distinguished apostle's woozy head. "Peter," we are informed by the wry tense declensions, "was not easily aroused." A while later the tense announces that "by this time Peter was beginning to come into possession

39. Acts 12:7.
40. Acts 12:8.
41. Acts 12:8.
42. Acts 12:6.
43. Gen 39:12.
44. Gen 39:12.
45. Eddleman, *Acts 12*, 162.

of his faculties," and a while after that "Peter was regaining awareness of what was taking place though he had not as yet assessed it."[46]

Though he dutifully tags along in the wake of the angel rushing from the jail, Peter still "wist not that it was true which was done by the angel; but thought he saw a vision."[47] Eddelman thinks Peter is not sleepy so much as stunned at the "suddenness and radical nature" of the event. That's not surprising for the "immediate aftermath of being aroused from sleep and of being projected into an escape from prison over four security guards."[48] But it is surprising enough to be pretty funny, especially considering "Peter himself had not yet become fully aware that this was sensory perception."[49] Not until he is outside on the street by himself, the impatient angel long gone to less exasperating rescues, does Peter "come to himself."[50] And only after he has taken his own sweet time to scratch his head and rub his chin and do a Chevy Chase double-take to make sure he has thoroughly "considered the thing"[51] does Peter rouse enough to realize he has actually escaped from prison.

That Lou Costello portrait of a man sleepwalking through his own life-and-death rescue doesn't end at the prison gates. Peter gets no respect even from servants. Fresh from his miraculous jail break by means of supernal aid, he knocks at Mark's house, where the faithful are gathered praying, ironically enough, for his release. "And as Peter knocked at the door of the gate, a damsel came to hearken, named Rhoda. And when she knew Peter's voice, she opened not the gate for gladness, but ran in, and told how Peter stood before the gate."[52] The agitated damsel leaves the prophet—who this very morning had prison doors opened for him by a conscientiously attentive angel—to cool his unheeded heels outside. The guy who had no trouble breaking out of prison is having difficulty making it in to his friends' house. Luke proclaims, with what has to be a twinkle in his eye, "Peter continued knocking."[53] The scenario is equally amusing whether the compulsive knocking is a matter of lingering grogginess or of apostolic chagrin.

46. Eddleman, *Acts 12*, 162–63.

47. Acts 12:9.

48. Eddleman, *Acts 12*, 163.

49. Ibid., 163.

50. Acts 12:11.

51. Acts 12:12.

52. Acts 12:13–14.

53. Acts 12:16.

The humor of the episode, like a lot of New Testament humor, beams all the more brightly from the somber context of high seriousness. Astute commentators have noticed how implicitly "the rescue of Peter recalls Jesus' resurrection."[54] The parallels are striking: "the rescue take[s] place at Passover," and the subsequent events of Peter's rescue and Jesus's resurrection are not only similar but occur in similar sequence, most strikingly when "the first witness to Peter's release is a woman (12:13–14), whose report, like that of the women who went to Jesus' tomb, is not believed." Scripturewise readers "would have been cued" by the description of Peter's rescue "to notice both exodus and resurrection motifs."[55] It's a serious tribute to the resilience of New Testament humor that any levity at all can penetrate such a thicket of weighty theological implications.

Peter's Rodney Dangerfield act persists throughout Acts. He's all thumbs in his handling of religious challenges. As late as the council at Jerusalem, after much disputing with Jewish Christians, Peter, official head of the hierarchy, stands up to cut the ecclesiastical Gordian knot of church contention with his climactic pontification. But his keynote speech inspires something short of a standing ovation—audience response is underwhelming. We are informed precisely of the anticlimactic impact of Peter's oration on the congregation: "Then all the multitude kept silence, and gave audience to Barnabas and Paul."[56] Apparently the only person present who pays attention to Peter's speech is James, who reiterates to the multitude exactly what Peter said, a redundancy apparently necessitated by the fact that no one paid any mind the first time. That picture of nobody listening to Peter, of the revered head of the church being honored more in the breach than in the observance, is double-edged in its humor. At the same time it smiles empathetically with Peter, it grins impishly in the direction of the other half of that New Testament odd couple: Paul.

Man of Many Words

Acts' satire of Paul is even more understated than its spoof of Peter, and even more exaggerated. That's doubly witty because the portrait of Paul is in its entirety a portrait of his overstatement. Acts focuses inordinately on "the

54. Garrett, "Exodus from Bondage," 656.
55. Ibid.
56. Acts 15:12.

act of proclamation"[57]—after all is said and done, more is said by the apostle than done. Paul is, in the sparkle-in-the-eye perspective of Acts, precisely what we perceive him to be throughout the whole of the New Testament, though we may be reluctant to put it so bluntly as Acts does: Paul is a man of many words.

In its stress upon Paul's much speaking, Acts is fitting prelude to the seemingly never-ending Pauline epistles—over a third of the "bulk"[58] (the term is more precise than it may sound) of the New Testament. Again and again Acts underlines the bottom-line point: Paul talks too much. His extreme volubility is indicated by constant innuendo suggesting in ironically understated terms, by hint and insinuation, that he's chattering like a jaybird. A few verses almost anywhere in Acts' persistent portrait of Paul's speechifying demonstrates the ongoing joke on apostolic longwindedness: Paul reasons with the Jews for three Sabbaths, "as his manner was."[59] Paul "disputed . . . daily."[60] When the Lord, who really by now ought to know better, enjoins Paul to "hold not thy peace,"[61] Paul takes him at his word and preaches for "a year and six months,"[62] apparently nonstop. When Paul lays hands on his converts we can tell it's at the apostle's bidding that the Holy Ghost comes on them, because "they spake with tongues" in echolalic reflection of their loquacious teacher.[63] Encouraged by that verbal success, Paul "spake boldly for the space of three months."[64] And again in the next verse we see him again "disputing daily,"[65] and in the *next* verse are informed "this continued by the space of two years."[66] Paul declares that his disciples should "remember"—and if they forget we can be sure he'll be sure to find a few words to remind them—"that by the space of three years I ceased not to warn every one night and day."[67]

57. Reasoner, "Theme of Acts," 640.

58. Votaw, "Peter and the Keys," 10.

59. Acts 17:2.

60. Acts 17:17.

61. Acts 18:9.

62. Acts 18:11.

63. Acts 19:6.

64. Acts 19:8.

65. Acts 19:9.

66. Acts 19:10.

67. Acts 20:31.

Night and day, day and night, Paul distinguishes himself as the talky apostle. He's easy to recognize anywhere in Acts—the one with his mouth open. He's so infectiously loquacious that people surrounding the apostle sometimes catch the talkativeness disease from him: A "damsel possessed with a spirit of divination"[68] follows Paul around testifying profusely of their mission, "and this she did many days."[69] Paul is evidently piqued by this "extremely annoying"[70] verbal competition, in his typical *will everybody please just shut up and listen to me* style. He gets so increasingly frustrated with this woman who won't cease speaking—"anyone who has been heckled at length while speaking can sympathize with Paul"[71]—that he finally resorts to verbal miracle, casting out the talkative spirit.[72]

Meanwhile Paul himself just can't shut up. Imprisoned on charges of preaching, his incorrigible response is to convert the jailer.[73] He and Silas decide to pray aloud and sing, oblivious to the painful acoustical reality that it's midnight and they're in the closed confines of prison. "The prisoners," Luke informs us laconically, "heard them."[74] When church leaders send him away by night for the express purpose of avoiding rabidly anti-Christian rabbis, the outspoken Paul, unable to forego any opportunity to talk, winds up in a synagogue preaching to Jews.[75] Not surprisingly, word seems to be getting around about Paul's propensity for much speaking. "When Paul was now about to open his mouth," judge Gallio in hasty self-defense disarms the impending Pauline disquisition: "If it be a question of words and names . . . look ye to it. . . . And he drave them from the judgment seat,"[76] just in the nick of time, before synchromesh-tongued Paul can get his mouth in gear yet again.

The understated fun Acts has with the loquacious apostle reaches as far as Lystra, where superstitious citizens become convinced Paul and Barnabas are "the gods . . . come down to us in the likeness of men." They figure Paul must be "Mercurius"—Mercury, the messenger of the gods, infamous

---

68. Acts 16:6.

69. Acts 16:18.

70. Arrington, *Acts of the Apostles*, 170.

71. Klauck, *Magic in Early Christianity*, 261.

72. Acts 16:18.

73. Acts 16.

74. Acts 16:25.

75. Acts 17:10.

76. Acts 18:14–16.

as a big talker. They type cast Paul in that motor-mouth role "because he was the chief speaker."[77] It's a clever ironic touch—Paul's preaching here specifically castigates pagan gods, and does it so eloquently he is mistaken for one: the talkative one. Paul himself occasionally seems to recognize a high degree of difficulty with wordiness in his voluble style. He prefaces his defense to Felix with the plea "that I be not further tedious unto thee, I pray thee that thou wouldest hear us of thy clemency a few words."[78] We can empathize with Felix, bored before the diatribe begins—we've heard it before, one of those "to make a long story short" promises that always come too late.

All of this playing upon Paul's perennial much-speaking frames that delightful slapstick incident in Acts 20 when Paul in typically fine verbal fettle at a church meeting "continued his speech until midnight."[79] "And there sat in a window a certain young man named Eutychus, being fallen into a deep sleep: and as Paul was long preaching, he sunk down with sleep, and fell down from the third loft, and was taken up dead."[80] Loathe though we are to laugh at Eutychus's fatal misfortune, it's hard not to relish that picture of the Apostle of the Lord having to interrupt his interminable sermon to raise from the dead the young man he has literally bored to death by his "long preaching."[81]

The incident must have certified even for Paul that his speechifying could get so garrulous as to be legally punishable—sermonic accessory to murder. So has he from this life-threatening tragedy learned his lesson, this apostolic windbag? Has he realized that verbosity can bore people not merely to tears, but within an inch of their lives? Does Paul repent at long last of his congenital wordiness, never again to talk a fellow Christian to death? We thought not. That very night, two scant verses later, Acts informs us with tongue firmly in cheek that our hero "talked a long while, even till break of day."[82] The tongue is so far in that dignified cheek under the twinkling eye of Acts it's hard to tell whether it "stands in any way to the positive side of Paul's credit as a speaker that only one listener died."[83] Perhaps we

77. Acts 14:11–12.

78. Acts 14:4.

79. Acts 20:7.

80. Acts 20:9.

81. Acts 20:9.

82. Acts 20:11.

83. Statement by D. J. Scheerer, one of my students, in *English 350: The Bible as*

should be grateful, in the presence of a tongue that longwindedly lethal, so few lives were lost.

It's a pretty good joke, certainly a consistent one—and an intricately extended one in its complicated crescendo to that Eutychus punch line. Acts' satire of Paul is pushed inexorably toward that sort of extreme. The incessant piling up of example after example is laughably over the top in directions that border on burlesque. Acts resorts at times to bodily humor too broad to be considered subtle, as with those hyperactive sons of Sceva. But its amusements are usually satirical, like those that light up Paul. If there were such a thing as sophisticated slapstick, Acts' unremitting portrait of Paul as the man who talks too much—the apostle who's so filled with so much of the word of the Lord it just keeps gushing out, the preacher so inspired he can leave no thought unspoken—might qualify.

Lightbulbs Going On Over Our Heads

Acts rests its case. Paul talks too much. Peter fumbles and stumbles and bumbles. Acts presents those characterizations in humorous light to literary purpose. The New Testament engages in what can be seen under the literary microscope to be deliberate amusement. Even more clearly than its presence is its purpose—the humor is aimed to enlighten us. All that teasing of Peter and tweaking of Paul isn't there simply for the fun of it: the whimsy, as always with New Testament humor, as always with humor almost anywhere in the Bible, accumulates to insight.

At a very deep level—almost a subliminal level—smiling at Peter and laughing at Paul may illuminate in addition to their personalities their ecclesiastical roles and, at still deeper levels, the theological significance of these early church leaders. Most Christian theologians attach more importance to Paul than to Peter in their impact on the primitive Christian church. There is agreement close to consensus that Paul's missionary and doctrinal contributions did more to shape the early church, mainly—and this isn't much of an oversimplification—on the grounds that Paul talks more than Peter does. He certainly does. Scholars tend to put the point more politely: "Paul measured larger than Peter" because "the epistles of Paul, which constitute one-third of the New Testament in bulk . . . give

---

Literature course. Brigham Young University: Winter Semester, 2007.

us acquaintance with Paul and Paul's message in a remarkably full and accurate way."[84]

We get it: Paul talks more. Paul manages as much as ten times as much verbiage in the New Testament as Peter. But the humor tends to question that honorific reading of Paul. If "the judgment of history pronounces Paul the greater of the two, in spiritual insight, in moral courage, in practical wisdom, in Christian theology, in missionary labors, in service to humanity"—or, to get right down to cases, particularly in terms of verbal stamina—"our information concerning the two men is unequal. It may come about that Peter will be more highly estimated as the history of the period becomes clearer."[85]

Peter, less sophisticated and much less verbal than Paul, is quite likely in charge in the early church. It would be a fundamental biblical contradiction if God's spokesman were to be heard simply for his "much speaking," as the mistaken "heathen" assume when they pray.[86] Proud as Paul is of his inveterate vociferousness, and grateful as we are for its flowering in such magnificent scriptural moments as his paean to love that "never faileth,"[87] there is strong ironic undercurrent in Acts to suggest that his elaborate sermons, like the perorations of many a modern preacher, may not be unmitigated blessing, may sometimes show off as much as they edify. Peter doesn't speak as indefatigably nor with as much polish. But these persistently satirical portrayals of Paul in Acts recommend that when Peter speaks, Bible readers do well to listen. That writ-in-humor principle may apply beyond Acts to the words of all God's good servants—the most insistent sermonizers may warrant less of our attention.

In his second short epistle (Peter writes only the two, with the possible implication for more loquacious preachers that brevity may be the soul of wit) Peter comes close to accusing the junior apostle of assuming he's senior just because he's talked more. Peter's sidelong rhetorical glance at Paul here may even suggest that those voluminous Pauline letters, instead of always dazzling with brilliance, sometimes baffle with bull. The quieter apostle points out that the voluble apostle "in all his epistles"—Peter's right: there are a ton of them—can be dense going: there "are some things [in

---

84. Votaw, "Peter and the Keys," 10.

85. Ibid.

86. Matt 6:7.

87. 1 Cor 13:8.

them] hard to be understood."[88] All in all "the history of the attempt to understand this enigmatic apostle [that would be obfuscating Paul as opposed to transparent Peter] and his letters reads like a history of attempts to put him in his place."[89] Not a bad idea, but it could prove an exercise in futility. Theologians talking Paul into anything would be like Elmer Fudd outwitting Bugs Bunny.

When Would Jesus Laugh?

Insight that manages to be that significant, growing out of satire as subtle as the humor of Acts, is a dramatic indication that New Testament humor is intentional. It is purposeful, pointed. And it is pervasive. Though we selected Acts at random to search for humor—in fact, tried to set the humor threshold high with it because the book has always felt so Pauline pompous—Acts may have proven to be, after a closer look, the funniest book in the New Testament. That necessitates a less obvious example from a definitively unlikely source: that most seriously mystical and somberly philosophical of gospels, John. And a particularly somber situation: Pharisees, eager to trap Christ between his natural compassion and that rigid Mosaic code that doomed adulterers to death by stoning, test his judgment by bringing before him a woman caught red-handed in adultery—"in the very act."[90]

In Chaucer that bawdy "in the very act" would be boisterously burlesque. It's far from ribald here. But even in this poignant context subliminal hints of realistic irony contribute to understanding the situation. Jesus stoops down to write with his forefinger on the ground.[91] The speculative potentialities of humor here raise the question of why, in such a dramatic all-eyes-upon-him moment, he would perform such a whimsical act. Why write graffiti while the authorities glare? Is Jesus stalling for time to come up with his clever reprimand? Is his playfulness smiling at the high seriousness of the Pharisees? Is his stooping an affront to their officious uprightness? Is his casual demeanor insulting their compulsive orthodoxy, implying that their obsessive concerns don't matter as much as they think they do? Is his sand-art nonsense sneering at the Pharisees' pride in their hair-splitting

---

88. 2 Pet 3:16.
89. Furnish, "Putting Paul in His Place," 3.
90. John 8:4.
91. John 8:6.

ratiocinations? Is his deliberate delay suggesting that their eagerness to convict, their rush to judgment, threatens any chances of justice? Is that doodling needling the judges, letting them simmer in their own judgmental juices?

That sort of evanescent hint of a situational smile is not going to score a ten on anybody's laugh meter; it would take much more explicitly funny insinuations to coax actual chuckles from such serious context. Still, humor appears to be implicit in the situation. A Calvin Grondahl cartoon pictures a student on a Christian campus, much the worse for wear from well-thrown rocks, lamenting to a campus policeman "All I said was 'Let him who is without sin cast the first stone.'"[92] The cartoon clarifies the classic conflict inherent in this legal fencing match between Jesus and the Pharisees: graciousness versus self-righteousness, radical individuality against institutional order, the revolutionary against the establishment, hippy dreamer against entrenched social tradition, Mel Brooks against everything normal.

Profound issues are being investigated by this simple scenario—questions about the value of institutional stability, about how wise it is to keep doing things the same ways we've always done them because they've always worked that way. Accompanying those ironic considerations are amusing resonances that tend to tease the powers that be, or think they are. Jesus comes close to sticking his tongue out at the Pharisees. He is provocatively anti-hierarchical in this scene. He refuses to defer to the learned accusations of the aristocratic elders, "as though he heard them not."[93] He listens attentively to the concerns of the woman with no cultural voice, the woman outlawed by institutional authority—morally disdained, socially outcast, legally indicted. "The heart of this story"[94] is the absolute "equality of the woman and the scribes." "Jesus nullifies the presumed control of the scribes and Pharisees and places them on the same level as the woman. In this text Jesus will address neither party according to conventional social expectations but will speak with each in his own time, in his own way."[95]

The Christ here is a classic trickster figure—a calculating troublemaker, deliberate upsetter of ecclesiastical applecarts. Jesus confronts conventional authority as cheekily in this passage as sassy Sarah contradicting the angel,[96]

92. Cracroft, "Humor of Mormon Seriousness," 17.

93. John 8:6.

94. O'Day, "John 7:53—8:11," 636.

95. Ibid., 636.

96. Gen 18:15.

audacious Abraham haggling with the Lord,[97] brassy Jacob disputing with Laban,[98] brash Joseph bragging to his big brothers,[99] iconoclastic Moses badgering Pharaoh,[100] scofflaw Samson insulting the Philistines,[101] upstart David leveling Goliath.[102] For all the seriousness of such intense situations, there is inherent humor in the way this classic biblical scenario's reversal of social convention overturns the way things have always been done, tips tradition right on its ceremonious head. We're as stunned at this kind of reversal of the expected as Goliath must have been, none of us ever having had anything like that enter our heads before.

The slightest possibility of humor in this overcharged context alerts us to significances we would otherwise miss. When the mob, "convicted by their own conscience, went out one by one," they exit "beginning at the eldest, even unto the last."[103] The distant outside chance of any hint of teasing here makes readers wonder what that slight detail signifies. Why the eldest first? Because they had sinned the most, those dirty old men? Or is that inference the self-absorbed defense of an immature reader? Could these old geezers, on the other hand, have exited early because experience had made them wise enough to recognize their own sinfulness? Or is that, on the other hand, the self-serving assumption of a senile reader? Those implicit possibilities, resonant with ironic implications, call in question fundamental premises. Humor, or even the possibility of humor, even in this somber circumstance, makes us weigh the bottom-line significance of that narrative trifle of elders exiting first: Is first the worst here, or the best of all the game? Are Pharisees really the best of us? Are sinners actually the worst?

New Testament humor, never obvious, is here so understated as to be no more than latent. But that ironic understatement points to the implicational heart of the passage: We are never in a position to judge anyone. Those pharisaic judges, representatives of the highest community standards—particularly in this context where they are the officially certified judges of someone as obviously guilty as a confirmed lawbreaker, witnessed

97. Gen 18:23–33.
98. Gen 30:25–34.
99. Gen 37:5–8.
100. Exod 7:10–13.
101. Judg 15:4–8.
102. 1 Sam 17:42–49.
103. John 8:9.

by reliable observers in the commission of the crime—stand quietly self-condemned, caught in the web of their own self-righteousness. There's such extensive *in flagrante delicto* in these circumstances we begin to wonder if there might be enough culpability to go around, start to ask ourselves whether this whole scenario of judgment is a setup. How do these respectable elders know the probable prostitute in the first place? How do they know such up-close-and-personal details of what she was up to and when she was up to it? How long did these peeping toms have to wait to see her "in the very act?"[104] Did this well-orchestrated entrapment require any degree of pimping or even participation to prime the prostitutional pump?

Goaded by such engaging implications, we might well wonder, closer to home, where we personally stand relative to the confirmed sinner. Are we with Jesus, casually stooping down with the iconoclastic rebel, party to his caste-leveling graffiti-writing insolence, skewering the community leaders, accomplice to his undermining of all conventional social values? Or do we stand with the upright defenders of community standards, the staunch elders of the old time religion? Will we be able to find in our personal stance, whatever it may be, the good sense and the good humor not to judge? Will we rise to this literary occasion to dance lightfootedly away from pharisaical rigidity and all the security of its conservatism, the safety of its status quo familiarity? If the Savior can doodle while dignitaries simmer (especially if he's ducking his head to hide a grin), if John (the gloomy Jeremiah of the New Testament) can hint any inflection of humor in this gravest of situations, we might learn from that.

When we read the Bible as if it were a Sunday school manual—or, worse still, as if it were a historic artifact—rather than the literary art that it is, we miss much of what is actually in it. Robert Alter talks of "The Art of Reticence"[105] in the Hebrew Bible, of how the Bible tends to tell us least about what it wants us to think about most. Humor observes that ironic "first shall be last, and the last first"[106] approach in textual action. Paul may get more New Testament media time than Peter, not because he is more important, but because he is in fact more peripheral. Peter does not demand our respect; Paul clamors much more noisily for our attention. But it may well be that Peter, ultimately, has more of significance to tell us.

---

104. John 8:4.

105. Alter, *Art of Biblical Narrative*, 114.

106. Luke 13:30.

The best things in the Bible—the humor, the deeper insight, the relevance to our lives—those "things that are more excellent"[107] are easy to miss, never "sounding brass or a tinkling cymbal,"[108] always still waters that run deep. Given our predispositions to read this text every way except the way that it presents itself to us, the literary aspect is easy to miss. The humor is even easier to miss. It's easy for modern readers to miss the illumination of the human condition radiating from the Bible, the spirit, the passion, the compassion, the humane humor of this magnificently understated writing.

The New Testament is remarkably good reading when we read it as it was written. Maybe we read it too dutifully, scholarly, maybe even too pharisaically: "If your nose is close to the grindstone rough / and you hold it down there long enough, / three things will all your world compose: / the stone, the ground, and your darned old nose."[109] Maybe we need to look beyond our theological noses more deeply into the New Testament. Maybe there's humor there. Maybe the humor matters. Maybe the implications of the humor are essential to its meaning. It might be that humor is so integral to the New Testament text that it's impossible to hear fully what the book is trying to tell us without hearing the humor.

107. Rom 2:18.

108. 1 Cor 13:1.

109. "Unknown Dobro Player," *Molly and Tenbrooks*.

6

"A Ruddy Countenance"

David as Trickster

OUR MOST TRADITIONAL TEXT, the Hebrew Bible, presents us with protagonists so untraditional it's sometimes hard to tell they are protagonists. We discover in this venerable relic of a heroic age heroes who look
none too heroic, who would comport themselves more appropriately in a
more modern more cynical text as antiheroes. The closer we look, the more
the Bible is characterized by unlikely protagonists, unreliable, untrust-
worthy, downright deceptive protagonists, heroes whose behavior seems
anything but heroic.

Jonah, for instance, responsible for the redemption of the entire Ninevite nation, tries to dodge his prophetic call.[1] Samson gives every indication of being less interested in the work of the Lord than in the intimate
workings of Philistine women.[2] Gideon, called to be a "mighty man of
valour,"[3] seems to the contrary downright cowardly, requiring sign after
sign before he manages to buck up courage enough to confront the Midianites[4]—and even then dares fight only by night.[5] Not merely lesser lights
of the Bible but its most magnificent luminaries—Abraham, Jacob, Joseph,

1. Jonah 1:1–3.
2. Judg 14:1–3; 16:1, 4.
3. Judg 6:12.
4. Judg 6:36–40.
5. Judg 6:27; 7:9.

even the mighty Moses—act a lot of the time in a lot of ways that seem the precise opposite of heroic.

Our Audacious Hero

Outstanding in that lineup of unlikely Old Testament heroes, the foremost candidate for heroic unlikeliness, is a biblical star as surprising as the phenomenon itself. David, the epitome of biblical heroism, is at the same time about as unlikely as a hero can get. Readers are prone to focus on his piety, as emphasized in the high-toned spiritual cast of his trash talk to Goliath: "All this assembly shall know that the Lord saveth not with sword and spear [and I'm just too darn humble even to mention slings] for the battle is the Lord's, and he will give you into our hands."[6] Yet however disinclined we are to notice, the Bible stresses as well—probably more emphatically—the shepherd boy's blatant ambition when he checks out the thoroughly secular rewards for killing Goliath: "The man who killeth him, the king will enrich him with great riches, and will give him his daughter"[7]—and checks that out again,[8] and again.[9] David's dramatically expressed heroic motivation is to battle God's battles for him. But there's clearly a little something in it for David.

Hero. And antihero. That would make him schizoid in modern terms. In the Bible it makes David profoundly paradoxical. In complementary tension with traditional Jewish and Christian readings of Davidic piousness, modern "hermeneutic of suspicion"[10] readings play up David's trickster aspects. "The traditional version characterizes David as a pious shepherd who rises to become the king of Israel. The critical version presents David as a cunning usurper who murders and schemes his way to a throne not rightfully his."[11] The Bible itself reconciles those readings in that liminal narrative territory and ambivalent moral dimension where "David can be both a hero and a usurper."[12] In the biblical view David is not simply good,

---

6. 1 Sam 17:47.

7. 1 Sam 17:25.

8. 1 Sam 17:27.

9. 1 Sam 17:30.

10. Bosworth, "Evaluating King David," 191–92.

11. Ibid., 191.

12. Ibid., 210.

nor only bad. David wears an angelically white hat at the same time he rides a devilishly dark horse, and he manages both magnificently.

Biblical authors present a David who is, in synergistic synch with his persona of intense spirituality and profound integrity, frankly on the make. He's a man who lives opportunistically, by his wits, capable of adaptation so supple it can stretch into deviousness. So much does the great King David thrive through self-serving trickery that Raymond-Jean Frontain sees deceptiveness as the essence of the man. The key to David's very survival, let alone his success in the biblical annals, may be "the drama of lies, feints, and repeated instances of deception that is enacted within 1 and 2 Samuel and the opening chapters of 1 Kings"[13]—in sum, David's entire career. Shepherd to king, David is chameleonic. He works both sides of all streets. Not satisfied with being "involved in many acts of deception," he's involved in both directions—"some he initiates, but he is more often on the receiving end."[14] Deceived and deceiving, fooling and getting fooled, David is every which way an antihero.

Looked at from that vantage point of heroic unlikeliness, edged as it is by biblical humor, David's often dissembling and sometimes erratic behavior focuses his character on a remarkable incarnation of biblical heroism: David looks a lot like a traditional trickster. Whether kicking his skirts too high dancing before the Ark,[15] dodging one roadrunner step ahead of Saul in the desert,[16] knocking down to size that proud giant Goliath deftly as Brer Rabbit defeating Brer Bear,[17] or outfoxing everyone from stately Saul[18] to charismatic Absalom[19] in winning and rewinning the kingdom, David is a "prankster."[20]

Trickster behavior, evident in everything he does, may be most obvious in his against-the-grain politics. Much of the humor of the "folk trickster" gets generated by his gadfly antics as "antagonist to the social establishment."[21] There is frequent and frequently ambivalent humor in

13. Frontain, "The Trickster Tricked," 172.

14. Marcus, "David the Deceiver," 164.

15. 2 Sam 6:16.

16. 1 Sam 22–26.

17. 1 Sam 17:49–50.

18. 1 Sam 18:12–30.

19. 2 Sam 18.

20. Jurich, *Trickster Heroines*, 33.

21. Ibid.

those political machinations, humor augmented by several levels of irony. David's trickster aspect is an equal-employment jester, "laughable for both how it succeeds in duping others and how it recoils to dupe the mischief-maker,"[22] David himself. Magnificent King David, in his Michelangelo's *David* mode, accompanying the revered Ark ceremoniously back to Jerusalem, forgets himself so far as to dance so vigorously he "shamelessly uncovereth himself." When the personification of Hebrew culture and the epitome of Israelite piety exposes the royal private parts "in the eyes of the handmaids of his servants, as one of the vain fellows,"[23] we cannot help but smile out of both sides of our mouth. On the one hand, the text enjoys the deflated spectacle of the burst balloon of political pomp and religious ceremony. On the other hand, the passage smiles at the clownish overenthusiasm of our charming hero. David's uncanny appeal is trickster paradoxical: the more we laugh at him, the better we like him.

Quintessential Trickster

Underneath the high-toned trappings of his glorious political and military success, the greatest king of Israel comes to incarnate at his core the role of the rascal trickster. The pattern of that role is as fluid as it is complicated. And it is remarkably complicated, a shifting kaleidoscopic of multiple-personality disorders. But any *Top Ten List of Trickster Characteristics* would have to include in its juggling act such common elements of the much-studied trickster phenomenon as [1] underdog, [2] outsider, [3] rebel, [4] border crosser, [5] situation twister, [6] taboo breaker, [7] shape shifter, [8] deceiver, [9] friend of the gods, and, ultimately and summarily and intriguingly for our purposes, [10] comic. Hynes considers any character who exhibits any one of those traditional characteristics a certified trickster.[24] David qualifies at the top of his trickster class, at any given point in his evolution from apprentice shepherd to journeyman warrior to five-star ruler incorporating many of those shades of trickiness, and at some points in his rainbow career shining in every dimension of that spectrum.

As with other ancient mythological tricksters like Loki or Odysseus or Krishna in his cowherd manifestation, or such ethnic tricksters as Coyote of the Navaho or Raven of the Pacific Northwest or Ananse the spider

22. Jurich, *Trickster Heroines*, 33.

23. 2 Sam 6:20.

24. Hynes, "Mythic Tricksters," 34.

trickster of the African Ashanti, or such modern trickster figures as Huck Finn or Butch Cassidy or Calvin of *Calvin and Hobbes,* David's central narrative function is disrupting social normality.[25] He undermines authority figures, rebels against sanctions, violates taboos, profanes sacred icons. He is quintessentially trickster in his upstart underdog status, where he overcomes such overwhelming odds we still call any narrative of impossible triumph a "David-and-Goliath story."

Further true to the trickster mold, David is an outsider, existing beyond culturally defined borders, moving freely across them. He is a deceiver and a manipulator who can twist situations, turning normal social expectations on their heads in ways that frequently trigger humor—his narrative is rich with the characteristic comic elements of the traditional trickster. There is even some biblical indication that David takes on the weirdly typifying trickster role of shape-shifter, at least to the extent that he alters his appearance and sometimes his persona to negotiate difficult situations. David is a disturbingly close friend of the gods, too, favored of the divine—God himself proclaims him, even after all his dastardly deeds with Bathsheba and Uriah, "a man after mine own heart."[26]

David doesn't do much resting on those divine laurels. His flights of angelic spirituality continually crash in shocking earthiness—he is both transcendent saint and consummate sinner. One minute he's giving the devil his due, the next yearning toward Yahweh. He rocks the boat of cultural convention so vigorously he tips fundamental gender expectations all the way over. In the Bible, tricksters are most usually and usually most definitively women. "Practice of deceit" in biblical culture "more explicitly serves the woman. . . . It is woman whose identity has been most compromised and is, thus, in most need of rescuing."[27] Despite those severe gender handicaps, David boasts personality assets—his ADHD energy, his manic charisma, his unmatched genius for stirring up trouble—that star him with Eve as the prototypical biblical trickster.

Like most other tricksters, David often becomes the victim of tricks in the very process of tricking tricky rivals, personifying in his rollercoaster ups and downs both "do unto others before they do you first" and "what goes around comes around." That capriciousness makes pinning down the storyline—let alone grasping the thematic implications of this preeminent

25. Hyers, *Spirituality of Comedy*, 177.

26. Acts 13:32.

27. Jurich, *Trickster Heroines*, 34.

biblical trickster—a lot like herding cats. His on-and-off haphazardness may also be what makes the bottom-line moral of the Davidic trickster story settle out with such serendipitous inevitability in the direction of "cast thy bread upon the waters: for thou shalt find it after many days."[28]

The most intriguing thing about David's trickster status, particularly in light of how subtle the phenomenon tends to be in its literary effects—and hence how little we've noticed it—is its prominence. The trickster element is anything but disguised, in no way veiled by the Bible. David, far from being camouflaged by a crowd of more conventional characters, is featured as the prime exemplar of a host of prominent biblical trickster figures, from con-man Jacob to riddling Samson to a shockingly witty Jesus. The phenomenon is so widespread it makes the whole culture a kind of composite trickster—Israel constantly outwits or more usually is outmaneuvered by Egypt and Edom and Canaan and Philistia and Babylon and Assyria and Rome. The universality of this trickster theme makes King David symbolic point man for his entire nation; if Israel was a cereal company, David would be its crazy Trix rabbit.

The Bible is all about the underdog—"the marginal's confrontation with oppressive authority, more specifically Israel's dealings with its Philistine enemies."[29] As the centerpiece of that celebration of underdogs everywhere, of unlikely heroes perpetually facing impossible odds, stands David, invariably outmatched. Nobody does vulnerability better. The prototypical embodiment of the archetype features adolescent David confronting seasoned bully Goliath, brawling "man of war from his youth,"[30] whose shield bearer, half his size, looks to be twice as big as young David. That against-all-odds quality makes David the ideal trickster, the consummate trickster, the star trickster, and that's in competition with such a vast array of trickster protagonists, particularly the panoply of female flimflammers and professional pullers of the wool over male eyes from Eve to Esther, Rahab to Ruth, Miriam to Mary Magdalene.

The appeal of David's frank tricksterism is played up unapologetically by the Hebrew Bible, which seems to view him as heroic not in spite of but because of his trickster nature. Biblical texts take the trickster paradigm so seriously, honor it so unquestioningly, as to validate King David by the same standard that got President Nixon impeached: trickiness. Biblical

---

28. Eccl 11:1.

29. Niditch, "Samson as Trickster," 608.

30. 1 Sam 17:33.

narrative props up David's favored status by promotion of his trickster aspects, often investing such value in that trickster manifestation as to certify his trickster acts as inspired—at their rule-busting best, divinely guided. In that same paradoxical last-shall-be-first manner, biblical narrative honors him by lowering the level of his adventures with humor. The Bible encourages us to laugh at David's comic image by way of inviting us to respect him not just in more detail, but in more depth.

Underdog

David acts out the trickster life from his earliest appearance as deadeye shepherd sharpshooter who on the dead run nails the giant right between the eyes, to his last sad fadeout as the impotent old king who "gat no heat."[31] The wording is from the King James Bible, whose literary superiority and evocative richness and, not incidentally, meaningful humor transcends more recent, more scholarly translations. Contrast that vivid image with the strikingly less lively and far less informative "though they wrapped clothes round him, he could not keep warm" from the New English Bible. Or "he could not keep warm even when they put covers over him" in the fine New International version. Or the equally bland if more tender "though they laid coverlets over him he could not keep warm" of the Jerusalem Bible.

All those modern versions limit their range by overlooking the trick-ster dimension, and with that limitation miss the attendant humor. The finest up-to-date translations ignore the implications of the warmth of the presence of that "young virgin"[32] Abishag in aging David's frigid bed, the ramifications of the servants' advising "let her lie in thy bosom, that my Lord the King may get heat."[33] The KJV's suggestion that leading-man-romantic King David in his dotage got no help from the Viagra treatment of the time, a more hands-on treatment than in our chemical times, is more than a matter of adding human color to the situation. David's ironic elderly incapacity may be the most important dimension of the passage's meaning. His lusty Don Juan vigor has declined to a pathetic impotence that invites smirking sympathy for the fading king, and for the inevitable tragicomic losses of all mankind. The spring-winter couple cuddled, but that's all the

31. 1 Kgs 1:1.
32. 1 Kgs 1:2.
33. 1 Kgs 1:2.

sexiest king in the history of the kingdom could manage. The hottest young thing couldn't warm old David up.

It's a hard-knock life, the trickster life, as fraught with being fooled as with fooling—like the lives of Jacob or Joseph or maybe even in some ways Jesus and probably all of us. For starters, little David is the ultimate underdog, the inauspicious apprentice who rises Horatio Alger-like above overwhelming circumstances, sheep herding then as now lowest profession on the socioeconomic totem pole. The low opinion of his own family makes that painfully clear. When David presumes to rise far enough above his stunted status to answer Samuel's call, his father dismisses him as "yet the youngest, and, behold, he keepeth the sheep."[34] His brothers don't think he amounts to much either, not even cannon fodder for the Philistines. In his older brothers' view he's good only for herding, and none too good at that—"With whom hast thou left those few sheep in the wilderness?"[35] But in the Bible as surely as in Saturday morning cartoons "there's no need to fear when Underdog is here."[36] As soon as we notice how long the odds are—David is the youngest of the brothers, a fairy-tale one-beyond-seventh son—we realize that the unfavorable circumstances could paradoxically propel this unlikely looking lad, brave little tailor among giants, to "not merely endure" but "prevail."[37]

Niditch argues that the trickster role itself is a subtype of the underdog role, a theme prevalent in the Bible because the Israelites saw themselves as perennial underdogs, ever embattled and disadvantaged, number two always trying harder.[38] The youngest son of Jesse, David is least likely candidate to attain the kingdom, not only in readers' eyes but in the sophisticated view of that astute seer Samuel. He doesn't even qualify as a candidate until Yahweh commands Samuel to ignore the clearly deficient "height of his stature"[39] that makes him runt of the litter among his strapping brothers. Israelites looked to their leaders for largeness, for Abe Lincoln and George Washington size. They were proud of the imposing height of their original

34. 1 Sam 16:11.

35. 1 Sam 17:28.

36. Searl, *Howling Good Time*, 24.

37. Faulkner, "Nobel Prize Acceptance Speech," 179.

38. Niditch, *Underdogs and Tricksters*, xi.

39. 1 Sam 16:8.

king, Saul, praised him as "higher than any of the people from his shoulders and upward."[40] David falls way short of the job description.

Yet he turns out, against those imposing physical odds, to be stunningly successful. David rises to become the greatest of Israelite kings despite that definitive deficiency of physical stature. Like that "tall pine" Lincoln, David "kept on growing."[41] When he faces off with the giant Goliath, the size and maturity differential is graphic: the huge Philistine "disdained him: for he was but a youth."[42] Goliath's less than gigantic "armor bearer" towers so imposingly over slight David that the movie version would require for David's part someone as diminutively youthful as Michael J. Fox.

David's unlikeliness as hero is stressed in ways other than size. It isn't only the lack of stature and experience that insults Goliath. His features, too, are inauspicious—David is something of a pretty boy. The rugged warrior Goliath trash talks him for being "ruddy, and of a fair countenance."[43] Too cute for a killer. The fair-haired lad looks anything but the warrior he turns out to be. Despite that unpromising appearance, this unsophisticated shepherd, this harp-playing and poetic and maybe just a little effeminate courtier, this untried warrior with armament as unprepossessing as his demeaningly rural and decidedly unmilitary demeanor, defeats the most imposing giant as readily as Jerry outsmarts Tom.

David's underdog status appears to facilitate rather than hinder his scrambling up the Palestinian winner's podium above vast Goliath and, for good measure, tall King Saul. There is clear comic contrast between Saul's imposing physique hiding shyly "among the stuff"[44] at his coronation and David's slight frame, in his audition for king, refusing with teenage overconfidence Saul's extra-extra-large armor. Even as a callow political neophyte, young David plays up all possible public relations angles with an aplomb that would impress Napoleon, histrionically predicting his victory—"all this assembly shall know."[45] With supreme confidence totally at odds with his vulnerable situation, "David hasted" and "ran toward the army to meet the Philistine"[46] headfirst into the fray. Frail David, who couldn't strike fear

40. 1 Sam 10:23, 9:2.
41. Sandburg, *The People, Yes*, 272.
42. 1 Sam 17:42.
43. 1 Sam 17:42.
44. 1 Sam 10:22.
45. 1 Sam 17:47.
46. 1 Sam 17:48.

into the heart of the local schoolmarm, is determined to take on all comers, to confront the mightiest champions of the most fearsome armies.

The resulting political sound bite, "Saul hath slain his thousands, and David his ten thousands"[47] quantifies how prodigiously the public reputation of unsophisticated David has grown. He's all the more popular a hero for his heroic unlikeliness. Adolescent David—unlike the typical trickster who ends up with perfectly appropriate poetic justice hoist on the petard of his own vanity—succeeds, succeeds beyond all expectation. His staggering political accomplishment is as overwhelming as the consequent social acceptance that lionizes him everywhere, especially among women. We would hardly expect him, in these circumstances where he is universally beloved, to maintain the usual social status of the trickster as outsider— outlandish stranger, outside-looking-in outlaw, "visitor everywhere, especially to those places that are off limits."[48] Yet as precisely on cue as if he'd read up on Hynes's outline of the literary trickster scenario, David manages to get exiled by Saul so he can roam widely and wildly outside Hebrew society. The imperial motivation for running him out of town could be scripted from the trickster paradigm—Saul is provoked by David's trouble-making proclivities, his Tom Sawyer trickster talent for imbroglio.

That trickster gift for disruption makes David not only an outlaw but a fomenter of outlaws, ultimately their leader. MacDonald describes him at this juncture as a "freebooter." "Our modern word for him" on this "side of his life, would be 'racketeer.'"[49] Dodging the Israelite army, David shifts roles into his Robin Hood mode. At his Butch Cassidy Hole-in-the-Rock hideout, the "cave Adullam,"[50] David gathers around himself a band of disgruntled outcasts: "everyone that was in distress, and every one that was in debt, and every one that was discontented, gathered themselves unto him; and he became a captain over them: and there were with him [a ragtag band of] about four hundred [ragged] men."[51]

Few though those numbers are—he's still dramatically underdog to mighty King Saul—David's feisty little outlaw band tripwires more disruption for Saul's kingdom than entire enemy armies. Saul gets so frustrated by the gadfly unrest he becomes obsessed with ridding the kingdom of David,

47. 1 Sam 18:27.
48. Hynes, "Mythic Tricksters," 34–35.
49. MacDonald, *Hebrew Literary Genius*, 41.
50. 1 Sam 22:1.
51. 1 Sam 22:2.

who leads his increasingly grim king on a Roadrunner chase through the Judean desert, always enticingly close, always maddeningly out of reach. With Saul breathing down his neck, David, trickster friend of the gods, is warned by the Lord in the cliffhanger nick of time to flee.[52]

When the treacherous Ziphites finger his location to Saul, David still manages to skip a scant step ahead.[53] The enraged king stays on his scent so doggedly that David the border crosser slips over into Philistine territory to avoid capture, allying himself with Achish and the Philistines, bitterest enemies of the Israelites.[54] It is trickster typical that David's locale, wherever he might flee, is always the liminal—not just the badlands of the Palestinian desert, but the border between acceptance and rejection by Hebrew society. His escapades are in every way outlandish. His very identity is all over the map. One scholar wonders whether David at this point is "renegade to his people or a fifth column in the Philistine army?"[55] Or, as befits the consummate turncoat trickster, both.

Twister, Taboo Breaker, Shape Shifter

As Wile E. Coyote, Genius, keeps rediscovering to his recurrent chagrin in his Roadrunner pursuits, it's hard to run a good trickster to ground. David, with his usual topsy-turvy style, may be out, but he's not down. For all the pressures on him, for all his shiftiness under those pressures, David keeps an eye focused firmly upon Saul's throne. The situation-inverter "overturn[s] any person . . . no matter how prestigious."[56] For David that "no matter how high" challenge targets the king. In the tricky process of supplanting Saul, the pretender to the throne comes at times perilously close to mocking him, a matter not merely of bad public-relations strategy but high treason. When the king blunders into the cave where the outlaw hides, hapless Saul is too slow on the uptake to notice he is there.[57] The pretender to the throne, confronted with direct opportunity to kill his rival, instead assassinates his dignity, ritually insulting Saul by cutting off the border of his regal robe

---

52. 1 Sam 23:11–13.

53. 1 Sam 26:1–4.

54. 1 Sam 27:5.

55. Schemesh, "David in the Service of King Achish," 73.

56. Hynes, *Mythical Trickster Figures*, 37.

57. 1 Sam 24:3.

in what looks more like a trickster move than the considered tactics of an ambitious politician.

Adding political injury to insult, the king-in-waiting waves the regal remnant, a red flag before the royal bull: "Behold, this day thine eyes have seen how that the Lord had delivered thee into mine hand . . . and I said, I will not put forth mine hand against . . . the Lord's anointed."[58] It is painfully clear here, to Saul and all the rest of us observing David's clever jibes, whose side God is on, who has the better campaign manager, the better speech writer. David's brandishing of the regal trophy trumpets triumphantly that he is not just rubbing salt in the royal wounds but co-opting the royal prerogatives, controlling the regalia he anticipates will be his. In this context of toying with Saul's kingliness, the aspirant to the throne comes close to sarcasm in his much speaking of his respect "for the Lord's anointed."[59] With ill-disguised self-assurance that he is about to be king himself, David displays more respect for the "Lord's anointed" next in line than for the present king; he seems more concerned about the kingly role he's about to arrogate than he is about King Saul.

That desecration of the royal reputation will come back to haunt him when he is himself king. Taboo violation, central to the mythological trickster roles, stands at the heart of biblical characterization of David. The trickster "seems impelled inwardly to violate all taboos, especially those which are sexual, gastronomic, or scatological."[60] In the scatological dimension we see David peeking out of a corner of a cave watching austere head of state King Saul relieve himself.[61] In the gastronomic mode we observe David's gauche eating of the sacred shewbread.[62] But it is in the disturbing Uriah incident, the watershed of Davidic narrative, that David reveals himself most dramatically as a breaker of momentous cultural taboos.

It is not just that as king, embodying in his very person the sanctity of Israelite law, he flagrantly breeches the strong taboo against adultery. David's attempted cover-up enmeshes him in violation of an even more severe taboo, the most serious Israelite prohibition: murder. In a further slide down the slippery slope of taboo breaking, David calls Uriah back from the battle in a misguided effort to cloud the paternity issue—about

58. 1 Sam 24:10.

59. 1 Sam 24:6, 10; 26:9, 11, 13, 16; 2 Sam 1:14, 16.

60. Jurich, *Trickster Heroines,* 42.

61. 1 Sam 24:3.

62. 1 Sam 21:6.

as close to a *Jerry Springer Show* episode as it's possible to get in ancient Israel. Loyal Uriah tricks the trickster by refusing to go home to his wife, his dogged devotion to his fellow soldiers casting an ever more shameful light on the king's casual betrayals. David's chagrin drives him so far over the edge of cultural taboo he puts out a contract on a trusted ally, a close neighbor who is probably a good friend as well, ordering the man he cuckolded sent to the front lines to be killed (in a final lethal irony) defending his king's interests.[63]

General Joab seizes the sleazy opportunity to trick the trickster commander. "Joab does not miss this chance to play a harmless but stinging joke on the king"[64]—not so harmless, but certainly stinging. Joab "baits a seriocomic trap for the king."[65] The canny general sets him up, instructing his messenger that when David is debriefing him, "if so be the king's wrath arise"[66]—that is to say, if the royal prima donna repeats his "why so many casualties?" speech—"then say thou, Thy servant Uriah the Hittite is dead also."[67] The dark humor here puts the trickster in his place by means of clever blackmail: *Careful of your criticism of me,* Joab is smirking: *I've got something on you.* "Judging by the zest with which he plays" this trump card, "Joab himself must have savored the irony."[68]

The trickster here clearly tricks himself, both in violating the Israelite law of which he is foremost representative and in prostituting his royal power in the process. Distressing though all this is, tragic though it is, it is so insistently ironic—so blatantly "who should know better than David?"—that there may be even here undertones of humor. This dismal climax is the culmination of the long series of David's taboo-violating tendencies that began when we saw him earlier eating the sacred shewbread and accelerated when the Israelites marched the Ark triumphantly into the City of David, David exposing his royal self dancing before the Lord, indecent in the presence of the holiest of Hebrew symbols. That worshipful hootchy-kootchy performance is simultaneously ecstatic (*ekstasis:* Greek "to step outside the norm," or *dance* outside) and unseemly enough to rip

---

63. 2 Sam 11:8–15.

64. Sternberg, *Poetics of Biblical Narrative*, 215.

65. Ibid.

66. 2 Sam 11:20.

67. 2 Sam 11:21.

68. Sternberg, *Poetics of Biblical Narrative*, 244.

a permanent breach between David and his official legitimate claim to the throne, Queen Michal, royal daughter of Saul.[69]

The seriousness of his violation of Hebrew taboo is highlighted by the utter estrangement it precipitates between David and his regal bride despite their crucial political relationship, a relationship the more significant because she was his first love. First love no more, the crown princess is put as rudely in her place as a peasant: "Therefore Michal the daughter of Saul had no child unto the day of her death."[70] The Michal who in a total turnabout now "despises" her husband has come a cool distance from the woman who related so enthusiastically to David that she abetted his trickster activities against her own father, fostering such far-out trickster work as shape-shifting. In their honeymoon days Saul's daughter, getting wind of the king's plan to assassinate her husband, enabled David's escape through the window of their palace apartment. Michal, in a Three Stooges coverup, shaped goat's hair in her husband's place in the bed, using the dummy—that staple of trickster misdirection from Balaam's ass to Charlie McCarthy—to cover David's getaway from the king.[71] Though shape shifting is the least evident of trickster characteristics in the Davidic narrative, David resorts more than once to significant disguise, as when he tries on Saul's oversize armor and his royal role in anticipation of facing Goliath,[72] or morphs malleably under Samuel's anointing hands from callow shepherd to king-in-waiting,[73] or poses as a madman among the Philistines.[74]

David's shape shifting extends further in the direction of the ludicrous. He romps through a range of roles that make him something like all things to all people, assuming more personas than Bugs Bunny befuddling Elmer Fudd. With the possible exception of Woody Allen as the multiple personalities of *Zelig*, David may hold the record for chameleonic character responsiveness to shifting environments. With Saul he is loyal Hebrew.[75] With Achish the Philistine, he is Hebrew deserter.[76] With Samuel, David is

---

69. 2 Sam 6:14–23.

70. 2 Sam 6:23.

71. 1 Sam 19:12–17.

72. 1 Sam 17:38.

73. 1 Sam 16:13.

74. 1 Sam 21:13–14.

75. 1 Sam 22:14.

76. 1 Sam 29:6.

humble shepherd.[77] With Joab, he's street-smart strategist.[78] With his rowdy band he's one of the guys.[79] With the Judahites, he's supreme monarch.[80] With Jonathan, he's devoted friend.[81] With his children he's absent father.[82] With Michal he is clownish husband.[83] With Abigail he is gallant lover.[84]

His role playing is protean. This Hebrew everyman comes close to being every man. "He was a many-sided man; a great lover—almost a romantic lover, a great warrior, a man of counsel and purposed plan, a man of wide experience in the adversities and successes of life, a man of close friendships, a man who slipped and fell and rose and went on, a great sinner and a great repenter."[85] That gift for shape-changing may be key not only to David's picaresque narrative—"the ragged irregularity"[86]—but also to his character. His dreams of what he might become were unlimited; his attempts to be everything he could be were unprecedented. He was an incarnate biblical version of the least assuming and what might be the most inspiring success story ever told: *The Little Train that Could*.

Deft Deceiver

But it is deception, next to comedy the most prominent of trickster characteristics, that plays the pivotal role in this narrative. This persistent trickster manifestation is so compelling a force in David's life it transcends morality, and this in an Israelite world, which is felt by most readers to be the wellspring of morals. Marilyn Jurich thinks the Bible's inordinate respect for Davidic deceit goes so far it "cannot be understood in terms of its relation to truth or falsehood."[87] The focus of the deception becomes not so much its falsity, rather its efficacy in creating "a sense of personal difference

---

77. 1 Sam 16:11.

78. 2 Sam 11:14–17.

79 1 Sam 22:1–2.

80. 2 Sam 2:4.

81. 1 Sam 18:3–4.

82. 2 Sam 13.

83. 2 Sam 6:20–22.

84. 1 Sam 25:39–42.

85. MacDonald, *Hebrew Literary Genius,* 43.

86. Ibid., 41.

87. Jurich, *Trickster Heroines,* 33.

and independence from society"[88] for the trickster. That valuing of individuating deception creates a kind of morality of differentiation. Ultimately
trickster success is a matter of establishing the trickster's uniqueness; the
more eccentric—for David, the more shifting and dissembling (and, it often
follows, the funnier)—the better.

David works the system as cunningly as Ferris Bueller on his day off.
He invests his irrepressible energy and his inimitable ingenuity and all
the intensity of his unique spirituality in running circles, deliberately silly
circles, around the Saulide monarchy. That rapid shifting of moral gears
as the trickster gyrates in and out of ethical territory may explain why
reactions to such quixotic passages are so individualized, why some of
us are more amused than others. The uncanny habit biblical story has of
seeming at the same time either "comic or more serious" may in its invitational openendedness provide a reader-response index to "how the reader/
listener registers the story."[89] The comic dimension is so psychologically
sensitive here, so litmus-like, that we are not reading the humor so much as
the humor is reading our attitudes.

Alone and on the run from Saul, David in high trickster mode saves
himself from starvation by lying. He lies not just to any man on the street.
He shanghais a priest to play straight man to his ethically edgy comedy act.
Suspicious as to why a noble of Saul's court would be traveling without reti-
nue, priest Ahimelech probes for indications of mischief. David's repartee
is quick-witted: "The king hath commanded me a business and hath said
unto me, Let no man know any thing of the business whereabout I send
thee, and what I have commanded thee."[90] This prevarication is no mere
slip of the tongue, no little white lie, but a deliberate, determined deception to pull politically lethal wool over the eyes of the holy man. Under
the pretense that he's on a secret errand for the very king from whom he is
fleeing, clever David scams sustenance—taboo food, the sacred bread eaten
exclusively by God and his sanctified priests. And David.

More and more the deceptive trickster, David ups the ante by relieving
the sanctuary of its most treasured relic, the sword of Goliath. Fraught with
ironic significance, the weapon that was earlier wielded against a mighty
owner is filched yet again for use against the power from whom it is stolen.[91]

88. Ibid.
89. Ibid.
90. 1 Sam 2:12.
91. 1 Sam 21:8–9.

A tactician canny as David has plenty of motive and opportunity during these lengthy machinations to notice Saul's shifty servant Doeg eyeing him, and a politician astute as David would deduce that the Edomite spy will inform Saul.[92] Yet David with nonchalant trickster insouciance goes through with the scheme, letting the consequences fall where they may, apparently unconcerned about what deeply concerns readers—that the stratagem may cost Ahimelech's life. We are right to worry; Saul's reaction surpasses our worst fears. David the survivor as always survives, but the king immediately murders Ahimelech in vengeance for David's deception, for good measure slaughtering his entire community of priests.[93] David as usual leaves bodies in his wake, and as usual the bodies point to others as the killers.

If Ahimelech, with benefit of prescient priestly capacities, falls afoul of David's deception, we can be sure he will not be the only victim. In the very next scene David again bites the hand that feeds him, initiating a series of deceptions of the Philistines who have granted him refuge. When Prince Achish's servants recite the refugee's résumé as the Israelites' most respected warrior, David, whose father obviously raised few fools, recognizes that the court of the Philistine prince may not be the safest place for a Hebrew hero. So he cannily "feigned himself mad in their hands, and scrabbled on the doors of the gate, and let his spittle fall down upon his beard."[94] Achish fails to see through David's act, probably because of its crazy trickster daring—a high-ranking Israelite would be unlikely to wander alone through hostile Philistine territory unless he really *were* mad.

Not satisfied with deceiving Achish, David fools the entire force of Philistine princes. Marginally safer among the Philistines now he has made himself so *persona non grata* with Saul, the trickster crosses the border again. In return for a place to settle, the vagabond supplies raiding spoils to Achish, tricking the Philistine lord into believing so thoroughly in his loyalty that Achish crows over his newfound ally, "He hath made his people Israel utterly abhor him; therefore he shall be my servant for ever."[95] Achish would no doubt have been less enthused had he realized David was raiding Philistine villages rather than Hebrew ones, but the trickster made sure he would never know: he left no witnesses.[96] Achish's fair-weather friend

92. Frontain, "The Trickster Tricked," 178–79.

93. 1 Sam 22:18–19.

94. 1 Sam 21:13.

95. 1 Sam 27:12.

96. 1 Sam 27:11.

repays his trust with an all's-fair-in-love-and-war con that yields sixteen months' worth of protection for Brer Rabbit and political egg on the face of Brer Fox.

That's mere warmup for the most dramatic deception. When Achish orders David to assist the Philistine attack against the Israelites, rather than protesting, David fakes excitement. He exults vociferously over the prospect of battling his countrymen, shrewdly anticipating that suspicious Philistine princes will never trust him in a fight against his own people.[97] Those wily Philistine warriors outsmart themselves by commanding Achish to "Make this fellow return . . . and let him not go down with us to battle, lest in the battle he be an adversary to us . . . [and] reconcile himself unto his master . . . with the heads of these men."[98] David throws himself into his "please let me fight" act with a fervor Brer Rabbit could admire, and the "don't throw me in the briar patch" reverse psychology works perfectly.

Trickster Through and Through

Such skilled manipulations lead to overwhelming political success for David. The shepherd boy becomes arguably the greatest figure in Israel's illustrious history, certainly his nation's greatest king, the man whose military and political success is certified by expansion of his country's borders and its economy and its international influence to the greatest extent in its long history. As David shape shifts from underdog sheepherder to mighty king, his trickster aspects naturally recede into the background. But David's essential deceptiveness doesn't diminish with his waning years. When his son Absalom conquers the kingdom, David, reverting to his bottom-line strategy, falls back on trickery to survive. In a last-ditch attempt to forestall being killed by his own son, David plots with Hushai to disrupt the plans of Absalom's advisor Ahithophel and convince the rebel king to pause in pursuit of David. The ploy gives David time to escape, the stratagem succeeding so well that Ahithophel the rejected counselor, the counselor outcounseled, kills himself out of professional respect.[99]

At critical junctures, as when Saul murderously pursues his son-in-law the dauphin, the shepherd-king's trickiness gets so acute it infects those around him. Like Michal with the goat-hair scheme, Saul's son Jonathan,

97. Frontain, "The Trickster Tricked," 177–78.
98. 1 Sam 29:4.
99. 2 Sam 15:32–37; 17:1–14; 23.

too, acts as co-trickster, accessory to David's evasion of the king. Jonathan's friendship is so compelling he bends his inflexible integrity and lies to his father, telling him that David has returned to Bethlehem for a sacrifice, then hides his friend in Saul's own fields to protect him from the royal wrath.[100] Jonathan's service as intermediary trickster for his friend amps up during David's exile—he acts directly as David's spy, even covenants explicitly to help him become king in the place of Saul,[101] stunningly generous behavior for the rightful heir to the throne.

David's trickster aspect is most energetic when he is most under duress, as with tricksters generally. But he is unusual among tricksters, perhaps unique, in that he works his tricks his entire life, and the tricks continue to work for him. Some commentators see David's deceivings as less successfully long-term. Frontain argues in "The Trickster Tricked: Strategies of Deception and Survival in the David Narrative" that whereas David is effective in his early deceptions, once he is established in authority he winds up getting tricked himself.[102] Nathan thoroughly tricks David, for example, with the parable of the ewe lamb.[103] Joab directs the woman of Tekoah to fool David with a false story to get David to invite Absalom back into his household.[104] Most significantly, Prince Absalom outmaneuvers his father at his own charismatic public-relations game when he popularizes himself with the people, stealing "the hearts of the men of Israel.[105]

Frontain is right that all of these are classic trickster-tricked reversals, worthy of the most exalted Hebrew Bible hero. How much they trick David is another question. David's reputation maintains Teflon imperviousness. No matter how dirty his hands get in the political mud fights, he remains the fair-haired boy. Nathan's parable, devastating as it is personally, has no discernible effect on David's political position except to increase his popularity. The woman of Tekoah's story merely enables the king to do what he wanted to do anyway—invite Absalom to return. Absalom's deception is of more consequence, coopting the kingship and threatening the royal life, but its results are less definitive. While the treachery temporarily drives David into exile, the trickster champion trumps his son with his Hushai

100. 1 Sam 32:42.

101. 1 Sam 23:16–18.

102. Frontain, "The Trickster Tricked," 183.

103. 2 Sam 12:1–7.

104. 2 Sam 14:1–21.

105. 2 Sam 15:6.

trick. David matches trick for trick, winds up with the throne again, and unlike ill-fated Absalom, dies never having been irreversibly outdone. Even more definitively over the long-term struggle of his life than in the specific confrontations that comprise it, David ultimately outfoxes his foxiest opponents.

Yahweh as Trickster?

Seeing David in all his deceiving, shape-shifting, taboo-violating, rebellious border-crossing, situation-inverting, underdog, comic glory, the question for a modern reader is not whether David is successful as a trickster, but why that makes him more heroic. Part of the answer may be found in David's divinely-certified status. It is clear that David holds special favor in the Lord's eyes—God calls him, well after his most devious acts, "a man after mine own heart."[106] Biblical writers affirm David's trickster behavior as heroic because they see it as enjoying the imprimatur of God. What is more, they see Yahweh as not merely winking at David's dubious tactics, but sometimes explicitly approving them, sometimes inspiring them, sometimes even initiating the deceit.

It's at that point where David's only-too-human tricksterism attains to a kind of divine comedy. At that divine-intersecting-human juncture, "God cannot—so to speak—help seeing the ridiculous and comical" in the resistance of those who "intend to hinder Him in completing His own plans."[107] Transcendent irony and sometimes downright comedy can be observed in his playful reaction, "may be seen from certain tricks that God plays against His enemies"[108]—or even sets up for his friends. Jonah schooled by the intriguing means of whale regurgitation[109] is no more striking an instance of divine practical joking than the walls of impregnable Jericho tumbled by nothing but the noise of rams horns[110] or the insult-added-to-injury hemorrhoids inflicted on the unfortunate Philistine soldiers who dare to commandeer the holy ark.[111]

106. Acts 13:22.
107. Jonsson, *Irony in the New Testament*, 48.
108. Ibid.
109. Jonah 2:10.
110. Josh 6:1–16.
111. 1 Sam 5:6.

Yahweh does more than approve David's trickery of Saul; he enables it, as when his favored David sneaks into Saul's camp by night and steals the royal spear and cruse of water to demonstrate his power over the king's life. That deft theft of Saul's insignia may be David's idea, but it is miraculously aided: "no man saw it, nor knew it, neither awaked: for they were all asleep; because a deep sleep from the Lord was fallen upon them."[112] That's aiding and abetting. The diety who causes that deep sleep of Saul's army approximates, if not a Mafioso boss puppeteering the bank robbery, at least a getaway car driver, a contributing accomplice to David's deception.

That is not an isolated instance of divine assistance of Davidic deceit. Yahweh is equally supportive of David's trickery of Absalom. When David sends Hushai to contradict Ahithophel's advice, thereby allowing David to escape from Absalom, the recorded reason that Absalom and "all the men of Israel"[113] respect Hushai's recommendation over Ahithophel's is that the Lord himself fosters this popular support—he "had appointed to defeat the good counsel of Ahithophel, to the intent that the Lord might bring evil upon Absalom."[114] In response to David's request to "turn the counsel of Ahithophel into foolishness,"[115] Yahweh explicitly expedites David's machinations.

The Almighty sometimes takes that tendency to back David's trickery so far as to initiate the deception. When the Lord commands Samuel to find the new king among the sons of Jesse, the prophet worries that Saul will find out why he has gone to Bethlehem, and more likely than not have him executed. So the Lord, in a sleight-of-hand move clever as any of the tactics of his favored David, commands Samuel to bring a sacrificial heifer to Bethlehem as cover. When the elders of the city bustle out to meet Samuel, God's prophet mouths the God-given alibi: "I am come to sacrifice unto the Lord: sanctify yourselves and come with me to the sacrifice."[116] Saul, decisively hoodwinked by this ecclesiastical duplicity, never suspects the secret anointing which precipitates his downfall. Modern readers, inside parties to the deception, may wonder, may even smile, at the irony of a morally heroic life initiated in and sustained by deception, deception which seems to be backed and even at times inaugurated by David's God.

112. 1 Sam 26:12.
113. 2 Sam 17:14.
114. 2 Sam 17:14.
115. 2 Sam 15:31.
116. 1 Sam 16:5.

David isn't the only Hebrew whose trickery is underwritten by the Lord. The most divinely supported of all biblical characters may be the patriarchs, who live by tactics that seem from a modern ethical perspective decidedly deceptive. Fearful that the Egyptians will kill him to appropriate the beautiful Sarah, Abraham successfully passes his wife off as his sister,[117] then pulls the same shifty trick on Abimelech, the king of Gerar.[118] In both these intriguing instances, those who are deceived earn Yahweh's punishment, maybe even his scorn. Deceiver Abraham on the other hand gets rewarded with sheep, cattle, slaves, and silver.[119] It's hard to avoid the conclusion that Old Testament morality blesses characters clever enough to instigate a successful trick, and punishes characters dumb enough to be duped—in much the way modern life seems to. Modern bumper stickers state more bluntly that life isn't fair, but the Bible appears to be operating with similar respect for the premise.

Jacob, the master trickster of the patriarchs, manipulates Esau out of his birthright.[120] Then with the help of Rebekah, to whom the Lord himself reveals that "the elder shall serve the younger,"[121] Jacob puts on goat skins to steal his brother's blessing from blind Isaac, the doltish ruse founding the Israelite nation on deception.[122] That's just the beginning of the deceptions in the Jacob saga. Laban tricks the trickster Jacob by substituting Leah for Rachel,[123] but this turns to Jacob's advantage when Leah proves the more fertile of the sisters.[124] Laban tricks Jacob out of his wages, yet by substituting the second-rate but more prolific black sheep and spotted goats, Jacob amasses a fortune at Laban's expense.[125] Jacob attributes this tricky ploy, as David so often does and Rebekah also did, to Yahweh's inspiration. "The angel of God," Jacob argues with the silken-tongued confidence of a television evangelist, "spake unto me in a dream."[126] Even if the Lord didn't help

---

117. Gen 12:11–13.

118. Gen 20:1–2.

119. Gen 20: 14–16.

120. Gen 25:29–34.

121. Gen 25:23.

122. Gen 27:1–41.

123. Gen 29:21–26.

124. Gen 30:19–20.

125. Gen 30:31–43.

126. Gen 31:12.

dupe Laban, the Bible certifies Jacob's deceptive behavior with impressive success.

Jacob's sons carry on the tradition of success-by-deception established by the founder of their nation. When Shechem rapes their sister Dinah, they answer "Shechem and Hamar his father deceitfully,"[127] consenting to Dinah's marriage on condition all the men of the city convert by circumcision. While the unfortunate men are incapacitated from the surgery, burlesquely enough "on the third day when they were [most] sore," Simeon and Levi unceremoniously take advantage of their delicate condition to slaughter them.[128] Jacob's other sons join these dubious elder brother role models to deceive their father in getting rid of Joseph.[129] Nor is the fair-haired favorite of Genesis, Joseph himself, exempt from the trickster game. A shape-shifter who keeps both his Israelite and his family identity hidden, Joseph in his vizier-of-Egypt disguise plays dramatic tricks on his brothers—he falsely accuses them of spying, frames them with planted evidence, finds pretext to imprison Simeon and imperil Benjamin.[130]

It's not just that God aids and abets tricksters in the Bible. He gets pretty tricky himself. Bible readers observe "certain tricks that God plays."[131] He plants the forbidden fruit tree "in the midst of the garden"[132] where the kids can't help noticing it, and as a result—like children told not to put beans in their noses—they are much more likely to succumb to the forbidden lure than if the parents hadn't brought it up. Though there's often something edgily amusing about these divine tricks, there's nothing trivial. They can be momentously paradoxical, as when God uses the same sea that frees the Hebrew nation to entrap the chariots of Pharaoh. They can be cosmically ironic, as when he allows the Master of the Universe to be brutally killed so that ordinary lowlife human beings might live more fully.

Trickster Hero

By describing David's trickster nature in such detail, biblical authors tie him into the Old Testament trickster tradition, associating him with the

127. Gen 34:13.
128. Gen 34:25.
129. Gen 37:23–28.
130. Gen 42–43.
131. Jonsson, *Irony in the New Testament*, 48.
132. Gen 2:9.

trickster patriarchs and judges. David's feigned madness before King Achish has much the same motivation as Abraham's bizarre lies to Pharaoh about Sarah—survival. Yahweh's assistance of David's stratagem against his son Absalom is reminiscent of the manner in which he inspires Rebekah to steal the family blessing for her son. David wins Michal and vast wealth from scheming Saul in the same sort of way Jacob outwits scheming Laban to win Rachel and Leah and vast wealth. Even the strange bride price of two hundred "foreskins of the Philistines"[133] recalls in its sex-edgy humor such singularly echoic events as Jacob's weird breeding practices with Laban's flocks, and Samson's paying off his wedding bet by knocking off Philistines. Trickster behavior, far from disqualifying biblical heroes, validates them.

Justifying his deceptions as Yahweh-inspired does more than alibi David. Including God as abettor and sometime initiator of trickster actions proposes the essential morality of what appears to modern readers to be questionable behavior. It underwrites acts that can seem at times ethically ludicrous and are always iffy—"God played tricks on creation."[134] "It can be argued that Jacob and Rebekah deceive Isaac because they know that Jacob is preferred of the Lord over Esau—they merely follow the Lord's desires."[135] David also deceives because he is attempting to honor what he is convinced are the Lord's wishes, shifting the ultimate responsibility for his actions to Yahweh himself. There is a sense in which David, anointed king by the Lord's prophet, is forced to trick—first to replace Saul and then to retain the throne—in order to fulfill God's designs. This biblical proposition is not mere political propaganda spun to leave David's image less tarnished from less honorable deceptions like getting Ahimelech killed. It is sincere effort to justify David's trickster behavior, casting it as an attempt to do the Lord's will.

There's another way all this emphasis on tricksterism, as it complements humorous effects, makes David look better. "Early examples of the trickster," according to Ann Engar, "exemplify Greek glorification of intellect."[136] The Hebrews may be taking that Greek glorification a step further, beyond the intellectual to the spiritual dimension. We have in David and in other Old Testament protagonists a new kind of hero, superior not only in intelligence but in spiritual sensitivity. It may be that trickster heroes

133. 1 Sam 18:25.

134. Berkove, "Trickster God in *Roughing It*," 85.

135. Engar, "Old Testament Women as Tricksters," 156.

136. Ibid., 143.

in the Hebrew Bible "more closely at times understand God's purposes."[137] That's significant because the tricksterism, particularly at its most humorous, represents an interiorization of value from physical power to intellectual power to moral power, as if we were to move from the raw brutality of Brer Bear through the cleverness of Brer Fox to the subtler awareness of Brer Rabbit.

So even as the Bible's stress on David as trickster makes him more heroic, that trickster emphasis simultaneously brings him down to a more human level. "As a deviant person, Trickster levels hierarchy and reverses status."[138] That turning of values on their heads is typical of the trickster; it's a thoroughly "subversive role." "Laughter is liberating," and the trickster's "on the fringe" antics become "the source for laughter."[139] The trickster is as comic as heroic, which may explain why the David narrative is rich in comic images, so rich it would appear impossible to overlook the cream of those comic elements rising to the top of the story. Yet some readers do. The myopia seems mainly a matter of simplistic assumptions about limitations on how much heroism and goodness humorous behavior can include. Hyers reminds us that "it is assumed" that biblical writers "were a humorless lot."[140] That means that "comic themes and devices are also not easily seen because of the prevailing assumption that such elements do not exist in Holy Scriptures. A person who is not open to the possibility of comic elements is not likely to be looking for instances or to see them, even by accident."[141]

Clowning Around with the Bible

However much it is overlooked, humor is ubiquitous in the Bible. The trickster dimension alone is so prevalently displayed it takes some serious eye closing to ignore the rainbow of its comedy shining through the changing biblical weather. Engar traces trickster outlandishness in "not only the humor of Rachel pretending to be menstruating, but also Jacob dressed in animal skins pretending to be his brother, Lot's daughters being so concerned about the imminent destruction of the world that they

137. Ibid.
138. Jurich, *Trickster Heroines,* 34.
139. Ibid.
140. Hyers, *God Created Laughter,* 4.
141. Ibid.

get themselves with child by their father, Boaz's surprise and trembling at seeing Ruth lying on the threshing floor, and Judith's prayer before she cuts off Holofernes' head."[142] The impact of that humor alters more than facial expressions. Tricksters in the Bible put so many noses out of joint, twist so many stiff necks, that they reshape the face of the world.

That kind of disjunctive comedy is epitomized everywhere in David's story. Imagine fledgling David, still wet behind the ears, diminutive and rosy cheeked, drowning in the official battle armor of Saul (the armor of a man who stands a head taller than the rest of the Israelites), marching off to confront giants while the towering leader, meanwhile, cowers incongruously in his tent.[143] Imagine little David scampering across the field to saw off Goliath's head with a sword he is barely big enough to wield, while slack-jawed Philistines look on speechless.[144] Envision Saul's bungling men storming too late into David's bedroom, momentarily persuaded by the goat hair sticking out from underneath the blanket that David is sick indeed.[145] Catch a glimpse of David's *Honeymooners* relationship with Michal from the perspective of *God Knows*: "And out the window I went, like some hairy-legged clown in a dirty burlesque."[146] Picture the comedy of David's Robin Hood character, darting over the countryside making life miserable for Sheriff-of-Nottingham Saul, a distressed and increasingly frustrated Saul, a Saul reduced to such foolishness he wanders unwittingly into David's cave, mistaking it for an outhouse.[147] Contemplate David the respected warrior acting crazy, drool dribbling down his beard in front of the entire city of Gath.[148] Watch him begging not to be thrown into the briar patch and laughing all the way home as the Philistines forbid his fighting in the battle David wants desperately to avoid.[149] Take a gander at the king of Hebrew Lotharios so smitten by one glimpse of naked Bathsheba he risks the kingdom for her.[150] Consider the noble king dancing down the street,

---

142. Engar, "Old Testament Women as Tricksters," 148.

143. 1 Sam 17:38–39.

144. 1 Sam 17:49–51.

145. 1 Sam 19:12–17.

146. Heller, *God Knows*, 161.

147. 1 Sam 24:1–4.

148. 1 Sam 21:13–15.

149. 1 Sam 29:3–11.

150. 2 Sam 11:2–4.

exposing himself by Radio-City-Rockette kicks too high for his too-short robe as the sacred ark is paraded into the city.[151]

To see the humor in the David narrative is to begin to understand biblical motivations for emphasizing David's trickster nature. The cleverness of the trickery that creates the humor "mitigates the moral judgment against the means the trickster uses," so that we laugh at the "extremes to which [he] goes in carrying out [his] plan."[152] "There is no feeling of moral indignation at such roguery, because laughter over the success of the trick displaces all moral resentment."[153] We are not nearly so upset as Michal at the unseemliness of David's prancing before the Ark, because we find more humor in it than she does. We mute somewhat the collateral-damage horror of Ahimelech's murdered priests out of respect for David's shrewd survival tactics. In his despicable plot against Uriah we are both more condemning of David and more likely to identify with him when we are wryly shaking our heads at the lengths to which a cheater will go to cover his tracks.

The authors clearly want us to admire their hero as they do. They seem to want us at the same time to see King David as he really is, in the raw. Humor manages that amalgam. The trickster is myth brought up close and personal, an "archetypal image of the human in a realistic sense rather than paradigmatic sense." With tricksters "we identify more totally than with those heroes that are beyond us."[154] The over-the-top drama of his life goes far toward making David the greatest of Hebrew kings. Yet his everyman trickster nature allows the man in the ancient Hebrew street—and people in twenty-first-century streets—to see him as one of themselves. However high his divinely-appointed regal status, David remains a character we can laugh at, and that makes him as accessible as the laughable characters we encounter every day, including ourselves.

The trickster humor of biblical characters relates them to us, almost homogenizes us with them. Humor brings the noble souls of the Bible down to our level. Better yet, the democratic movement of humor, as it makes kings condescend to common experience, makes commonplace folk more kingly. That means we too can aspire to David's compromised glory as king of the rednecks. Turning our Davidic experience, tricksterly enough, precisely on its head, Bible humor lifts us up by lowering the level. We find

151. 2 Sam 6:12–16.

152. Engar, "Old Testament Women as Tricksters," 156.

153. Gunkel, *What Remains of the Old Testament*, 183.

154. Hyers, *Spirituality*, 187.

within ourselves through the illumination of trickster humor what noble David, quintessentially the man of the people, found—both our folksy commonality and our regal potential.

God works in mysterious ways his wonders to perform. Actually, in light of a literary reading of the antics of the Davidic saga, he works by remarkably realistic means. These narratives look like more than stories that God is rumored to have had a hand in. They dramatize not only David's glorious successes but his all-too-human failures, showing him off as king and showing him up as trickster. The Samuel books, at the same time they celebrate David as Israel's golden boy, frankly reveal his warts. David's killing shot to the head of indomitable Goliath, absolute miracle, is simultaneously feet-on-the-ground realistic—thoroughly practiced in thousands of slingshot shots in the sheepherding wilderness, carefully prepared for by selection of the best military equipment and five-smooth-stone ammunition, brilliantly executed by element-of-surprise, speed-over-strength, superior-technology tactics. There is strong indication in both historical and psychological detail that this narrative, like biblical narrative generally, represents actual experience. There is telling evidence here, most telling in the situational humor, that something very like these edgy and unpredictable and altogether human events really happened.

7

"And Who Is My Neighbor?"

Odd Couples in Genesis

B IBLICAL CHARACTERIZATION IS EXTRAORDINARILY succinct. "It is a commonplace," Leland Ryken reminds us, "that the stories of the Bible tend to be told in a very spare, unembellished style. . . . We are told only the most important things."[1] Much of the impact of that streamlined style "stems from what is left unsaid, leaving a dense background of motivation and response open to inference."[2] Erich Auerbach showed us how unique that literary technique is, how strikingly that biblical understatement contrasts with wordier classical literature, where "clearly outlined, brightly and uniformly illuminated, men and things stand out in a realm where everything is visible."[3] In the Bible, on the understated and concentrated and ambiguous other hand, "we are compelled to get at character and motive as in impressionist writers like Conrad and Ford Madox Ford, through a process of inference from fragmentary data."[4]

Hebrew narrative is legendarily reticent, Hebrew prose pithy. Hebrew language itself is a concentrated shorthand compared to English—only eighty-six hundred total terms in the succinct diction of the Old Testament, contrasted with too many to count in the vast English vocabulary,

1. Ryken, *How to Read the Bible as Literature*, 39.
2. Schwartz, "Free Will and Character Autonomy," 53.
3. Auerbach, *Mimesis*, 83.
4. Alter, *Art of Biblical Narrative*, 126.

estimates ranging from fifty times the number of terms in the Hebrew Bible dictionary to as many as a million English words. In those tight linguistic confines, it is hardly surprising that Hebrew characterization is compact. What is surprising is how much literary juice that linguistic concentration squeezes. Less is more in biblical style—the sparseness of the writing is inversely proportional to the expansiveness of its effects. That compression is particularly productive in the Bible's shorthand characterizing. The Bible creates complex and subtle character portraits with the barest brushstrokes of description, breathes the breath of fulsome literary life into its characters through whispers of descriptive detail. The force of the Bible's compressed characterization has been recognized for as long as the book has been read. But it is yet to be appreciated how much the distilled wisdom of biblical wit matters to that vibrant characterization, how crucial a coloring comedy contributes to the Bible's subtle literary palette.

Less May Be More

King David provides dramatic evidence of the complexity of biblical characterizing—he ranks among the most complicated characters in literature. David holds so vivid a place in our cultural memory that the most captivating of artistic representations look like a faint shadow of the biblical original. Not even the great character actor Gregory Peck could fill the bill in Cecil B. De Mille's *David and Bathsheba*, and Richard Gere's more sophisticated, more recent film portrayal of *King David* doesn't come close. Even Michelangelo's celebrated sculpture can't match up to our iconic view of David, and wouldn't even if it were circumcised. Yet that insistently concrete image of David shining in our cultural memory depends upon a single sentence of physical description in the Bible, a sentence that sounds too generic to be memorable, let alone generative of the kind of ramifying specificity that can be observed in the biblical David: "He was ruddy, and withal of a beautiful countenance, and goodly to look to."[5]

Elijah has become so culturally real to Jewish culture, so intimate a part of Jewish imaginative heritage, that a place is set for him at every Passover feast. Youngest children entertain a realized persona of the prophet so persuasive they peek throughout the celebration to see whether the level of the wine in his cup recedes. Elijah's rough character has been elaborated in such detailed complexity that in some Semitic circles this most

5. 1 Sam 16:12.

cantankerous of prophets has become something of a Jewish Santa Claus. Yet the Bible provides for descriptive introduction to this intricate literary presence only that Elijah was "a Tishbite . . . of the inhabitants of Gilead."[6] That's not a lot to hang a characterizational hat on: Hebrew *Tishbite* might or might not mean "hairy." And even if it does, that slight detail could be the undistinguishing generic label of the Near Eastern "wild man" who lurks in his hairiness in the wilderness.[7] That cliché caricature—which on the surface of it doesn't seem to do much more than lump the prophet into a hairy stereotype with antisocials as diverse as Esau and Ishmael and Samson—somehow serves to differentiate and distinguish and unforgettably individuate a personality as memorable as Elijah.

That less-is-more syndrome works even with Moses, where it's more surprising because he gets more air time than any other character in the Old Testament. Talmudic legend credits Moses personally with all six hundred thousand words of the Torah. He is assumed to have authored not just Genesis, the foundational book of the Bible, but for good measure the voluminous tome of Exodus, Leviticus with its endless recitings of the technicalities of Israelite law, the innumerable genealogies of Numbers, plus Deuteronomy, a book some scholars think contributes as much to Old Testament theology as Paul's epistles to the New. Yet we have of direct physical description of this voluble biblical author only Moses's stuttering reference to himself as "slow of speech, and of a slow tongue."[8] That laconic self-description is not just sparse; it's patently counterintuitive, contradicting all that we know about the prophet. How does the Bible manage with such slight touches of descriptive detail to give us portraits of its characters so vivid we can be convinced Charlton Heston is the only possible Hollywood Moses?

It's an astonishing literary feat, that creation of such rich characterization through such limited materials. The Bible's capacity for complex and vital and nuanced and fulsome characterizing by minimal means approaches the miraculous. The Genesis creation scenarios are a world away from creation *ex nihilo*, presto-change-o notions of making something from nothing. But Genesis artistry sculpts complicated mountains out of simple molehills, works a kind of prestidigitation of prose that seems to shape universes out of thin air, weaves worlds out of the thinnest of thin

---

6. 1 Kgs 17:1.

7. Mobley, "Wild Man in the Bible," 220.

8. Exod 4:10.

words. Ambiguity appears key to that preternatural process, but that only compounds the artistic mystery: how can haziness make so much of so little? The stylistic miracle is enough to make a reader wonder how the Bible is consistently able "to evoke such a sense of depth and complexity in its representation of character with what would seem to be such sparse, even rudimentary means."[9]

Biblical narrative provides "nothing in the way of minute analysis of motive or detailed rendering of mental processes; whatever indications we may be vouchsafed of feeling, attitude, or intention are rather minimal."[10] And that absence of psychological analysis is not its only deliberate constraint on its characterization: "All the indicators of nuanced individuality to which the Western literary tradition has accustomed us . . . would appear to be absent from the Bible. . . . In what way, then, is one to explain how, from these laconic texts, figures like Rebekah, Jacob, Joseph, Judah, Tamar, Moses, Saul, David, and Ruth emerge, characters who . . . have been etched as indelibly vivid individuals in the imagination of a hundred generations?"[11]

Dynamic Duos

One of the ways the Bible manages its characterizing so effectively so efficiently is by the clever literary technique of contrasting characters. The Bible features an inordinate number of close complementary characters, sometimes intense friends like David and Jonathan, sometimes hostile brothers like Cain and Abel, sometimes actual twins like Jacob and Esau. Even when they are not twins they are what my cousin calls *twinners*, siblings or spouses or friends who share parallel situations but whose paradoxical dispositions and demeanors forge relationships that highlight their differences more than their similarities—a matched set of misfits. Twinners mix like oil and water. Genesis pairings establish the model for the rest of the Bible by their dramatic entrance, stage left, like the animals into the ark, complementary sets of salt-and-pepper-shaker people: Adam and Eve, Cain and Abel, Abraham and Sarah, Isaac and Ishmael, Abraham and Lot, Isaac and Rebekah, Jacob and Esau, Jacob and Laban, Jacob and the wrestler angel, Jacob and Rachel, Rachel and Leah, Joseph and Judah.

9. Alter, *Art of Biblical Narrative*, 114.
10. Ibid.
11. Ibid.

That two-for-the-price-of-one characterizing etches a *Mad Libs* pattern into the biblical text so habit-forming that readers itch to fill in any blanks. Meeting a pristine example of obedience such as Noah, for instance, Bible readers crave a contrasting example of disobedience, a counter character to balance the biblical scales. The subliminal balancing act may account for Noah's wife's shrewishness in the medieval mystery plays, maybe even motivate her unprovoked violence, her readiness to give gentle old animal-nurturing Noah "a clout over the head."[12]

That odd couple seesaw makes for exhilarating rides of reciprocal characterization. Given a character driven by ambition as single-mindedly as David, we are relieved to find on the immediate horizon a complementary counter-character like Jonathan, so generous he is willing to give his best friend the throne he himself was to inherit, even though that friend is the kind of friend who is willing to take it from him. The literary force field formed by the revolutions of biblical odd couples is so gravitationally robust that when it finds a complementary character missing, it encourages us to make her up. Sweet wife Eve is legendarily pure, saccharine sweet, all domestic innocence, so the Talmud fills in that character gap with sophisticated Lilith, Eve's sexy evil twin.

Those strange couplings may be as significant in the values they espouse as in their artistic impact—there may be important inherent message in this literary medium. Hebrew culture has often been accused of exclusivity, of shunning the non-chosen. But this double-dipping characterizing emphatically concerns the other, welcomes "the stranger that dwelleth with you."[13] That makes odd couple characterization not just tolerant but democratic. This characterizing by contrast is the precise opposite of a snobbish club: anyone can participate. We all in fact do. These Hebrew dialogues of character are universally inclusive—anyone from any cultural disposition or political perspective or religious attitude can relate to these close-to-home conflicts.

The closer we look in Genesis, the more mismatched matches we see: Simeon and Levi, that dynamic duo who put the Shechemites to the sword;[14] Sarah and Hagar, Abraham's dueling wives;[15] Bilhah and Zilpah,

---

12. Baugh, *Literary History of England*, 280.

13. Lev 19:34.

14. Gen 34:25–29.

15. Gen 16:1–5.

Jacob's fertile concubines;[16] Ephraim and Manasseh, Joseph's rival sons;[17] Er and Onan, sons of Judah destroyed for sexual misconduct;[18] Pharez and Zarah, sons of Judah born out of sexual misconduct.[19] To the farthest corners of the book that sets the pattern for the Bible, we see pair after intriguing pair: the two incestuous daughters of Lot;[20] the two angels who visit him in Sodom;[21] Lamech's wives, Zillah and Adah;[22] Adah's creative sons, Jabal and Jubal;[23] Tamar who tempts Judah in Genesis 38, and Potiphar's wife who tempts Joseph in Genesis 39.[24]

For all that insistent pairing, those Genesis couples are anything but matched sets: never Tweedledum and Tweedledee clones, always Dean Martins and Jerry Lewises. The pairings are so dissonant they've earned a place in popular culture as modes of opposites, paradigmatic odd couples: Cain and Abel, Jacob and Esau, Rachel and Leah—"Leah was tender eyed; but Rachel was beautiful and well-favored."[25] Contrast as a means of characterization is hardly unique to Hebrew literature. Character foils that illuminate other characters by contradicting them hold time-honored as well as up-to-the-minute place in literary tradition. But Genesis deploys the simple convention of contrasting characters with unparalleled subtlety and scope. Both the scope and the subtlety of these bifocal glimpses into the human condition are illuminated and augmented by humor.

The Odd Couple

Take, for example, the brothers Jacob and Esau—twins whom we might expect to share much in common, to be interdependent in their relationship, mutually mirroring in their behavior. Yet Esau and Jacob are about as ironically un-identical as it's possible for twins to be. Rebekah is warned by the Lord before the boys are even born that she will give birth to "two

16. Gen 30:4–12.

17. Gen 48:9–14.

18. Gen 38:6–10.

19. Gen 38:27–30.

20. Gen 19:30–36.

21. Gen 19:1.

22. Gen 4:19.

23. Gen 4:20–21.

24. Noble, "Esau, Tamar, and Joseph," 221.

25. Gen 29:17.

manner of people."²⁶ These founders of competing races, the progenitors of the Israelites and of the Edomites, are very nearly separate human species. Genetically close though the brothers are, Genesis makes again and again the point of their differences. Jacob himself views his fraternal twin—with whom he shares so much DNA nature and so much patriarchal nurture—from a perspective of opposition: "Esau my brother is a hairy man, and I am a smooth man."²⁷ The demeaning distinction goes beyond mere insult of Esau's hairy-chestedness, beyond the setup for the burlesque joke of imitating the macho older brother by the contemptuous expedient of donning animal furs—not quite a gorilla suit with Esau's name on it, but we get the point.

Jacob, in direct contrast, is smooth in every way, smooth "of skin and character"²⁸—smooth talker, smooth actor, suavely polished to the point of a little slipperiness. That sophistication typecasts him in terms of cultural cliché as "dwelling in tents,"²⁹ identifies Jacob with a civilized setting "which in this case serves as a double entendre for pastoralism as well as the moral qualities associated with interiority."³⁰ The reader alert to possibilities of humor will pick up on that intriguing "interiority" to notice that the nomadic tent is female territory. Jacob "remains in or around the tent preparing food while his brother goes off hunting in the field. In short, he is depicted in ways that are reserved elsewhere in Genesis exclusively for women."³¹ Genesis isn't intimating that Jacob is light in the sandals. His masculinity is emphatically affirmed—he is, after all, sire of the entire Israelite tribe. But the Bible, with its characteristic characterizing honesty, is frank about putting Jacob in his place: looking down all he likes on his brother's uncouth wildness, he's still a mama's boy. Esau stands foursquare in the masculine realm, as his father's favorite. Jacob, his mother's pet, is relegated to the female venue.

The characterization is both impeccable and impeccably fair, as balanced as it is vivid. Jacob may be less macho than his older brother, but that probably makes the younger kid, in the Bible's patriarchy-deflating terms—and, when we think about it, amusingly catty terms—more thoughtful,

26. Gen 25:23.
27. Gen 27:11.
28. Seeman, "Where is Sarah Your Wife?" 118.
29. Gen 25:27.
30. Seeman, "Where is Sarah Your Wife?" 118.
31. Ibid.

more meditative, more introspective, more self-aware. These biblical twin-ner syndromes perform a minuet of "relational and oppositional images." "The more interior actor" occupies a position of "structural inferiority and formal dependence"[32] in this nomadic setting—he's more effeminate. But he's also smarter. The Saul role here is commandeered by Esau, but that leaves Jacob free to be a David.

That's the way the balance of personality power works with these unidentical twins, possibly the way it works in all sibling rivalries: Jacob tends to be everything that Esau is not, and vice versa: "Esau was a cunning hunter, a man of the field; and Jacob was a plain man, dwelling in tents."[33] "And Isaac loved Esau, because he did eat of his venison: but Rebekah loved Jacob."[34] Every detail in the narrative differentiates the dissimilar broth-ers, down to their distinctive choices in spouses. When Esau steps outside the clan to take Hittite wives "which were a grief of mind unto Isaac and Rebekah,"[35] we can be sure that Jacob will seek a wife from among kinsmen, as his parents prefer. And we can be equally certain that at the very moment when he's falling passionately in love at first sight—"Jacob kissed Rachel, and lifted up his voice, and wept"[36]—he will check out his intended's ge-nealogical credentials with nerdy I'm-the-responsible-son thoroughness, making sure who she is, making sure of her pedigree, and making sure her blood lines match his maternal concerns—"Rachel the daughter of Laban, his mother's brother."[37]

That characterizing by juxtaposition is literarily efficient—two charac-terizations for the price of one. Aristotle would have admired the efficiency. He would have liked even more the inherent playing with paradox in the odd-coupling phenomenon, and especially liked the potential for humor in it; Aristotle thought "paradox related to the humorous"—"a device for illu-minating, as with a sudden flash, a neglected aspect."[38] Everything Genesis highlights about either odd character reflects upon the other, enriching the portrait, often through accents of humor. When Jacob is described, we are being told simultaneously what Esau isn't, so that we need not be informed Esau is something less than obsessive about work once we've noticed that

32. Ibid., 119.
33. Gen 25:27.
34. Gen 25:28.
35. Gen 26:35.
36. Gen 29:11.
37. Gen 29:10.
38. Jonsson, *Irony in the New Testament*, 21.

Jacob is workaholic. Picturing Esau as an unkempt, uncultivated, easygoing Walter Matthau sort of a guy from *The Odd Couple* movie, it's almost impossible not to picture Jacob as his counterpoint: a compulsive, driven, perfectionistic Jack Lemmon.

Their very names reflect the essential contrast. *Esau* means "red"—as in the color of the hair that distinguishes him, as in the earthily red lentils for which he sells his birthright, as in the soil of the Edomite nation he founds. In a telling synecdoche, the name makes the man his dominant physical characteristic: with Esau, what you see is what you get—*all* you get. Esau is not just red necked; he's red all over. His soul is redneck, low-class churlish. We hear from Esau the kind of "everybody's always picking on me" complaining we'd expect to hear in a trailer park. "Esau bitterly complains" about everything from how famished he feels to "his loss of status to his younger and shrewder brother."[39]

Jacob, on the other hand, is not so much what he looks like as what he does—in compulsive contrast with lackadaisical Esau, Jacob is not how he appears but how he acts. "Number two," as Avis used to advertise, "tries harder." *Jacob* means "supplanter," appropriate title for this embodiment of ambition we see struggling with his big brother as early as the womb and as an adult wrestling the very angels, wresting from odds-on favorites birthrights and blessings and new titles and vast herds, supplanting the expected heir as energetically as he later outwits and out-manipulates his cunning cousin Laban to become wealthy. Jacob gets it done. "The shifting portrait of Jacob—from victimizer (of Esau) to victim (of Laban) to survivor (he outwits Laban in the end)—finally coheres in that last portrait. Jacob is a survivor."[40] Genesis dramatizes totally opposite types, almost different species in those telling titles of tenacious *Jacob* ("he who grabs by the heel") and unshaven *Esau* ("shaggy").

Discerning insights are illuminated in Genesis by simple literary mirrors. Biblical stereotype, caricature verging at times on cartoon, can foster subtle effects. But however articulate, however sophisticated, the caricature retains something of a country grin, an insistent aura of Don Quixote and Sancho Panza—or Laurel and Hardy or Burns and Allen or Abbot and Costello or Maggie and Jiggs or Mutt and Jeff or Amos and Andy or Andy Griffith and Don Knotts—strange-bedfellows burlesque. Jacob in smelly animal skins disguised hilariously as Esau could not put his

---

39. Malul, "Succession in the Jacob-Esau Narratives," 196.

40. Schwartz, "Free Will and Character Autonomy," 67.

dysfunctional-family inheritance case to feeble-eyed Isaac with blunter nor more insulting accuracy: *Dad, you're blind as a bat in your choice of inheritors. Your favorite, as you can smell, stinks.* "The smell of my son," biased Isaac reluctantly admits, "is as the smell of a field"[41]—but then he and I, unlike you and your prissy mother, like that field smell.

Lot's Lot

Oddly matched as they are, Isaac's dissimilar sons are not exceptions in the Bible. Jacob and Esau, with their characteristic differences, typify a paradigm so pervasive in Genesis it lights up the farthest reaches of the Bible. The spotlight of character contrast, shining through the odd-couple spectrum, refracts a rainbow of biblical personalities. Odd couples turn the kaleidoscope of biblical characterization. Their contradictions create the intricacies of atmosphere. Their conflicts drive the narrative. At the deepest levels, literary and psychological, their profoundly problematic relationships reach beyond the coloring of characterization and the enlivening of event to illuminate theme. That binocular brand of bargain-basement epiphany reveals itself vividly in the odd-couple pairing of wise old Abraham and his new-kid-on-the-block nephew Lot.

Lot figures at first in the narrative as the patriarch's sidekick, tagging along like an Abraham knock-off, almost an Abrahamic clone, in the nomadic travels through Canaan—until he distinguishes himself by a crucial differentiating choice. When Uncle Abraham generously offers Lot his pick of grazing lands, Lot responds ungenerously, grabbing the best land, "the plain of Jordan," which is "well watered everywhere."[42] Genesis underscores immediately the results of Lot's greed and Abraham's generosity. "After that Lot was separated," from the patriarch, "the Lord said unto" gracious Abraham: "Lift up now thine eyes, and look from the place where thou art northward, and southward, and eastward, and westward: For all the land which thou seest, to thee will I give it, and to thy seed for ever."[43] Lot, "separated"[44] from his generous mentor, has made here a wet-behind-the-ears move as immature as Esau's mistake in selling his birthright, and very like it. Ditching his uncle to grab the land, Lot by his small-souled

41. Gen 27:27.
42. Gen 13:10.
43. Gen 13:14–15.
44. Gen 13:11.

selfishness cuts himself out of a huge chunk of likely inheritance.[45] Like Esau and the impatient prodigal son, he can't postpone gratification long enough to allow vaster potential benefits to accrue. It's clear at the outset that Lot is never going to amount to much, won't end up with a lot. He cashes in early.

Lot's selfish choices, we are ominously informed, set the direction of his life; he "pitched his tent toward Sodom," where "the men of Sodom were wicked and sinners before the Lord exceedingly"[46]—where things are bound to go from bad to worse in a landslide of accumulating misfortune; where he will soon be kidnaped by the warring local kings;[47] where he will be cowed into severe moral compromise by the Sodomite mob;[48] where he will barely evade the sky-is-falling brimstone storm that bakes his wife to a fare-thee-well,[49] a mere cinder of her former self. The tone of this crescendo of disaster is not so much tragic as pathetic, shameful, even humiliating. Hard to miss, for standup-comedian example, how the Rodney Dangerfield "Take my wife. Please" tone of the loss of Lot's recalcitrant spouse[50]—like the macabre offer of his own sexually vulnerable daughters to protect the virtue of powerful angelic visitors,[51] like his outlandish incest with his daughters that results in sons who are also his grandsons,[52] like so much else in these odd couple narratives—leans as much toward the ludicrous as to the tragic. That is not to suggest these quirky situations lack genuine pathos. The humor seesaw lifts on both ends. The comic deflation, as it augments the facetiousness of these strange shenanigans, simultaneously amplifies the seriousness of the tragedy.

Kenneth Gros Louis summarizes the alternating-current reciprocity of this weird pairing: "The destinies of Abraham and Lot are moving in different directions because of the values on which they base their lives."[53] Abraham, generous as Old Man River, just keeps rolling along, but "Lot, concerned primarily for himself, is shrinking as an individual, being

---

45. Helyer, "Separation of Abram and Lot," 78–79.

46. Gen 13:12–13.

47. Gen 14:12.

48. Gen 19:4–8.

49. 19:24–26.

50. Gen 19:24–26.

51. Gen 19:5–8.

52. Gen 19:36.

53. Gros Louis, *Literary Interpretations of Biblical Narrative*, 64.

reduced to the narrowness of his vision. His life fulfills his being, as he moves away from Abraham's grand vision to the Jordan Valley, to the city of Sodom, to the little city of Zoar, to the cave in the hills, to the smallness of his own family and the inbreeding of his own descendants through his daughters." In climactic commentary on the entropic devolving of his life, Lot's death knell sounds like an echo of nothing: "The space within which he lives literally gets smaller as the narrative progresses until he literally disappears; we never hear of his actual death."[54]

Lot gets wrapped up so tightly in himself he shrivels up and blows away. "Abram, on the other hand, expands in space and then in time, his descendants to be numerous as the dust of the earth."[55] Lot's selfishness shrinks his limited world as dramatically as Abraham's generosity stretches his expansive universe. Promised for starters that his seed will be "as the dust of the earth,"[56] magnanimous Abraham is blessed with more and more extensive guarantees until his promises include descendants as numerous as "the stars of the heavens."[57] As if that were not enough reward for the patriarch's openhanded largesse, God's blessing for him ultimately incorporates both dimensions—"as the stars of the heaven, and as the sand which is upon the sea shore"[58]—and by implication everything between, heaven and earth.

The ramifications of the odd-couple technique are as profuse as the cornucopial outpouring of Abraham's blessings. Biblical character couplings create double-barreled effects, effects that add up to more than the sum of their separate parts. Like such compelling narrative doublets as the two creation accounts in Genesis 1 and Genesis 2, the dual versions of Deborah's triumph in Judges 4 and Judges 5, or the competing reports of the conquering of Canaan in the book of Joshua and the book of Judges, these revisitings of the same circumstances from shifting perspectives project a vast spectrum of possibilities. They show us not only Abraham in light of Lot, or Jacob as illuminated by Esau. They envision what every character concerned could come to be, conjuring up a range of possible behaviors stretching from relatively simple personality oppositions as far as profound character potential. Odd couple characterizing does something

54. Ibid.
55. Ibid.
56. Gen 13:16.
57. Gen 15:5.
58. Gen 22:17.

even more cosmic. It forges room, between the acts of Esau and the facts of Jacob, for God.

The divine dimension looms large in Abraham's world, a world expansive as the cosmos after the Big Bang, all the more magnificent for its contrast with Lot's incessant shrinking. Abraham's life has more in it because God is in it. Abraham clings to his impossible dreams because he can glimpse "the perspective of the omniscient God, whose vision encompasses the distant future and whose omnipotence can shape that future."[59] Lot, his vision "confined to the present, a world circumscribed by the conditions he apprehends and not the miracles he is powerless to achieve,"[60] can stir his imagination barely enough to see in any sort of fourth-down-and-long situation a single constrained option: punt. That contrasting characterization shows why Abraham's vision is limitless, Lot's limited, and that makes clear the inherent moral of the story—selflessness is expansive, selfishness ingressive.

Genesis plays up that point with its contrast between Abraham's feast for the messengers from God and Lot's abstemious hosting of angels at the gates of Sodom: "Both men are seated: Abraham at the door of his tent;[61] Lot at the gate of the city.[62] On observing the approach of some strangers they arise, greet them, and bowing to the ground graciously extend an offer of hospitality. Even their speeches correspond closely."[63] But their hospitality doesn't correspond. Genesis stresses how differently these yin/yang heroes react to those parallel opportunities. When guests arrive, Abraham generates a flurry of giving, "running from his tent door to greet his vis[i]tors, hastening to his tent to tell Sarah to 'make ready quickly three measures of fine meal, knead it, and make cakes,' selecting a calf, tender, and good,"[64] serving his guests while they eat sumptuously in the shade of his tree. In contrast to Abraham's magnanimous largesse, "Lot, we recall, serves his guests unleavened bread"[65]—his "feast,"[66] as he calls it, consists of crackers, apparently without tea.

---

59. Schwartz, "Free Will and Character Autonomy," 55.

60. Ibid.

61. Gen 18:1.

62. Gen 19:1.

63. Alexander, "Lot's Hospitality," 290.

64. Gros Louis, *Literary Interpretations of Biblical Narratives*, 70.

65. Ibid.

66. Gen 19:3.

Given the rare opportunity to host angels, the sort of "a man's reach should exceed his grasp"[67] opportunity that comes once in a lifetime even for a patriarch, Lot spares the expense. No wonder his niggling, penny-pinching, what's-in-it-for-me, small-souled disposition can't generate much growth of character, not even from all that familial potential, all that right-stuff Abrahamic character DNA. Lot is so self-absorbed, so much the victim of the "man wrapped up in himself makes a mighty small package"[68] syndrome that he eventually evaporates from the Genesis narrative altogether, just fades away, his obsessive greed displaced completely by Abraham's organic bounteousness.

Abraham, on the great-souled and always-growing other hand, is all generosity. He refuses the kings' ransom offered to him, due him by the conventions of war.[69] He yields graciously to the patently unfair domestic demands of Sarah.[70] He indulges in random over-the-top not-to-say-weird behaviors like sharing his wife with Pharaoh and Abimelech, where the patriarch seems to modern eyes generous to a fault.[71] He gives and it is given unto him, "good measure, pressed down, and shaken together, and running over."[72] It is Abraham's unstinting generosity in everything he does that expands his world ultimately as wide as "the stars of the heaven, and as the sand which is upon the sea shore."[73] The character contrast is definitive, Abraham casting his bread freely on the waters, Lot with his eye narrowly on the main chance.

That debate of personalities contributes more than vivid characterization. This odd couple contrast, Lot's greediness a black hole that eventually engulfs him, Abraham's generosity a radiance that reaches infinitely outward, is an open invitation to ponder the Abrahamic graciousness and the Lot-like self-interest in each of us. The Bible recommends that kind of introspection. It urges soul searching, not idealistically but pragmatically, in the throes of real human experience rather than from the reassuring bias of theoretical self-justification. The Bible admires experience as C. S. Lewis does, because "it is such an honest thing. You may take any number

---

67. Browning, "Andrea Del Sarto," 354.

68. Rogers, *Simple Homely Truths*, 127.

69. Gen 14:21–24.

70. Gen 16:5–6.

71. Gen 12:14–15; 20:2.

72. Luke 6:38.

73. Gen 22:17.

of wrong turnings; but keep your eyes open and you will not be allowed to go very far before the warning signs appear."[74] Biblical odd-couple humor grounds us in human actuality to bedrock where we can be sure "the universe rings true."[75]

Burns and Allen

The biblical convention of contrasting characters is most productive not in the vivid precision of its characterizing, as with Jacob and Esau, nor even in the engaging relevance of its themes, as with Abraham and Lot. Bible story is at its best in raising profound questions, as it does compellingly in the case of the oddest Genesis odd couple, Isaac and Rebekah.

Before we meet Rebekah, Isaac has been clearly characterized for us by contrast—actually, in Isaac's case, by default. Isaac is, in a word, passive; not so much an active agent as an object acted upon. In the roll call of Genesis characters, he answers almost inaudibly, contributing so little action to the narrative that he's barely present. It takes a jocular miracle to get him here at all. He is named *Isaac*—"laughter"—because his parents chuckle at the rare notion that their promised son might actually come to exist, given Sarah's postmenopausal condition and Abraham's conjugal challenges in a culture without benefit of Viagra. In a manner not exactly calculated to contribute to Abraham's confidence in the bedroom, Sarah raises the touchy question of just how, under present marital conditions, Isaac is expected to get here: "Shall I have pleasure, my lord being old also?"[76] Given the impossibility of his begetting, let alone his birth, the advent of Isaac strikes Sarah—as it strikes any reader with any sense of realistic humor—as highly unlikely.

Readers with any sense of humor wonder too, with Sarah, just how fully Isaac is present even when he gets here. Isaac comes across as such a quiescent, tent-bound semi-invalid some scholars diagnose him as diabetic. Others think his low-key characterization so feeble that he might be made up, a figment of the cultural imagination invented to fill the gap between world-shaping Abraham and dynasty-creating Jacob. "He is presented as a largely passive figure around whom events occur, or whose actions comply with the plans set in place by others."[77] We see nothing of his youth except

74. Lewis, *Surprised by Joy*, 177.
75. Ibid.
76. Gen 18:2.
77. Boase, "Isaac in Genesis," 313.

hints of his being picked on by half-brother Ishmael, a vivid Mr. Hyde to Isaac's vague Dr. Jekyll. We see in his young adulthood only his role in Abraham's great trial, where Isaac, though in his vigorous thirties while his father has reached the doddering hundred-teens, displays his usual passivity not as dynamic sacrificer but rather so acquiescent a sacrifice that only the intervention of angels can save him. And then there's the non-drama of his love life, performed by proxy, featuring in its starring role an Isaac so unassertive he does his courting by deputy.

Delicate young bride-to-be Rebekah, on the other hand, proves so energetic that when Isaac's John-Alden surrogate requests a drink this dynamic woman-child draws water for "the camels also, until they have done drinking."[78] If a camel's water tank is as capacious as it looks from the outside, water for "all [the] camels"[79] of the caravan is a whole lot of water, and the woman who descends and ascends the steep stone steps of the well bearing on her head the heavy pitcher to fetch that water is a whole lot of woman. Even at this tender age we can see she's a go-getter. It doesn't take much of a crystal ball to glimpse in the casual hints of psychological insight in this single foreshadowing what a mature Rebekah will look like: "Rebecca's masterminding is made much of: she insists twice that Jacob obey her orders (at verse 8 and 24), and she even takes the blame on herself explicitly, 'Upon me be your curse, my son' (27:13). She is the active subject who directs each step of the plot."[80]

Dynamic Rebekah, likely not much older than the threshold of nubility, braves the fearsome desert, risks her life on a throw of the marital dice with a man she has never met, ventures from her childhood for the first time in her life to face the vagaries of first-date betrothal, to a man at least twice her age, probably three times as old.[81] Twelve-year-old Rebekah can handle it. Customarily the man would have been expected to endure that daunting wilderness traveling, but effervescent Rebekah shows no signs of fatigue or even diminished enthusiasm from her arduous desert trek in Isaac's stead. Characteristically, she leaps down from her camel, eager to meet her husband-to-be, and finds him, characteristically, meditating "in the field at the eventide."[82] By the time of that first encounter, we've a

78. Gen 24:19.

79. Gen 24:20.

80. Schwartz, "Free Will and Character Autonomy," 58.

81. Gen 24:55–67.

82. Gen 24:63.

fairly good idea from these odd-couple snapshots who will wear the pants in this family. Those incisively characterized energetic qualities of Rebekah in odd-couple conjunction with those contemplative qualities of Isaac convince us even before they get together that she is likely to be the actor, he the acted upon even in such a crucial patriarchal prerogative as fatherly blessing. It's clear before the couple's earliest meeting whose favored child will end up with the birthright.

On the Other Hand

Those thin candles of odd-couple characterizing radiate a surprising amount of light. The rapidly sketched dynamism of the damsel Rebekah shapes not only how we see her but what we think about what she does. Regina Schwartz in her spirited defense of female autonomy in the Bible suspects as I do that too many "scholars transfer the culpability from Rebecca to God too readily. Is not the theft of the blessing her scheme?"[83] It's not just that Rebekah is autonomous. Her independence infuses her narrative with profound significance. Her soap-opera confrontation with unassertive Isaac over their sons' blessing raises intriguing questions about relationship dynamics. Who behaves best? My sympathies are drawn like a magnet to the can-do high-energy Rebekah. Where are the sympathies of Genesis, of the God who stands behind the narrative? Is the Bible approving a person who pesters as annoyingly as Delilah nagging Samson until the Lord in exasperation shares his secrets? Does Scripture underwrite someone who takes matters into her own hands to make certain that God's intent, as revealed to her, prevails? Does the Bible back a woman who seems by implication of her extensive manipulations to doubt whether God can handle it himself? Is dynamic but manipulative Rebekah being applauded, or even endorsed, or even approved?

Or does the text side with the person who faithfully and trustingly and stoically awaits God's will—passive but patient Isaac? We feel automatic respect for the mother who dramatically gets the things done that need to be done in the family. Do we feel any appreciation for the father, overshadowed by her dramatics, left in the wake of her energy, who knows like his father before him what all good husbands know: when to leave well enough alone? This odd coupling poses significant dilemma. Is it better, like Rebekah, to

83. Schwartz, "Free Will and Character Autonomy," 58.

eagerly enact the will of God, even, if need be, by deception? Or is it better, like Isaac, to trust in God, albeit passively—do they serve better "who only stand and wait"?[84] The text makes clear that Isaac ultimately not only recognizes but certifies the rightness of his sons' blessing: "Yea," he says of Jacob well after his theft of the blessing, "he shall be blessed."[85] Does the God who promised Rebekah that Jacob would be blessed approve the duplicity with which she makes sure the promise comes to pass? On the ever-present biblical odd-couple other hand, would *laissez-faire* Isaac have been spirited enough to bless rightly if his wife had not forced his hand?

The flint of Rebekah's intense action, striking the steel of Isaac's quiet patience, sparks burning questions from those divergent lifestyles. We admire the feisty manipulations of the Rebekahs (though they seem arrogant in their presumption that God needs their devious assistance) as much as we respect the quiet faith of the Isaacs (though they seem feeble in their lack of concern for furthering the Lord's work). The dialogue of odd couples makes us wonder, wondering with our left brains if we might do better to be a little more like proactive Rebekah, wondering with our right brains if we might do better to be a little more like trusting Isaac. It is at that deeper level of questioning, deeper even than character or thematic implication, that there is so much going on in these simple oppositional patterns. Biblical authors, with their "eye for the ludicrous side of life, as well as for its more sober aspects," managed with that binocularly inclusive perspective—it feels almost polyocular, like a fly's eye—to be "faithful to nature. They reported what they saw."[86]

They saw a great deal. There is so much in these Genesis odd couplings—so much subtle characterization, so much thematic insight, so many profound questions—that we begin to wonder whether there might be significance in the pattern itself, might be meaning in the consistent recurrence of these character pairings. Could it be that Genesis is suggesting to us through its recurrent odd couples that there may be more than one way to skin a cat, more than one way to get the right boy blessed? If there is reader-response message in the paradox of this always latently and often actively humorous medium, the moral may be "to be sensitive to the experiential side of the Bible," "to resist the tendency to turn every biblical

---

84. Milton, "When I Consider How My Light Is Spent," 1397.

85. Gen 27:33.

86. Shutter, *Wit and Humor of the Bible*, 27.

passage into a theological proposition."[87] Looked at through the lens of its humor "the one thing that the Bible is not is a theological outline with proof texts."[88]

There may be, the biblical humor seems to urge, more than one way to work righteousness. Rebekah manages to get Jacob the blessing in her pro-active way. But the trusting approach of Isaac contributes in its way, too, to the blessing. In fact Isaac contributes so substantively to the blessing of his less favored son that under pressure from Esau for a counter blessing he de-clares unequivocally his fervent conviction that Jacob's blessing stands—"I . . . have blessed him? yea, and he shall be blessed."[89] Isaac takes that failsafe faith so far as to re-bless his last son,[90] just to make sure he's first. Clearly both of these very different parents' very distinctive parentings contribute crucially to getting the good job done for their children.

We are left by all these Genesis odd couplings to struggle as fiercely as Jacob and Esau in Rebekah's womb, debating with our inmost selves about which of our ambivalent personality characteristics may be most appro-priately championed by these biblical surrogates, trying, to save our souls, to figure out which disposition ought to prevail in us. What succeeds best: energetic pragmatism or trusting idealism? Or, to biblically complicate the complicated question, is some precarious balance of both better? "Most like an arch this marriage," John Ciardi decides: "two weaknesses that lean / into a strength. Two fallings become firm."[91] Are our characteristic halfway measures, even those with competing incompatibilities, more complete in concert?

Again and again the Bible confronts us with that kind of compelling question, engages us in philosophically momentous and profoundly per-sonal moral choice. The light comedy of these sitcom odd-couple situations in the Bible can serve as a catalyst for deeply realistic value-relevant inter-nal debates about our very lifestyles, the moral considerations accented by the piquancy of the humor. Which is worse, the Bible asks in its odd-couple parables, to be prodigal or self-righteous? Which is better, to be orthodox Israelite or repentant Ninevite? Which is the worthier, which the happier

---

87. Ryken, *How to Read the Bible as Literature*, 18.

88. Ibid.

89. Gen 27:33.

90. Gen 28:1.

91. Ciardi, *The Collected Poems of John Ciardi*, 196.

lifestyle: Adam's steadfast loyalty to things as they are, or Eve's risky venture toward a wider world?

Whose is the better way, Genesis wonders with its cosmic comic smile, Jacob's impressive amassing of great wealth, and the clever way he leverages it to reconcile to his brother? Or is his proffered gift to Esau, "all this drove,"[92] actually a bribe? Is it expiation for guilt over theft of the birthright? Is our hero as materialistically opportunistic as he appears, trying to buy his brother off? And what is going on with his dark-side twin, the brother we thought was cast as villain here, who seems now so incongruously above such ulterior motives? Might Esau's irresponsible rejection of Jacob's responsible wealth be the better, less materialistic, way? Something in our moral selves may lean away from sophisticated Jacob toward guileless Esau, in all his redneck simplemindedness, when he brushes off his twin's calculated tactics: "I have enough, my brother."[93]

Easygoing Esau

When the brothers warily approach reunion after long years of hostile avoidance, Jacob, apparently for fear of Esau's revenge, prepares meticulously. Cautiously as Ebenezer Scrooge's accountant, the birthright boy orders his multifold familial blessings in inverse sequence of value, handmaids first because they are most dispensable, Leah and her ample and hence disposable brood midmost. Last and most protected he places, with her favored children, beloved Rachel, "well favoured" Rachel,[94] the love of his life, the woman for whom passionate "Jacob served seven years . . . and they seemed unto him but a few days, for the love he had to her."[95] And then the patriarch complicates that clear tapestry of priority, with its frank graph of what matters most to him, by placing in the safest place of all, at the secure end of that echelon of measured caring, himself.[96]

That emphatic subliminal satire punks esteemed Jacob, the revered *Israel,* father of the nation. Jacob rebukes himself by his behavior, lays out for us in overdrawn circus-clown detail that extravagantly frank portrait of his tactical nature, his entrepreneurial eye out for profit, his compulsive

92. Gen 33:8.
93. Gen 33:9.
94. Gen 29:17.
95. Gen 29:20.
96. Gen 33:1–15.

accountant mentality, his self-obsessed, selfish self ensconced at the center of the web of his worried world. The scenario is as bad-violin plaintive and as wryly funny as Jack Benny's perpetual penny-pinchings. We have to laugh to keep from crying at the sight of such transcendent values—the family, the integrity of the self, life itself—systematically devalued by such materialistically trivializing concerns. Jacob is incorrigibly "me first." And yet, so *responsible*—the kind of guy we trust with our clans, our companies, our nations.

Meanwhile carefree Esau runs as enthusiastically and unthinkingly as that overgenerous father of the prodigal son,[97] his sole concern to meet "my brother,"[98] little brother Jacob—Esau "embraced him, and fell on his neck, and kissed him."[99] That's silly as well as extravagantly noble, of course: unsophisticated Esau fails completely here to take advantage of his hard-earned emotional and considerable financial leverage over his cheating and condescending brother, misses totally his chance to get back some of his own. In this climactic confrontation of the brothers' long imbroglio, steeped as their dubious relationship is in the Machiavellian machinations of all that festering family baggage, readers expect just what the civilized brother expects—something out of a Hatfield-and-McCoy feud. Instead of the climactic duel of that lifelong quarrel, rather than the final fatal falling of the Damoclean sword that has hung over the entire relationship, with Jacob we find instead, substituted stunningly for the former life-threatening bully, a big brother who's just happy to see us. We get the joke: raging bull becomes Ferdinand. We pick up quickly on Esau-related amusement because Esau is the displaced, the dumb other. Hardly dummies ourselves, we see right through dumb-guy jokes.

But humor where a smart guy is outsmarting himself may be another matter for us. "I'm never quite so stupid," Linus of *Peanuts* shakes his cartoon head, "as when I'm being smart."[100] Jokes on smart guys, like Leah tricking her wily way into a frustrating marriage,[101] or Jacob and Laban with their revolving-door reciprocal outfoxings over the flocks,[102] or Joseph

97. Luke 15:20.
98. Gen 33:9.
99. Gen 33:4.
100. Short, *Parables According to Peanuts*, 72.
101. Genesis 29:30.
102. Gen 30–31.

and his tattletale "evil report"[103] that turns his brothers against him, are harder for us to get, because we're smart guys. We overlook the Jacob joke, because when it comes to Jacob, the joke is on us. We have trouble seeing, the Bible may be saying, that our success in the world may be far from the outward sign of inward grace we Puritan descendants take it to be, far from God's gold star on our foreheads. The most accusatory irony underwriting the Jacob/Esau saga is that our personal caravans of Jacob wealth may be exactly what anyone not acculturated into seeing otherwise would see them to be—the certification, the made-in-America stamp, of our spiritual poverty.

Our Jacob justification for taking poor people's money is that they don't deserve it, maybe don't even value it. Like too-easy Esau, they're just not as appreciative of material quality as we finer folk. If money mattered to them as much as it matters to us, they'd have some. Our sophisticated acculturation in moral economics makes it easy for us to laugh at Esau—so oblivious, so crass, so gauche. Esau just doesn't get it. It's harder for us to laugh at sophisticated Jacob, though he may be far more deserving of being laughed at, and though his behavior is probably precisely what we sophisticates ought to be laughing at, since his failure to get the joke is so much like ours. But it's hard for us to laugh at Jacob. If we laugh at Jacob, we laugh at ourselves.

That juxtaposition of the contrasting assets and competing liabilities of tenacious Jacob and "let it be" Esau provokes readers. As it often is with biblical odd couples, the contrasts in the relationship are so inherently dramatic that audience identification with either or both of the characters, even amid this labyrinthine inner debate, is almost automatic. Our reader involvement is more than a matter of empathy, more than the way that "with our smiles or laughter we show our sympathy." "We are actually taking part,"[104] trying on roles, "identifying with characters," rather than "simply being told a series of facts."[105] In that trying out of lifestyles, Genesis is cross-examining us, here and at every odd couples turn, with its implicit question: *Who do you want to be?* Robert Browning understood how vital this ongoing dilemma of day-by-day character-constructing weighing of

---

103. Genesis 37:2.

104. Jonsson, *Irony in the New Testament,* 19.

105. Ryken, *How to Read the Bible,* 34.

the lessers of evils and the best of betters can be, for Genesis narrative and for our real-life experience: "Life's business being just the terrible choice."[106]

Jesus Against the Pharisees

Odd couples abound in the Bible everywhere, some of those in the New Testament odder than those in the Old. The oddest New Testament odd coupling is probably not that Mutt-and-Jeff pair of New Testament missionaries, tight-lipped Peter and motor-mouth Paul. It's not those mismatched visionary bedfellows John the Baptizer and Jesus the Healer. It's not Peter and Judas. It's not the Sons of Thunder, boisterous James and his brother John, the gentle "disciple, whom Jesus loved."[107] It's not the uneasily-yoked gospel authors, not matter-of-fact Mark stumbling in harness with mystical John, nor legalistic Matthew looking down over his accountant spectacles at humanistic Luke. It's not Mary and Elizabeth, nor Mary and Martha, nor Mary Magdalene and Mary the mother of Jesus. It's not Jesus and Judas, nor Jesus and Lazarus, nor Jesus and Mary, nor Jesus and Peter, nor even Jesus and Satan.

The strangest New Testament odd couple is Jesus and the Pharisees. Both sides of that strange equation are deeply religious. Both are profoundly dedicated to the good of the people. Both Jesus and the Pharisees are devoted teachers of crucial social and moral values. Yet the two sides are so at odds that nothing can convince them to be civil, not even religious emergencies like a woman taken in adultery[108] or lame folk in need of immediate healing[109] or pressing questions of how much should be given for charity.[110] They cannot agree even to disagree, even when they agree in areas as potentially uniting as their mutual loathing for Roman occupation.[111] Even in matters that matter as much as a long tradition of professional rabbinical courtesy, nothing can convince them to be civil. Of all the odd couplings in the Bible, that of Jesus and his fellow rabbis is the most quarrelsome.

Some readers see Scripture as proscribing a straight and narrow path of pious rectitude leading with unvarying precision to never-ending bliss

106. Browning, *Ring and the Book*, 112.

107. John 20:2.

108. John 8:3–6.

109. Mark 2:6–12; 3:1–6.

110. Luke 11:42.

111. Mark 12:13–17.

(with never a blip or a shadow or any kind of concern) in a four-square heaven where we concourse day and night perpetually with perfectly cloned angels, all of us singing never-endingly our perfectly pitched eternal note of praise in the unchanging choir in the sky, weaned away forever from our idiosyncrasies, from the annoying anomalies of such mutable distractions as gender, having shed with our flawed skins our very personalities and everything else that made us unique or in the slightest degree interesting.

The Bible sees it differently. For the Bible, that harp-playing notion of heaven is not just unrealistic. It's a notion of hell: "Hell, sleek hell, hath no freewheeling part."[112] That idea of a perfect existence with no surprises is like a great-aunt's parlor, everything so orderly that nobody can have any fun in it. The Bible suspects heaven might be more fun, and funnier. Maybe things are so spontaneous and nonexpectational and free that everybody is having a good time. The Bible's view of the best life is less proscriptive than orthodox views, more invitational. What it invites us to is not so much obedience as fullness of life, not narrowness but abundance, not correctness but expansiveness, not strictness but generosity, not righteousness but love. Instead of directing us to be a certain kind of Catholic or evangelical or even nondenominational Christian, the Bible urges us to be all we can be. "All we can be" can be pretty odd, about as odd as both sides of an odd couple.

In the Bible's view, it's a good idea to be Daniel. When in Babylon, it's a good idea to avoid the very appearance of evil, to be rigidly orthodox, publically circumspect, unwaveringly righteous, even at risk of your life. The Bible further suggests, on the directly contradictory other hand, that it's a good idea to be Esther. When in Persia, it's a good idea to be compromising, assimilative, to insinuate yourself into a culture, keeping your values not just low-key but incognito until you are in a position to make a difference in that culture, even at risk of your own life. It's all good, the Bible says—good to stand up for what we believe, good to disguise what we believe for a good cause. The Bible's odd-couple riddles propose some radical paradoxes: Rebecca does well with her manipulative style, Isaac does well in his lackadaisical manner. Samson's violently rebellious way against the Philistines is a good way, and so is Jesus's passive resistance to the Romans. Biblical do-your-own-best-thing wisdom insists it can be exemplary to be unyielding Daniels, laudable to be compromising Esthers.

112. Kennedy, "Nothing in Heaven Functions as It Ought," 33.

The Bible may even be suggesting to us, in its always inclusive way, that the best of us, like David or Moses or ultimately Jesus, are both.

The one thing among all those competing positive possibilities that the Bible doesn't want us to be is a Pharisee. The book's so dead set against Pharisees it's hard for readers to remember those dedicated shepherds of their flocks are good guys, really good guys, upholders of community values, champions of conservative principles. Yet the New Testament loathes their orthodoxy, particularly in contrast with that surprisingly radical Jesus, who wants instead of the old-time religion a better one. The Bible's problem with Pharisees seems to be the same problem it has with us—rigidity, lack of flexibility, a compulsiveness in defending our version of the faith that gets in the way of larger possibilities. St. Peter at the heavenly gates in a *Bizarro* cartoon tells a pharisaical applicant: "You were a believer, yes. But you skipped the not-being-a-jerk-about-it part."[113] The Bible urges us not to be satisfied even with excellent things, but to seek "the things that are more excellent."[114] Reading the Bible less pharisaically, opening ourselves to such expansive aspects as biblical humor, might be a good place to start looking.

I think the Bible is saying read as unpharisaically as possible. Read the Bible itself, for yourself. Read the Bible—not what the Vatican or the Southern Baptist Convention or the Methodist Synod thinks of the book—the book itself—not what Mary Baker Eddy or Billy Graham or Pope John Paul II or John Wesley or Martin Luther or L. Ron Hubbard or William Penn or Joseph Smith[115] or Joel Osteen says about the book. Do what all those great Bible readers recommend you do: read it yourself. If it's not funny for you, don't laugh. Don't so much as smile. If you find genuine humor in it, and the humor is meaningful for you, absorb as much of that Good Book good humor as you can into your life.

On Second Thought

In the Bible's balancing act of one unbalanced character against another we see a literary technique reminiscent of Hebrew poetic structure: *parallelism*. Parallelism is a kind of odd coupling of poetic lines featuring, in Bishop Lowth's famous description, "correspondence of one verse, or line,

---

113. Piraro, *Houston Chronicle*, Jan. 26, 2007.

114. Rom 2:18.

115. Smith, *New Translation of the Bible*, 7.

with another."[116] Between those lines, as in the character couplings in Genesis, there is a kind of dialectic. This structure of parallelism, according to Stephen Prickett, "whether fortuitous or providential, ha[s] shaped the whole structure of Jewish thought."[117] The "characteristic biblical mode of encounter with God is not, as one might expect, submission, but *argument*. Wrestling Jacob, or Abraham pleading for the cities of the plain . . . sets the tone for book after book of the Old Testament—culminating, perhaps, in the great debates of Job."[118] That dialectic, that literary wrestling, that contention of character against character and lifestyle against lifestyle is part of what makes biblical writing so paradoxically humorous and so question-provoking and so ultimately illuminating.

Genesis's odd couples look a lot like arguments—literary arguments, but breathtakingly close to literal arguments. They are literal not just in the sense that Cain and Abel and Abraham and Sarah and Joseph and Judah actually quarrel, but in the visceral immediacy with which we readers internalize their arguments. "Kierkegaard found in Plato's dialogues and Socrates' discussions examples of humour which purpose not to give a final answer to the questions but to stimulate thinking."[119] To really read humor, or anything else in the Bible or anywhere else, we must "be active—in visualizing, in imagining scenes, in entering into the spirit of events."[120] That spirit is easy to miss, and especially easy to miss when it's colored by anything other than the high seriousness, which we expect from this text. So often in biblical narrative "the comical element has vanished" for us simply because we overlook it, because of a gloomy modern disposition toward "sympathy with the tragic."[121]

Genesis's odd couplings may amount, bottom line, to smiling invitations to us to enter into the moral choices of its characters as if they were our own. Genesis may be urging us to examine aspects of our personal lifestyles in the light of the down-to-earth lifestyle choices of biblical personalities—not only Rebekah and Isaac, but Rebekah and Isaac as case studies of the active and the contemplative life. Not only Abraham and Lot, but our Abrahamic generosity pitted against our Lot-like self-interest. Not simply

116. Lowth, *Sacred Poetry of the Hebrews*, 258.

117. Prickett, *Words and the Word*, 110.

118. Ibid, 109.

119. Jonsson, *Irony in the New Testament*, 37.

120. Ryken, *How to Read the Bible*, 34.

121. Jonsson, *Irony in the New Testament*, 19.

Adam and Eve, but the status-quo Adamic traditional tendencies within us versus the go-for-the-gusto, risk-taking, innovative Eve attitude.

Odd couple humor in the Bible may plumb even deeper into our understanding of ourselves. It may go so far as to suggest that otherness itself, even the most radical otherness, is really part of us. "Otherness," as Levinas insisted, "is the manifestation of the infinite."[122] Maybe our most definitive differences at the deepest levels assert our essential sameness with others. Divide us as you will, biblical odd couple humor may be suggesting at heart we remain one.

Human meaning depends so definitively upon differentiation that when humanity discovered Lacanian difference and began to assert the meaning grounded in distinctions, we may have exiled ourselves from Eden. Maybe there is in that divisive tragedy an implication that the heart is more the solution to our dividedness than the head. Maybe we might manage better thinking if we were to think, as the Bible does, with our "hearts."[123] Maybe the only way back together, to true human intimacy, is to feel our way together by rediscovering that we share the same human heart, that our hope for unity and even integrity lies in love. However impossible it is to reason the shards of our fractured world or even of our Humpty-Dumpty selves back together again, we might yet feel our way back together. Human warmth, including human humor, might help us reconstruct ourselves.

Characters as different as Jacob and Esau are, after all, twins—close enough to be confused for each other by their own father; close enough despite all their differences to share in their individuated marrow identical genes; close enough for all their fierce competitiveness to come finally to love each other. If the ironic reason they couldn't stay together is that they were essentially too much alike, that may ironically hold out hope for them to finally find themselves in each other. Esau has come a long way since we and his brother last saw him, has come closer to being like his twin. He is, for instance, more sophisticated—the erstwhile rube rubs it in a little about his frightened brother's melodramatic precautions: "What meanest thou by all this drove?"[124] Esau is not wholly himself until he discovers the Jacob sensitivity within him. Jacob is not completely Jacob until he realizes his own Esau toughness in a struggle with a shadowy wrestler who might be or

122. Levinas, *Ethics and Infinity*, 106.
123. Prov 2:2, as throughout the Bible.
124. Gen 33:8.

might as well be his own brother. Genesis suggests here something like the psychological imagery of right brain/left brain. However oppositional the contrasts between the divisions of the mind, ultimately the effectiveness of their communal and even individual functioning depends upon corpus-callosum sharing.

More than Meets the Eye

People, too: "'Men work together,' I told him from the heart. / 'Whether they work together or apart.'"[125] That's truer of our laughter than it is of our work. And, like most everything else in the Bible, the odd-couple vision of unity in diversity, that *e pluribus unum* enigma of individualistic common-ality, raises more questions than it answers. The biblical "idea of humour," like everything else in the Bible, functions not to provide final answers, rather "to stimulate thinking."[126]

The focus of that thinking, bottom-line, is *us*. What remains to be discovered by us, the Bible may be suggesting in its persistent odd-couple patterns, is that the divisions that tear our worlds apart are not so much between us as *within* us. Cartoon *Pogo* smiles at the irony of that: "We have met the enemy, and he is us."[127] That's why humor is such a compelling means of assuring that we're all in this together. Humor connects us, reminds us how fundamentally we are brothers, related as profoundly for all our differences as Jacob and Esau. Humor is superb at allowing the reader "to recreate the story in his or her imagination."[128] That may explain why, as some of our most rigorous scholars suspect, "the original tone of the Jacob-Esau-Laban story cycle was humorous" before its rollicking foundations were "gradually revised toward a more lofty and religious tone."[129] Laughter, the Bible could be suggesting at its deepest levels, conjoins us. Humor is by its nature shared insight. Humor makes our very separations shared. It makes our isolation communal. It can even, at its deepest levels, reveal that the most fundamental othernesses are within us.

We tend to find about as much humor in biblical texts as we look for. Some of the most sensitive readers of the Bible have "closed their minds to

125. Frost, "The Tuft of Flowers," 19.

126. Jonsson, *Irony in the New Testament*, 27.

127. Kelly, *Pogo*.

128. Ryken, *How to Read the Bible as Literature*, 33.

129. Ibid., 9.

its comic possibilities," creating for themselves "an impression of a stiff and serious document that never relaxes into a smile."[130] Such a superb reader as George Steiner can announce complete "absence of purely verbal wit in the Old Testament."[131] Yet equally-superb-reader Samuel Sandmel's *The Enjoyment of Scripture* spends most of its time enjoying "comic episodes, ranging from scenes like the murder of Eglon by Ehud to whole books, such as Jonah and Esther."[132] Appreciation of that humor is not just a more sensitive way to read, not just a more enjoyable way; it's a more *meaningful* way. The more alert we are to the possibilities of biblical humor the more aware we are of biblical meaning. Bible humor is not merely for laughs, but to induce us "to think again about how [to] read it, alerted to the dynamic surprises of Scripture."[133]

Genesis's odd couples may ultimately be arguments, ultimately for the reader internal arguments, about what we might be—a sort of systole and diastole of the soul. We are not only in our relationships strange halves of odd couples, as my wife will emphatically testify. We have within our individual selves competing aspects of personality every bit at odds as the couples in Genesis. We are ourselves, as dramatized by those odd couplings, walking dialectics, open-ended discussions, infinite possibilities. Walt Whitman caught glimpses of that untapped potential within us: "I am larger, better than I thought, / I did not know I held so much goodness."[134] Biblical odd couples announce by their very existence, let alone their dialogues and debates and disagreements, that there may be more in us than we knew.

Shel Silverstein, with similar whimsical profundity, his eyes "greyish blueish green" and hair "reddish blondish brown," realizes in the physical ambiguity within his own person the odd couplings latent within each of us. He realizes, too, the infinite possibilities those dilemmas of the soul imply: "All the colors I am inside / Have not been invented yet."[135] The contrasting characters of Genesis, by virtue of their very oddities, their very contradictoriness, provide envelope-pushing paradigms by which readers might

---

130. Landy, "Humor as a Tool for Biblical Exegesis," 99.

131. Steiner, *After Babel*, 22.

132. Landy, "Humor for Biblical Exegesis," 99–100.

133. Ibid., 100.

134. Whitman, *Leaves of Grass,* 151.

135. Silverstein, "Colors," 24.

reinvent themselves. That odd-fellow reinventing can at times be genuinely funny. It's always genuinely meaningful.

8

"Man Thinks, God Laughs"

Humor as Morality

ANY READING OF ANYTHING worth reading, especially humor, most especially biblical humor, "should begin in delight and end in wisdom."[1] We've prospected for biblical delight and wisdom strategically by means of the textual explorations of *Illuminating Humor of the Bible*, covering only 30 percent of the Bible's sixty-six books, yet all of its diverse genres, most at some depth. Those wildcat drillings into biblical humor, if they haven't hit many gushers of hilarity, have tapped consistently into reliable currents of biblical amusement. Everywhere we've looked in the Bible, we've found humor. How meaningful is it? Has the discovery of all this scriptural humor, however delightful, unearthed any wisdom?

The humor of the Bible focuses more than dedicated readers might have suspected—more than some of us might have liked—on the failings of the faithful. It's not that bad guys don't get their just deserts in Scripture: Sisera bites the Hebrew dust he crushes under his iron-wheeled chariots.[2] Haman is literally "hoist with his own petard,"[3] hanged "on the gallows that he had prepared"[4] for his enemy. Proud Pharaoh does a belly flop from the

---

1. Frost, *The Road Not Taken*, xxix.
2. Judg 5:26–27.
3. Shakespeare, *Hamlet,* 3.4.206.
4. Esth 7:10.

pinnacle of the world into the mud at the bottom of the Red Sea.[5] The tyrant of magnificent Babylon sinks so low he finds himself foraging for grass with cattle.[6] The arch architect of evil, wiliest of serpents, enmeshes himself in the coils of his own Machiavellian machinations.[7] Justice conspires consistently with poetic justice to give biblical villains exactly what they have coming to them—almost always humiliatingly, and sometimes hilariously. In its deflation of the magnificently villainous, the Bible holds to the C. S. Lewis principle that "the Devil is (in the long run) an ass."[8]

But calculated evil is seldom as funny as bumbling goodness pratfalling over its own fine intentions. Biblical narrative invests less of its careful comic timing in wreaking disaster upon dastardly villains than in tripping up good guys. The Bible loves to throw pies in the faces of its protagonists. The holier the hero, the more unholy the glee the text takes in farcically plastering him with coconut cream. Scripture seldom makes light of its favorites, but it frequently has fun with them, particularly when they're taking themselves too seriously. Centuries before social protest came into cultural fashion, biblical writers were routinely upsetting the smug decorousness of the status quo, turning over applecarts of convention, relishing social inappropriateness, dancing with David before the sacred Ark. Bible heroes, in their unrelenting realism, do such quirky things that their bizarre behavior quite frequently makes them funny.

That short circuit between what we expect from Bible exemplars and what we get is a shock awaiting reader psyches, a palm buzzer that can shake us up whenever we shake hands with a biblical character. The Bible we consider a cathedral of reliability turns out to be more of a funhouse of surprises; what we expect is everywhere ambushed by what actually is. Unassertive Eve changes everything.[9] Noble Noah is revealed as a lush.[10] Staunch Abraham is so fearful of Pharaoh he proffers him his stunner of a wife.[11] Dignified Sarah giggles at the solemn pronouncements of angels.[12]

---

5. Exod 14:28.

6. Dan 4:33.

7. Gen 3:14–15.

8. Lewis, Preface to *Paradise Lost*, 95.

9. Gen 3:6.

10. Gen 9:20–21.

11. Gen 12:11–13.

12. Gen 18:12.

Isaac, not content with playing favorites, favors the wrong twin.[13] Jacob, foundation of the Israelite nation, cons everybody he meets, from his twin brother to angelic ambassadors.[14] Shy Rachel shamelessly steals her father's beloved household idols, covering the theft by sitting on them and claiming it's that time of the month.[15] The founding father of the circumspect Jews, kosher Judah himself, sleeps with his daughter-in-law—Genesis's ungainly attempt to pretty up the public relations of that unseemly coupling in the Judean dust makes it sound all the worse to us: he mistakes her for a prostitute, and pays her well.[16] Simeon and Levi hack up the entire tribe of their sister's suitor after they've sweet-talked the prospective in-laws into circumcision—under pretense, of all things, of cementing bonds of brotherhood—casually murdering them at the pinnacle of their groin pain, "on the third day, when they were sore."[17] Jacob, instead of disapproving their murderous behavior, worries about his local reputation: "ye have troubled me to make me stink among the inhabitants of the land."[18] The pick of the Genesis litter, Joseph, gets so uppity-little-brother full of himself we can understand why older brothers want to be rid of him, how in reaction to his arch condescension they relish the poetic justice of selling him as a slave.[19]

And that's merely the prologue of the pattern. The smudges on the white hats of the Bible's heroes get ever more incongruous with distance from these Genesis instances. Madeline L'Engle, from her novelist's-eye view, summarizes the paradox—God's chosen are laughable, uniformly flabbergasting choices:

> It seems that God goes to great pains to choose the most unqualified. Would you choose a one-hundred-year-old man and a woman beyond menopause to start a nation? The disciples were not really very qualified, and they let Jesus down pretty badly and deserted him. Gideon said "But I come from the least family of all and I'm the least of my family," and yet Gideon was chosen to save the nation. Moses stuttered. Heaven knows that if Paul came up before a church calling committee, he would never get chosen.[20]

13. Gen 25:28.

14. Gen 25–33.

15. Gen 31:34–35.

16. Gen 38:18.

17. Gen 34:25.

18. Gen 34:30.

19. Gen 37:18–20.

20. L'Engle, "Interview with L'Engle," 3.

All humanity can relate. We can identify with protagonists whose very ordinariness enables them to do extraordinary things. Bible narrative feels like real experience, where we're as likely to be the butt of a joke as to be the David Copperfield "hero of my own life."[21] L'Engle finds the paradox of such consistently ludicrous choices for such crucial callings by an omniscient Chooser "consoling"—"all of the people that God chooses, that God asks to do something, are people that are singularly unqualified." That's paradoxically encouraging to us because in a very real sense "not one of us is qualified."[22]

The divine moral of that reiterative story of unlikely heroes seems equally encouraging: God cares more about the workers than the work. The biblical God, as revealed in the humor of his book, is less concerned with getting things done than with encouraging people to do things they didn't think they could. The Bible's characterizing is dramatically dynamic, focused not on the righteous consistency we like to think so important, but on human growth. God seems less intent on putting people in their proper places than on extending their ever-loving possibilities. The Bible has as much fun as Shakespeare with "what fools these mortals be."[23] But the Good Book is laughing with us, not at us. The Bible is genially encouraging ludicrously limited folks, the kind of folks we find ourselves through the lens of biblical humor to be, to be better, to be all we can be.

Laughter as Revelation

The shock of Bible humor can wake us up to life's possibilities. Optimally, our "eyes shall be opened"[24] when Genesis throws the cold water of humor in our faces, opened as widely to reality as Adam and Eve's eyes after Eden, not just to vaster vistas but to wholly new views. Biblical laughter can stretch the range of our understanding as far as the most paradoxical possibilities, from the ridiculous to the sublime. It can make us aware of "the laughter of mocking irony at the pretensions of those who consider themselves only splendid," and simultaneously alert us to the opposite "laughter of joyful irony with those who consider themselves only ridiculous."[25] Bibli-

21. Dickens, *David Copperfield*, 9.
22. L'Engle, "Interview with L'Engle," 3.
23. Shakespeare, *A Midsummer Night's Dream*, 3.2.115.
24. Gen 3:5.
25. Good, *Irony in the Old Testament*, 246.

cal laughter can reveal us to ourselves holistically, reveal at the same time our pathetic pretenses to the emperor's new clothes and our vast unguessed potential. "Thou art Peter, and upon this rock I will build my church."[26] It's a good joke, the pun on *petros* working in both Greek and Aramaic. *Rocky*, like in the movies—the nod toward granite reliability slyly intimating, simultaneously, the probability of rocky roads ahead, a less-than-smooth way forward. The ambivalent nickname foreshadows in Peter's particular rockiness slippings and stumblings of faith, trippings over incompetency, roadblocks of outright denial. There is the same kind of ironic encouragement in nicknaming Simon *Peter* as when Gideon, cowering in his shed, is addressed by an angel as "mighty man of valor."[27]

The unlikeliness that characterizes biblical heroes makes them revelatory. Revelation is by its nature unlikely, not just unpredictable—"the wind bloweth where it listeth"[28]—but improbable. Revelation, to be revelation, has to tell us something different from what we already know. Intersecting as it must the improbable and the possible, revelation is necessarily paradoxical. That inherent paradox may be what makes biblical revelation so breathtakingly heterodox, so miraculously inclusive, what makes the recurrently surprising answer to the Bible's open-ended multiple-choice questions almost always—"all of the above." The tripwire of humor triggers transformative explosions in our perspectives and our expectations, rearranges personal parameters, urges toward "newness of life."[29] Straining to discover the possible in the improbable, to uncover the sublime in the apparently ridiculous, Scripture is always pushing the envelope of what can be.

A slant window opens onto the illuminating humor of that revelatory process when David converses with the Lord (in Joseph Heller's amusingly insightful *God Knows*) about what to do with the conquered town of Keilah. General Joab is comfortably confident that the Keilahites will back their recent liberators—David, not so much. The king wants a little divine advice:

> "Will Saul come down to Keilah after me as Thy servant believes?"
> "You bet," said the Lord.
> "And will the men of Keilah deliver us into the hand of Saul?"

26. Matt 6:18.
27. Judg 6:12.
28. John 3:8.
29. Rom 6:4.

"It's funny you should ask."

"They will?"

"They will deliver thee up."

"Then we'd better get away, right?"

"You don't have to go to college," said the Lord, "to figure that one
    out for yourself."[30]

The process of revelation, Bible style, comes down to thinking outside
the box, being open to new possibilities, thinking what hasn't been thought
before. That's why God so often initiates such startlingly revolutionary
thinking. Humanity can get in on those revelatory revolutions as well;
conversations with God can lead people to think in different directions,
to think almost as differently as he does, as David does here. Humor is
more than mere aid to revelation; it is an aspect of the process. The humor
demonstrates that revelation is not theoretical nor magical but literal. In
scene after biblical scene, Bible humor reveals divine influence magnifying
actual human experience.

Most life-changing among the revelations poured out upon readers
by the biblical floodgate of humor is a better way to read. Those who take
Scripture seriously as revelation would do well to try to read it as if it actually
were. Reading a text the same way, however many times, however mindful
the repetition, stimulates little new insight. Blinders of codified theologies
coerce an unfortunate number of readers to reread in mind-numbing old
ways always, never seeing anew. If the Bible is only infallible or simply inerrant, the whole truth laid out once and for all, there's really no need to read
it except to remind ourselves of what we already know. If, on the other
hand, Scripture reading can include the possibility of communication with
God in the manner of David's—actual conversation that might actually
reveal something to us—something personal perhaps, maybe something
never before thought of, at least by us—the more we read it, and the more
differently we read it, the better.

Humor Works

Humor's solid earthiness makes for a down-and-dirty hands-on approach
to reading the Bible. Humor yields real results, coming to grips with actual as opposed to theoretical truth—like Linus's *Peanuts* parable: "I love

---

30. Heller, *God Knows*, 188.

mankind. It's people I can't stand."[31] That pragmatism may explain why humor, however little respect it gets as proper worship in the more reverent corners of our culture, works so well as "pure religion and undefiled before God." Humor is actively disposed "to visit the fatherless and widows in their affliction."[32] Humor works best with what may count most—not the propounding of theology but the practice of it. It is significant how often the Bible "hath shewed thee, O man, what is good"[33] through humor. Humor emphasizes the essential scriptural moral—not so much knowing what to do, "but to do justly and to love mercy, and to walk humbly with thy God."[34]

Humor works. Humor works in the Bible the way humor works everywhere, cutting us enough slack in our know-it-all certitude to give us space for flexibility, allowing us enough elbow room in our orthodox constraints to grow. When we're laughing at ourselves we're seeing possibilities for being better. Humor is character building. "The biblical understanding of individual character," as foremost biblical literary scholar Robert Alter and I see it, is dynamic, developmental, unpredictable: "a center of surprise." Bible heroes can't stand still long enough to be static. Their "changing nature of character is one reason why biblical personages cannot have fixed Homeric epithets (Jacob is not 'wily Jacob,' Moses is not 'sagacious Moses')."[35]

Character in the Bible is "often unpredictable, in some ways impenetrable," morphing in and out of its "penumbra of ambiguity."[36] The shifty potential of that biblical character revolves centrally around humor, as when that superlative opportunist Jacob transforms himself into whatever personality role works in whatever Harold-Lloyd-hanging-from-the-clock situation he gets himself into, as much the chameleon as Peter Sellers morphing with multiple-personality-disorder dexterity into different personas in *Dr. Strangelove*. Jacob is all things to all people. One moment he's a coddled mother's pet.[37] Then he's a clever adolescent outwitting his older brother.[38] The next time we see him he's a visionary mystic watching angels

31. Short, *Gospel according to Peanuts*, 122.

32. Jas 1:27.

33. Mic 6:8.

34. Mic 6:8.

35. Alter, *Art of Biblical Narrative*, 126.

36. Ibid., 129.

37. Gen 25:28.

38. Gen 25:29–34.

ascend into heaven.[39] Immediately after, he's a hard-bargaining lawyer cutting a canny deal—with God, of all people—for frankly materialistic "bread to eat" and "raiment" and safe passage "to my father's house in peace."[40] Then he's a desperate romantic so passionate in his courting he "served seven years for Rachel; and they seemed unto him but a few days, for the love he had to her."[41] Then he's an entrepreneur, cleverly manipulative in his business competitions with Laban.[42] Then he's a pit bull of a wrestler so tenacious he can squeeze a blessing out of a shadowy angel.[43] Then he's a paranoid narcissist hiding behind the protective wall of his wives and children.[44] Then he's a worried father, so concerned with his boys he inspires the same Judah who sold Joseph as a slave to volunteer for the prison term of his little brother Benjamin.[45]

No wonder Jacob is not just Jacob but *Israel*,[46] father of all Twelve Tribes, those drastically distinctive tribes so variously blessed by him in the climactic chapters of Genesis.[47] His QuicksDraw-McGraw morphings of character make Jacob the epitome of human being, poster boy for being all we can be. The father of Israel is, almost literally, everyman. If in fact Israelite blood is as widely dispersed in the world by the Lost Ten Tribes as biblical legend would have it, Jacob DNA may have wended its way as far as our lives. We may, in our personal moral marrow and our own distinctive character genes, literally embody Jacob-like possibilities, unlimited Jacob-engendered potential.

Bible humor pushes the envelope of character so vigorously it can stretch the reader's character. Bumping into diverse biblical models at the traffic jam of our mutual humanness makes for mind-boggling and eye-opening collisions with unabashedly human Bible role models. Father Abraham himself "was no saint and it is his various flaws and weaknesses that make him such an appealing character." And probably the most appealing

---

39. Gen 28:12.
40. Gen 28:20–21.
41. Gen 29:20.
42. Gen 30:25–43.
43. Gen 32:26–29.
44. Gen 33:1–2.
45. Gen 44:27–34.
46. Gen 32:28.
47. Gen 49.

aspect of Abraham's humanity is that "he had a sense of humor."[48] The venerable patriarch's most sublime conversation with heaven has a humorous tilt to it, as in his less-than-decorous response to the Lord's announcement of the imminent miraculous fulfillment of the ultimate covenant promise: "Then Abraham fell upon his face, and laughed."[49] The best of biblical characters are thoroughly human, pathetic one minute and arrogant the next, criticizing and complaining and controlling, lusty and miserable, jovial and jealous, and ecstatic and angry, even with God.

The ironic tremors from these seismic rumblings of scriptural character rattle the cages of orthodoxy. In the fiery crucible of experience in the Bible, souls metamorphose—not set in stone, not rigidly predestined, not fated, not so much as constrained by divine expectation. That naturalistic biblical portrayal of "man as a free agent"[50] reflects to the reader a stunning spectrum of psychological possibilities: "hope for the wrongdoer, from Adam to David in disgrace, pity for the lost and rejected, like Esau or Saul, dissociation from the outwardly well-conducted, like Laban in hospitality, even irony at the expense of God's own ministers and mouthpieces."[51] Far from reinforcing any kind of status quo, far from codifying rules of best behaviors or so much as a black-and-white set of expectations of what readers ought to be, Bible humor sets us free to be our unique best selves.

Reading the Bible by way of its humor is individuating. Many textual experts take Elisha to be a rerun of Elijah—*Elisha* is the southern version of the northern *Elijah*, and Elisha's bio is an episode-by-episode reiteration of Elijah's prophetic resumé. But that solemnly reductive reading, for all its redaction-theory credentials, won't stand up to the literary perspective, warmed by humor. Elisha is literarily characterized as a calmer, gentler prophet, stably and predictably introverted, in direct contrast with Elijah's bipolar extremes that swing wildly from starring dramatically as God's lightning rod[52] to pouting moodily in caves.[53] The two prophets are yet more definitively differentiated, and more humorously, by their contrasting tonsure. Elijah's surname, *Tishbite,* probably means "hairy," whereas Elisha is something close to a patron saint for those of us losing our hair.

---

48. Good, *Irony in the Old Testament,* 79.

49. Gen 17:17.

50. Sternberg, *Poetics of Biblical Narrative,* 157.

51. Ibid.

52. 1 Kgs 18:30–39.

53. 1 Kgs 19:9–10.

He distinguishes himself from Elijah and pretty much everyone else as the prophet insulted as *Baldy*—"go up, thou bald head; go up, thou bald head."[54] Humor, with its propensity for seeing people as they uniquely and amusingly are, sees more of what is in people and of what is going on in the Bible.

Laughing Our Way into Newness of Life

Humor strikes fire from character in biblical narrative at the juncture where the theoretical meets the actual, the transcendent becomes imminent. Biblical humor does more than characterize. It creates character. That's more than a matter of the Bible's implicit conviction that a sense of humor is more important for character than a sense of dignity. In the biblical balance scale of what really matters, a sense of humor may be as crucial to character as integrity. And it is even more crucial to what may matter more—repentance, the disposition to shape things as they are into what they ought to be. Biblical *wisdom*, the genre in the Bible where humor is most emphasized, argues a sense of humor as a kind of gyroscope for keep-all-the-balls-in-the-air balance and keep-on-trucking tenacity and keep-your-options-open spontaneity: "To everything there is a season, and a time to every purpose under the heaven . . . a time to weep, and a time to laugh."[55]

The practical impact of humor in the Bible involves more than that smorgasbord of lifestyle options. Biblical humor ultimately expands the soul. It is the nature of this cosmic laughter to foster bigheartedness—not theoretically, but viscerally, deep in us as the fountains of joy. Bible humor brings out the best in us. It urges laughter not as criticism nor condescension nor cruelty, but as largesse of the heart. This is soul-nurturing humor, making-the-most-of-things humor, creative humor, productive humor, generous humor, the sort of humor that can "give, and it shall be given unto you; good measure, pressed down, and shaken together, and running over."[56]

Bible-brand humor at its best goes beyond the *quid pro quo* tolerance of "her sins, which are many, are forgiven; for she loved much,"[57] beyond even the graciousness that "covers over a multitude of sins."[58] Humor at its

54. 2 Kgs 2:23.

55. Eccl 3:1, 4.

56. Luke 6:38.

57. Luke 7:47.

58. 1 Pet 4:8, NIV.

Bible best is a group hug. All who laugh have felt the mutuality of the experience, the contagiousness, the realization that we're all in this together. Laughter in groups, which is where it thrives, in fact where it mostly is, connects and bonds. It's a sharing of souls, capable of reaching out as far as complete acceptance: "Hath no man condemned thee? . . . Neither do I condemn thee."[59] Humor as heartfelt as the best of Bible humor includes all of us, spreads the joy, makes it possible that everybody "might have life, and that they might have it more abundantly."[60]

Jesus works that warm amplification of goodheartedness most vigorously in his parables, in those down-to-earth accounts he loves to push beyond our comfort zones. He pushes them really far. To evoke his vision of better possibilities, "Jesus indulges in the comic distortion of mundane reality."[61] Humor radiates from the mind-altering, certitude-unsettling, soul-shaking manner of his parable scenarios, where commonplace circumstances get jerked around so contrary to everyday experience they twist our minds into new dimensions. Our worst Samaritan enemies turn out to be our best friends.[62] Prodigal ne'er-do-wells celebrate at their fathers' parties while stay-at-home do-gooders sulk outside.[63] The homeless are welcomed into high society feasts, for the express purpose of annoying celebrities.[64] Young women who would have been the life of the party are refused admission to weddings because they forgot to bring flashlight batteries.[65] The agreeable volunteer never gets off the couch; the ornery naysayer saves the day.[66] Vineyard keepers resolve the nagging annoyance of attacks on their servants by sending their sons out to get killed.[67] Stewards are encouraged to protect their personal interests by preemptive embezzling.[68]

There is gritty realism in Jesus's parables, realism of a wildly innovative nature. The parables look at the most mundane of matters, but look at them in a way they've never been looked at before, with a kind of outlandish

---

59. John 8:10–11.

60. John 10:10.

61. Funk, *Parables and Presence*, 132.

62. Luke 10:25–37.

63. Luke 15:11–32.

64. Luke 14:16–24.

65. Luke 14:7–11.

66. Matt 21:28–32.

67. Mark 12:1–8.

68. Luke 16:1–12.

pragmatism that trespasses the borders of our received notions and shanghais readers into the surrealistic territory of humor. Parable humor am-
bushes moral complacency by means of a startling new system of moral
economics. We find ourselves in the parables in a whole new world of fiscal
reality that laughs off zero-sum limitations in favor of a win-win world,
where sons who waste their inheritance are rewarded for their prodigality
with more robes and rings and fatted calves,[69] where good retirement-fund
advice recommends putting all investment eggs in one pearl-of-great-
price basket,[70] where that's OK because in this economy barley seed can be
counted on to yield a hundredfold.[71] The fiscal bottom line of these startling tales posits a life where more time is invested in the search for a lost
coin than the coin is worth,[72] where late-day workers warrant the same full
wage as those who've labored since dawn,[73] where a widow's mite counts for
more than the vastest philanthropic contributions,[74] where otherwise sane
shepherds risk the safety of their entire herd to wander off after a stray,[75]
where Lehman Brothers-style investments of talents turn out to be more
rewarding than fiscal carefulness.[76]

Parables aren't satisfied with simply including humor, for the window dressing. They function by means of humor. They impact the rutted
routes of the psyche as shockingly as IED's. The explosive power of irony
in parables can blast readers out of complacency. "Laughter is the spark
which passes when imagination strikes the ground. When fact meets fancy
a fatted calf is killed."[77] Parables come by those lightning strikes of epiphany
as naturally as they come by their humor. "By its very nature metaphor
involves exaggeration, for it does not say something is like something else,
which can be true, but that something is something else, which cannot be
true."[78] By virtue of wildfire unexpectedness, surprise that is surprisingly
often sparked by humor, "a parable possesses power to shape and change

69. Luke 15:11–32.

70. Matt 13:45–46.

71. Mark 4:3–8.

72. Luke 15:8.

73. Matt 20:1–6.

74. Mark 12:42–44.

75. Matt 18:12:14.

76. Matt 25:14–30.

77. Zuver, *Salvation by Laughter*, 125.

78. Stein, *Difficult Sayings in the Gospels*, 72.

attitude," so much power it can introduce its readers to "a new possibility of existence."[79]

Laughter is good for the soul. It does more than make us feel better. It makes us better. "No man who has once heartily and wholly laughed can be altogether irreclaimably bad."[80] Laughter is soul-altering in the way hallucinogenic drugs are mind-altering, changing us, sometimes merely momentarily, sometimes irrevocably. Humor has in it the seeds of the most rejuvenating kind of repentance, in its most nurturing forms serving almost as "a midwife of souls."[81] William Hazlitt sounds biblical when he points out that "man is the only animal that laughs and weeps; for he is the only animal that is struck with the difference between what things are, and what they ought to be."[82] Laughter's innate capacity for motivating repentance, for helping us be better, makes humor potentially life changing. Humor can be "redemptive when it leads to comic self-discovery."[83] Part of the reason laughter makes us feel so much better is that it makes us better.

Makes us smarter, too. Bible humor opens our minds, extends our horizons—mostly, surprisingly enough for true believers, by challenging our credulity. "It ain't necessarily so, / It ain't necessarily so— / De t'ings that yo' li-ble / To read in de Bible— / It ain't necessarily so."[84] There's a lot of that "not necessarily" sort of thing in the Bible, things like *Pinocchio* whales[85] and patriarchal lifespans that span almost a millennium[86] and talking donkeys that would seem more at home in *Shrek*.[87] It's enough to make a Bible reader think. It's enough to challenge a Bible reader's faith, to try its mettle, to strengthen its sinews. It's enough to make a Bible reader struggle with the paradox of faith and doubt, to discover when they complement rather than contradict, to realize "there lives more faith in honest doubt, / Believe me, than in half the creeds."[88]

79. Stein, *Parables of Jesus*, 66.

80. Carlyle, *Sartor Resartus*, 26.

81. Zuver, *Salvation by Laughter*, 133.

82. Andrews, *Dictionary of Quotations*, 427.

83. Trueblood, *Humor of Christ*, 54.

84. Gershwin, "It Ain't Necessarily So."

85. Jonah 1:17.

86. Gen 5.

87. Num 22.

88. Tennyson, *In Memoriam*, 1221.

Humor helps us focus. In addition to making us think more broadly, Bible humor simultaneously concentrates our attention on what most matters. For all the befuddling complexity of its workings, humor, with the advantage of that Gordian-knot-cutting brevity that is "the soul of wit,"[89] can cut to the chase of the most complicated and crucial concerns. The triple-decker debate of Job through forty-two chapters of tag-team argument with Eliphaz and Bildad and Zophar and Elihu on the profound philosophical question of why bad things happen to good people can be difficult to compass, hard to grasp even in its broad essentials—and, as a result, hard to care about. But no one misses the same essential point in the shortcut terms of sarcasm: "Hast thou seen the doors of the shadow of death?"[90]—or, in Woody Allen's comic paraphrase: "I don't mind dying. I just don't want to be there when it happens."[91] Even in theologically obfuscating Job, Bible humor approaches miracle in its capacity to clarify at the same time it enlarges the view.

More than Meets the Eye

Humor enlarges everything. There's a whole lot of that humorous expansion going on in the Bible, much of it through irony—so much that many commentators admit humor in the Bible only in its ironic form, thinking the single thing among biblical writers that "might be called humor is their penchant for irony."[92] But it's generally conceded by those very reductivists that there's a whole lot of irony around—"dramatic ironies abound." Even in the unlikely purview of the austere prophetic writings "a persistent use is made of rhetorical ironies of all kinds—sarcasm, invective, mock-incomprehension."[93] There's so much of this brand of biblical humor that Good, who wrote the book on the subject, thinks "an essay on irony in the book of Genesis should probably be of book length."[94]

Bible irony can be as intense as it is pervasive. Elijah's send-up of the priests of Baal on Mt. Carmel heaps sarcasm upon sarcasm in its paean of merciless mockings: "Cry aloud: for [Baal] is a god; either he is talking, or

89. Shakespeare, *Hamlet*, 2.2.90.

90. Job 39:17.

91. Allen, *Insanity Defense*, 54.

92. Jacobson, *Story of the Stories*, 170.

93. Ibid.

94. Good, *Irony in the Old Testament*, 81.

he is pursuing, or he is in a journey, or peradventure he sleepeth, and must be awaked"[95]—the "intention is exaggerated to the point of . . . sarcasm."[96] That makes biblical irony, like most things literary in the Bible, go well beyond "a bit of effective storytelling technique."[97] It's anything but trivial. Irony reinforces an entire worldview: "In a universe where God's ways transcend human understanding and in which an unseen spiritual world is portrayed as being just as real as the physical world, it is inevitable that discrepancies in perception will keep entering the action."[98] Irony in the Bible underscores what might be the biblical bottom line: there's more here than meets the eye.

God's cosmic comic putdown of impatient Job, for instance, drips deliciously with sarcasm. And all that searching sarcasm, all seventy-seven scathing rhetorical questions worth, aims at the point where most biblical irony aims—that there may be more to things than we thought: "Dost thou know the balancings of the clouds?"[99] "Hast thou entered into the springs of the sea?"[100] "Have the gates of death been opened unto thee?"[101] "Hast thou perceived the breadth of the earth? Declare if thou knowest it all,"[102] you know-it-all.

Most biblical irony tends to be less blatant, as with Christ's at Capernaum. When the mob spurns his one-shot loaves-and-fishes miracle (which pales for the hungry crowd in comparison with Moses's provision of more exotic manna on a daily basis for decades in the wilderness), Jesus responds wryly "Your fathers did eat manna in the wilderness, and are dead"[103]—my provisions just might work out better for you, long term. The more subtle the irony, the more penetrating. If sarcasm hammers increasingly resistant surfaces with its mallet blows, the best biblical irony, more of a scalpel, eviscerates.

The least funny humor in the Bible is the most heavyhanded, as in the direct "so's your mama" prophetic invective of insults like "Ephraim

---

95. 1 Kgs 18:27.

96. Gable, *Bible as Literature*, 35.

97. Ibid.

98. Ryken, *How to Read the Bible as Literature*, 56.

99. Job 37:16.

100. Job 38:16.

101. Job 38:17.

102. Job 38:18.

103. John 6:49.

is a cake not turned"[104]—burned on the one side, raw on the other—not perhaps the best batch of fry bread, those Ephraimite rednecks with their farmer tans and their undercooked culture. Inclining away from the bludgeonings of prophetic sarcasm toward the sophisticated understatement of the wisdom books, we find ourselves in more subtle and more significant humor territory: "Of making many books there is no end; and much study is a weariness of the flesh."[105] This quieter irony is both more telling and more relatable for more of us. We'd have to be anti-Ephraim bigots to really relish "throw out those bad pancakes" insults. But we don't have to be an academic geeks to smile with the Preacher about the pains of obligatory study, especially when we're right now reading it in God's assigned study book. Ecclesiastes gives us a less obvious smile than Hosea, and a more meaningful one.

The humor in both cases is implicit. Biblical irony works by understatement. It leaves blanks for us to fill in. The wider the blank, the more reader experience that can be grafted into the text. Bible humor is participatory, invitational—do-it-yourself. By dramatizing the dissonance between appearances and reality, between what is and what ought to be, irony invites us to decide for ourselves what will be. The Bible and its humor leave a stunning degree of that decisive deciphering up to the reader. That's why the deeper the irony probes and the more significant its implications, the less obvious it is. Some of the most penetrating biblical irony concentrates itself in "fat chance" propositions, impossibilities embedded in straightforward statements that purport to propose practical action. "Thou shalt not covet,"[106] especially in light of the likelihood that the Hebrew meaning is closer to "desire," on closer examination seems as unlikely a proposal "as if the lawgiver was making a jest."[107] That submerged comedy is compounded by the even more unlikely and "even more comic words 'your neighbor's goods.'"[108] Funny thing is, that expectation is so impossible to meet, as we keep-up-with-the-Joneses moderns know full well, that any approximation to it is pretty good.

That "don't covet" directive ranks in the minor leagues of impossible commands in Scripture. The Bible pushes so hard toward impractical ideals,

104. Hos 7:8.

105. Eccl 12:12.

106. Exod 20:17.

107. Barnstone, *Other Bible*, 650.

108. Ibid..

toward impossible dreams, toward "song of songs"[109] and "holy of holies"[110] sorts of pinnacles of impossibility that there are times when its "words make sense only if they are exaggerated banter."[111] And those improbably bantering words tend to be, doubly improbably, among its most significant: "Let the dead bury their dead."[112] "Unto him that smiteth thee on the one cheek offer also the other."[113] "Whosoever looketh on a woman to lust after her hath committed adultery already with her in his heart."[114] "Love your enemies, bless them that curse you, do good to them that hate you, and pray for them which despitefully use you, and persecute you."[115] "Be ye therefore perfect, even as your Father which is in heaven is perfect."[116] The insistent irony in these extraordinary statements is so over-the-top it invites us not to laugh the implications off, but to stretch ourselves by reaching for the stars. This deep-down irony invites us to consider impossibilities, provokes us to ponder the imponderable, conceive the inconceivable, unscrew the inscrutable.

Blessed Are Your Eyes

Looking into the microscope of humor attentively enough can change not just what we're seeing but the way we see. Humor "creates a world of meaning" the reader can enter and use as a "lens through which [to view] his own world."[117] That humor-polished eyepiece can see into the heart of things, as deep as "the sense of ultimacy with which the Bible invests human experience. What in most literature would be portrayed as a purely natural occurrence—the birth of a baby, a shower of rain, the daily course of the sun—is portrayed in the Bible as being rooted in a divine reality that lends spiritual significance to human and natural events."[118] That penetrating view enabled by biblical humor enhances our perspective, ramps up our

---

109. Song 1:1.

110. Exod 26:33.

111. Trueblood, *Humor of Christ*, 65.

112. Matt 8:22.

113. Luke 6:29.

114. Matt 5:28.

115. Matt 5:44.

116. Matt 5:48.

117. Scott, *Jesus, Symbol-Maker*, 14.

118. Ryken, *How to Read the Bible as Literature*, 180.

view of life until it is "filled with meaning."[119] Humor enables the visionary advantage of what Russian formalists call "making strange,"[120] disorienting us to reorient us. Humor works for human vision both centrifugally and centripetally, focusing us as it blows our minds. Both directions, it can help us see ourselves better. It can help us see the church better, see that it is "not yet what it should be."[121] It can help us see God himself better, to "confront Christ as actually portrayed rather than as we have imagined Him to be."[122]

Those perspectives matter in the Bible. "For as he thinketh in his heart, so is he."[123] Biblical humor intimates that we shortchange ourselves when we limit our vision, when we confine our options by personal narrowness or the constraints of other people's orthodoxies. The Spirit we think we are familiar with—the computer-controlled air conditioning of our small-church gospel—may in fact be more like a wild west wind, a "rushing mighty wind,"[124] "a great and strong wind" that "rent the mountains,"[125] blasting down the high Himalayas of our hearts and into the farthest Siberian steppes of our souls. If life is as we see it, it is no small matter that the Bible helps us see it more richly, more deeply, more intensely, more dynamically, more gladly—more humorously. Bible humor awakens us to what Owen Barfield described as "fresh meaning."[126]

Seeing differently makes us different. "The neurotic who learns to laugh at himself may be on the way to self-management, perhaps to cure."[127] Appreciation of Bible humor could alter personality, reset the essential stance of a soul, adjust the GPS of a personal disposition from the tragic mode to the comic. The Bible narrative itself is "a story beginning in deepest despair" that works its way "to wholeness and well-being."[128] That "upward movement from misery to happiness"[129] migrates Scripture away from the inexorable downhill slide of tragedy toward a caravan of comedy,

---

119. Ibid., 181.

120. Erlich, *Russian Formalism*, 26.

121. Brown, *Critical Meaning of the Bible*, 44.

122. Trueblood, *Humor of Christ*, 19.

123. Prov 23:7.

124. Acts 2:2.

125. 1 Kgs 19:11.

126. Barfield, *Poetic Diction*, 201.

127. Allport, *Individual and Religion*, 92.

128. Gros Louis, *Literary Interpretations of Biblical Narratives*, 189.

129. Ryken, *How to Read the Bible*, 82.

upwardly mobile. And that positive, practical thrust into newness of life makes biblical humor imminently transcendent, capable of lofting us into "Somewhere Over the Rainbow" dream territory right in our own back yard. Bible humor works as a portable bridge between what we are and what we can be.

We can be happier. Humor, as most of us have noticed, makes us happier. Happier is what the Bible, in its weird discombobulating way, is urging us to be. "Authentic comedy raises life above the confines of the merely conventional to reintegrate it, on the other side, into a new and strange world."[130] Humor turns the world upside down, inside out. "Recognition scenes in the parables are humorous because they involve a reversal of the substantial, comfortable, patent nexus of . . . the received world."[131] That gear-shifting, life-affecting humor can reach a long way, from the ridiculous to the stunningly sublime. "It is hardly ever noticed that the inert figure on the cross has a smile on his lips" at the "joke"[132] of that ultimate reversal. "The kingdom Jesus anticipates is the present world stood on its head. John is deadly serious and consequently tiring. Jesus is funny."[133] Funk may overstate the cheerful tone of the crucifixion, but he's spot on about the cosmic paradox—the worst tragedy of all time turns out to be even better than it looked to be bad.

Everything in Bible reading turns out better with humor. Many think the Bible's "primary impulse" is "to provide instruction or at least necessary information, not merely to delight." But we "miss much that the biblical stories are meant to convey" if we miss the Bible's "play of exploration."[134] We miss much of the delight of its "delightful words."[135] We miss how intensely the authors, maybe even the Author, enjoyed the writing. We miss the best way to understand that writing—which is to read it as it was written, in the same spirit of expansive joy. Humor may not be, as modern culture seems to have assumed, "the invention of the devil as a tool for engaging in frivolity and encouraging sacrilege, thus making children wiggle in church and giggle during confirmation."[136] Nietzsche himself, thought by some to

---

130. Funk, *Parables and Presence*, 132.

131. Ibid., 131.

132. Ibid.

133. Ibid., 132.

134. Alter, *Art of Biblical Narrative*, 46.

135. Eccl 2:10, NEV.

136. Hyers, *God Created Laughter*, 14.

be of the devil's own party, points rather to somber Satan as the one who is "serious, thorough, profound, solemn"—all in all, grave, bringing us down with the heavy weight of seriousness: "through him all things fall."[137]

How Would Jesus Laugh?

Many dedicated Bible readers distill its complex moral and ethical ramifications down to a single pragmatic question: What would Jesus do? That implicit invitation to emulate the Lord in our personal lives provides a helpful window into the practical implications of the Bible. Jesus himself expected much of readers, explicitly expected us to become perfect, "perfect, even as your Father which is in heaven is perfect."[138] It may seem counterintuitive, even irreverent, to suggest anything as finite and flawed and definitively human as humor as a primary step in that perfection process. Yet humor is an improvable aspect of humanity, and an aspect that we have observed in *Illuminating Humor of the Bible* to be key to improvement of more serious aspects. And humor has the profound advantage of joining Jesus where he lives, not in our customary solemn notions, but in his actual presence in the Gospels.

What would Jesus do about humor? What he *did* do was laugh—a lot. The most exemplary personality ever, the ultimate model for our personalities, has a sense of humor that gets undeniably demonstrated again and again in the Gospels, at times hilariously. We largely overlook the "Laughing Jesus" of the Gnostics,[139] mostly miss "Jesus' capacity for fun, his comic sense."[140] But the "laughter of God"[141] is more than a figment of Gnostic imagination. Orthodox legend to the contrary, God, when we saw him up close, laughed so often and so energetically that he shocked the solemnly orthodox—Pharisees lodge public complaints about his partying no fewer than eleven times.[142] Christly laughter echoes through the Gospels. "In terms of sheer bulk, the humor of Jesus is of more than passing importance."[143] "Mark preserves four laughter-provoking sayings, Matthew

---

137. Nietzsche, *Thus Spoke Zarathustra*, 40–41.

138. Matt 5:48.

139. Freke, *Laughing Jesus*, title page.

140. Price, *Common Room*, 282.

141. Lanyon, *Laughter of God*, 9.

142. Most dramatically in Matt 9:11; Mark 2:16; Luke 5:34.

143. Webster, *Laughter in the Bible*, 116.

includes nineteen, and Luke includes at least twenty-one."[144] There are so many humorous references we can't know Christ completely— or even on balance—without knowing his humor. It's "an element in Christ's life which is so important that, without it, any understanding of Him is inevitably distorted."[145]

The obviousness of the humor in the Gospels makes our failure to apprehend it intriguing. We seem to have carefully quarantined our cultural conception of Jesus away from laughter, to a degree that may itself be laughable: "In two thousand years of Christianity, Jesus Christ has never been known to laugh."[146] That process of censoring the divine laughter begins as early as the Gospels themselves. The further the Gospel writers move from Jesus, chronologically and theologically, the less funny he gets. John, as opposed to those earlier Synoptic Gospel writers who had Jesus saying something funny in most chapters, "did not report even one saying that can be interpreted as humorous."[147] That may be a slight exaggeration, as we shall see with the story of the woman at the well, but the point is well taken. The modern church seems seriously determined to continue that depressing downward trend toward divine humorlessness.

Despite that dedicated anti-humor crusade inherited by us from John's Gospel, much of the humor remains. To the embarrassment of the wholesale censorship of the humorless gospel, there's humor everywhere else in the New Testament. That's particularly true in the Gospels themselves, where we are closest to Jesus's life. The initial and most momentous call to the kingdom, the world-shaking invitation to future pontiff Peter to join the Jesus quest, verges on jest. Given the ironic issues Jesus's fishy pun raises about the infamous reputation of fishermen for stretching the facts on everything from whether they're biting today to the size of the one that got away, "It's hard to think that they did not smile when He said 'Follow me, and I will make you fishers of men.'"[148] Hard to imagine, too, at the height of the rockstar fame that he never took too seriously, that Jesus wasn't smiling some when he wryly disparaged his legendary reputation

144. Ibid.

145. Trueblood, *Humor of Christ*, 9.

146. Hussey, "Wit of the Carpenter," 336.

147. Webster, *Laughter in the Bible*, 116.

148. Trueblood, *Humor of Christ*, 63.

for attracting audiences: "Wherever the corpse is, there the vultures will gather"[149]—more than one way to draw a crowd, folks.

Some of his "exaggerated . . . humorous saying"[150] gets chuckle-aloud risible in its entertaining overenthusiasm—that speck difficult to remove from our friend's eye because of the rafter obscuring our own vision;[151] those rich men finding it a relative relief to thread themselves through needles rather than squeeze their overfed bodies and bloated souls through the strait gates of heaven;[152] Pharisees who fussily strain out the gnats in their soup but enthusiastically gulp down full-grown camels that got there who knows how but obviously have to be swallowed with a remarkably high degree of difficulty, knobby-kneed humptybumpty camel ungainlinesses poking every which way past extraordinarily protuberant Adam's apples all the awkward way down those stiff-necked pharisaical throats.[153]

It's obvious Jesus laughed often, smiled more often. The most conservative scholarly estimate tallies at least forty-four humorous episodes in the four brief accounts we have of his life[154]—even though one of those accounts completely undercounts to the extent of no sense of humor whatsoever. That still adds up to a humorous incident in two out of every three Synoptic chapters, a high incidence for a Mark Twain novel, and a particularly impressive tally in a book we somehow manage to read as somber. If not a God of laughter, like Vishnu, Christ is definitely a laughing God.

"Again I Say, Rejoice"

To whatever extent God is a God of laughter, it might be interesting to address him as if he were. It would certainly be different. And there could be advantages to a more humorous approach to worship—clear advantages, like an integral drive toward expansiveness and experiment and innovation, like an inherent resistance to the rigid limitations of orthodoxy, like a natural thrust toward living reality instead of lifeless theory. Humor as an aspect of worship opens up fascinating options, and those may be the more personally applicable the less we are disposed to try them: "Those who find

149. Matt 24:28, NEB.

150. Trueblood, *Humor of Christ*, 62.

151. Matt 7:3–5.

152. Mark 10:25.

153. Matt 23:24.

154. Webster, *Laughter in the Bible*, 116.

no humor in faith are probably those who find the church a refuge for their own bleak way of looking at life."[155]

Christianity may not have tapped in as deeply as it might to the merrymaking dimension of worship. Religion can be a celebration: "They who know the truth are not equal to those who love it, and they who love it are not equal to those who delight in it."[156] Religion at its best is associated with joy, some of it so ecstatic it can move the topography: "Ye mountains, that ye skipped like rams, and ye little hills like lambs."[157] The Bible encourages our human capacity for ecstatic worship: "Rejoice in the Lord always: and again I say, Rejoice."[158] That may not be a mere matter of ritual. Rejoicing can rise to the level of a moral discipline that culminates in the Pollyanna Principle: gladness not as a result of goodness but as a cause of it. Ultimately, happiness may be a moral imperative. "There is no duty we so much underrate as the duty of being happy."[159] We should "rejoice and be glad all our days."[160] "We should make merry, and be glad."[161] Christian celebrants of the goodness of life are urged to go so far as to "rejoice, inasmuch as ye are partakers of Christ's sufferings . . . be glad also with exceeding joy."[162]

For all its religious-show-business aspects, and despite its distastefulness to folk as stuffy as high-society Michal, merrymaking like David's before the Ark is clearly worshipful. Dancing and laughing before the Lord, David in his unorthodox performance managed an enthusiasm out of the reach of more sober ritual.[163] That kind of enthusiasm is counterintuitive for many of us these religiously somber days. We feel more righteous about the Martha disposition in ourselves, "careful and troubled about many things."[164] Jesus himself encouraged the more spontaneous approach of Mary, the easygoing genial sister who "hath chosen that good part."[165] Maybe something about the gospel really is good news, "good tidings of

---

155. Short, *Parables of Peanuts,* 151.

156. Confucius, *Analects,* chapter 6, principle 18.

157. Ps 114:6.

158. Phil 4:4.

159. Stevenson, "Apology for Idlers," 22.

160. Ps 90:14.

161. Luke 15:32.

162. 1 Pet 4:13.

163. 2 Sam 6:12–15.

164. Luke 10:41.

165. Luke 10:42.

great joy, which shall be to all people."[166] Maybe the humor in Scripture is intimating that the good news is a kind of celebration. Maybe it's a feast we're invited to.[167] We might want to celebrate with the rejoicing prodigals rather than sulking outside the party with self-righteous elders so "angry" they "would not go in."[168]

Humor might work in worship better than we think. Humor is where the alternating current of divinity and humanity most electrically meet, as in Jesus's encounter with the Canaanite woman. It's an edgy conversation, charged with witty tension, which may be why "there is a more widespread recognition of this encounter as humorous than of any other particular part of the Gospel record."[169] Jesus's bluntness here shocks a lot of readers: "It is not meet to take the children's bread, and to cast it to dogs."[170] That response to the woman's heartfelt plea for help with her demon-possessed daughter is sharper than we're used to from the Savior. Either he is frankly insulting the woman, rudely refusing her the gospel, rejecting her on blatant racist grounds, or there is here "an element of banter."[171] The banter seems confirmed by Jesus's genial response, his accepting approval of the cleverness of the woman's quick-witted retort when its logic flattens his: "Yet the dogs eat of the crumbs which fall from their masters' table."[172] "He was delighted. One conceives Him laughing readily at His self-discomfiture."[173] Such sassy repartee doesn't fit our accustomed model of worship. But it's an interesting model. And the humor involved makes it an extraordinarily effective one. Few prayers of the profoundest reverence manage the honesty of communication, let alone the intimacy, that is accomplished by these impertinent jibes. Nor is the incident isolated.

Jesus's encounter with the Samaritan woman at the well resonates with his conversation with the other foreign woman, echoes it so closely as to confirm it. This bantering is edgier still, compounded by what sounds disturbingly like erotic overtones. The woman, at the romantically charged scene of Jacob's well, historical site of the betrothal of both Rebecca and

166. Luke 2:10.

167. Luke 14:7–11.

168. Luke 15:28.

169. Trueblood, *Humor of Christ*, 116.

170. Matt 15:26.

171. Trueblood, *Humor of Christ*, 123.

172. Matt 15:27.

173. Hussey, "Wit of the Carpenter," 335.

Rachel, puts mildly flirtatious moves on the Savior. He calls her on her presumption with the same witty sharpness he used with the other foreign female, proposing—in these circumstances surely not without a touch of teasing, and possibly some derision—that it might be a good idea for her to go get her husband. When she declares herself uninhibited by any encumbrances of the marital variety, he nails her with his "You said it, Sister" zinger: "Thou hast well said, I have no husband: For thou hast had five husbands; and he whom thou now hast is not thy husband."[174] This frank repartee at the courting well is far from the sort of refined interaction with the divine we normally attempt among our sanctified pews and altars. For one thing, it's funny. For another, it's real—its edgy unorthodoxy confirms it even for skeptical scholars like the Jesus Seminar as historical. For another, as with the Canaanite-woman conversation, it works. The humor-tinged interchange is about as intimately efficacious as human communication with God gets.

Humor as Grace

Humor's potent powers in the Bible go beyond communication with God, beyond even connection with God. Humor at its best functions as a kind of bargain-basement grace. "There is a state of grace which is an affair of the comic intelligence. Religion needs this 'sunlight of the mind' to keep her enthusiasms fruitful and the heart sweet."[175] The God who weeps with us in our mortal woes surely smiles sympathetically, too, at the comedy of our human foibles. The Bible's parody and lampoon and slapstick and sarcasm and wit and all those subtler ironies intimate a shared comic vision between heaven and earth. That divine rainbow of humor radiates through a broad spectrum of human laughter, "the laughter of unbelief, of despair, and of scorn, and the laughter of believing happiness are here uncannily juxtaposed, so that . . . one hardly knows whether belief or unbelief is laughing."[176] For all the ambivalence of that human laughter, its divine source is certain: "God gave us laughter."[177] God's laughter can function as

---

174. John 4:17–18.
175. Smith, "Comic Spirit in Religion," 191.
176. Norris, Amazing Grace, 358.
177. Ibid.

a kind of grace. It understands us. It cares about us. It makes our own best laughter "praise of God because it is a gentle echo of God's laughter."[178]

We undervalue laughter, underestimate the serious efficacy of humor. Milan Kundera quotes the "fine Jewish proverb": "Man thinks, God laughs."[179] Laughter may be a better way of thinking—humor ranks high among our most complex and subtle modes of thought: "Humor's the hardest thing to translate."[180] Maybe even for God. Laughter for God could trump not only our thought, but his, not just emotionally and spiritually, but intellectually. It may be that God's thought naturally culminates in laughter, soars beyond mechanical analytical intellect into organic holistic delight. "Man thinks, God laughs." He's obviously smarter when he's laughing than we are when we're thinking. Maybe he's smarter when he's laughing than he is when *he's* thinking. Whatever the profound implications of God's laughter, we are created in that jovial image. We are nurtured in humor and mature toward fullness of laughter. That raises the ante of our human capacity to catch God's subtle biblical jokes. Divine humor DNA in us may mean more than stimulation of our intelligence or encouragement of our emotional development or nurturance of our moral maturity. It may mean that laughing with God makes us closer to him, maybe even more like him.

That is intriguing theology, almost a theology of humor: "For after that in the wisdom of God the world by wisdom knew not God it pleased God by the foolishness of preaching to save them that believe. For the Jews require a sign, and the Greeks seek after wisdom: But we preach Christ crucified, unto the Jews a stumbling block, and unto the Greeks foolishness."[181] The more improbable the paradox, the closer the oddity comes to humor, the more it makes a certain kind of preposterous sense: "God hath chosen the foolish things of the world to confound the wise; and God hath chosen the weak things of the world to confound the things which are mighty; And base things of the world, and things which are despised, hath God chosen, yea, and things which are not, to bring to nought things that are."[182]

What if that profound foolishness could lighten up our psyches enough to "mount up with wings as eagles"?[183] Reaching toward the wisdom in the

178. Norris, *Amazing Grace*, 358.
179. Kundera, *Art of the Novel*, 58.
180. Mukherjee, *Jasmine*, 149.
181. 1 Cor 1:21–23.
182. 1 Cor 1:27–28.
183. Isa 40:31.

humor of the Bible might free up our spiritual imaginations, allow us the lightfootedness of grace and the heavenly expansiveness of room to move, to dance beyond the littlenesses of our perspectives, to swing the sweetness of our souls beyond the limitations of our certitudes. "The presence of irony is a possible touchstone to the presence of liberating faith."[184] That kind of humor-informed faith might open the prison gates of our most steadfast theologies, might provide "freedom spacious enough to permit both a self-irony that is not self-destructive and an irony on the world that is not arrogant."[185] Humor is minor miracle: "you never know why people laugh. I know *what* makes them laugh but trying to get your hands on the *why* of it is like trying to pick an eel out of a tub of water."[186] Laughter in its essence may ultimately share more in common with spirit than we've noticed: "The wind bloweth where it listeth, and thou hearest the sound thereof, but canst not tell whence it cometh, and whither it goeth: so is every one that is born of the Spirit."[187]

Laughter being such a breath of fresh air, we might read the Bible better if we were to read more attentive to its humor. We might with benefit of humor approach the ideal more realistically, with more spontaneity and less rigidity, more enthusiasm and less decorum, more unbearable lightness of being and less solemnity, less righteousness and more grace. Humor is not just warm and fuzzy. It works. Humor merges so companionably into the spirit it can be hard to tell where one ends and the other begins. Humor can function with our reluctant spirits as effectually as divine WD-40.

The honey of humor, for all its messiness, encourages happy outcomes better than the astringent vinegar of criticism. There's abundant practical precedent for the functionality of that bunglingly goodhearted humor approach, that "here's another fine mess you've gotten me into" paradoxical provocation for making things better: the Canaanite woman wittily negotiates for gospel scraps.[188] Paul, red faced, resurrects the unfortunate disciple he's bored to death by his "long preaching."[189] The prodigal son's prodigality hits pig-hugging bottom so hard it trampolines him right back home to his

---

184. Good, *Irony in the Old Testament*, 244.

185. Ibid., 245.

186. Anobile, *Flask of Fields*, 18.

187. John 3:8.

188. Matt 15:26–28.

189. Acts 20:9.

father's hug.[190] Abraham rescues Lot by the intriguing expedient of haggling with the Master of the Universe over Sodomites, ineffectively.[191] Joseph annoys his brothers so pestiferously with his self-serving dreams they sell him into slavery—in Egypt, exactly where he needs to be to save the family and the race.[192] Exactly where the Hebrew race needs to be to be enslaved so they can be freed by Moses.[193] Moses stutters his uncertain way to the totality of the Torah.[194] The exodus midwives save an entire generation of baby boys from Pharaoh's death sentence with the ridiculous excuse that Hebrew mothers are too "lively" for them, "delivered ere the midwives come in."[195] Jonah responds to the divine call by running the precise wrong direction in order to convert an entire nation of the unlikeliest converts in history.[196] Shadrach, Meshach, and Abednego emerge from "the midst of the fire" of "the burning fiery furnace" smelling like a rose—not even "the smell of fire had passed on them."[197] Job nags God into the most eloquent theophany of all time.[198] Jesus gets harassed so much by local religious authorities for "eating and drinking"[199] with those party animals the "publicans and sinners"[200] he becomes the Christian model of abstemiousness. One of the few men of his time to actually associate socially with women,[201] he gets for his pioneering feminist efforts cast retrospectively as the epitome of disinterest in females. Ranking high among the wittiest wisecrackers ever, he is relegated by our cultural memory to nothing but tragic roles.

The ironies get stacked so high in the Bible it would be funny if it weren't so serious. However outrageous the paradox, however understated the undertone of humor—the more so in fact the more understated it is—always the humor is meaningful, even life-affecting. The Bible is not kidding around. There is the profoundest cosmic irony in The Master of

190. Luke 15:14–19.
191. Gen 18:23–32.
192. Gen 45:5–8.
193. Exod 1:8–10.
194. Exod 4:10.
195. Exod 1:19.
196. Jonah 3.
197. Dan 3:27.
198. Job 38–41.
199. Matt 11:19.
200. Mark 2:16.
201. John 4:6–26; 8:1–11; 11:1–34; 19:25; 20:1–18, for instance.

the Universe reduced to the role of a mere man—a lower-class, Middle Eastern, possibly impoverished, and probably illiterate man at that—in an insignificant place, at an unremembered time. And David, almost as much the fair-haired boy of the Old Testament as Jesus is of the New, pulls off some downright outrageous escapades for a moral hero. David in his Mafia mode strong-arms the poor people of the Judean hills into paying for protection[202]—strong arms some of them, like Nabal, to death.[203] He upgrades his ambitious aspirations out of that lowlife neighborhood with the help of what looks suspiciously like timely and well-alibied contracts put out on political opponents.[204] In a religious society where ritual propriety is sacrosanct, he eats the sacred shewbread[205] and defiles the sacred Ark[206] and has too much blood on his hands to build the sacred temple.[207] He holds the Bible record for ineffectuality as a father,[208] against tough Old Testament competition. He sweet-talks his best friend into giving up the kingdom to him.[209] He takes way more wives than is good for a man, yet still feels the need to steal the wife of his loyal captain,[210] then, to cover up the royal adultery, have him murdered.[211] Yet he somehow manages, through it all, to be a "man after God's own heart."[212]

Saul makes mistakes far less egregious than David's, yet turns out far worse. Hard to tell how much sense of humor factors into that. But Saul definitely takes himself too seriously, at times to the point of paranoia. David's cheerful disposition, on the other hand, resonates with the old quip, "They'll never kick me out of the church. I repent too damn fast." The contrasting capacity of David and Saul for laughing at themselves reflects in their readiness for repentance. When Samuel confronts Saul about ceremonial misdemeanors, Saul gets defensive: "Not my fault. The people made

---

202. 1 Sam 25:6–8.

203. 1 Sam 25:37–38.

204. 2 Sam 2:15–16; 3:27; 4:68, for starters.

205. 1 Sam 21:6.

206. 2 Sam 6:14–16.

207. 1 Kgs 5:3.

208. 2 Sam 13.

209. 1 Sam 23:17.

210. 2 Sam 11:3–4.

211. 2 Sam 11:14–15.

212. Acts 13:22.

me do it."[213] When Nathan accuses David of stealing Bathsheba—"thou art the man"—David repents on the spot: "I have sinned against the Lord."[214]

A sense of humor by no means makes a person righteous, obviously makes none of us sin-proof. Though it sometimes urges us away from evil,[215] humor can't guarantee our goodness. But it might make us less stiffnecked, less proud. It might help with repentance. Saul, bless his huge but humorless heart, never quite got it. David did. The moral of Bible humor is that we can get it. Humor, whimsically idiosyncratic by its nature, doesn't work for everybody, doesn't work for anybody all the time, and doesn't work for any of us in the same way. But that very self-selectivity means that when it works, it really works. I'm hoping exactly what I think the Bible is hoping: I hope the humor works for you.

---

213. 1 Sam 15:14–15.

214. 2 Sam 12:7, 13.

215. Lewis, *Screwtape Letters*, 5.

Bibliography

Achtemeier, Elizabeth. "Women." In *The Oxford Companion to the Bible,* edited by Bruce M. Metzger and Michael D. Coogan, 806–18. New York: Oxford University Press, 1993.

Ackerman, James S. "Satire and Symbolism in the Song of Jonah." In *Traditions in Transformation: Turning Points in Biblical Faith,* edited by Baruch Halpurn and Jon D. Levenson, 74–119. Winona Lake, IN: Eisenbrauns, 1981.

Ackerman, Susan. "Digging up Deborah: Recent Hebrew Bible Scholarship on Gender and the Contribution of Archaelogy." In *Near Eastern Archaeology* 66 (2003) 172–84.

Alexander, T. Desmond. "Lot's Hospitality: A Clue to His Righteousness." *Journal of Biblical Literature* 104 (1985) 289–91.

Allen, Leslie C. *The Books of Joel, Obadiah, Jonah, and Micah.* The New International Commentary on the Old Testament. Grand Rapids: Eerdmans, 1976.

Allen, Woody. *The Insanity Defense: The Complete Prose.* New York: Random House, 2007.

———. "Random Reflections of a Second-Rate Mind." In *The Best American Essays 1991,* edited by Joyce Carol Oates and Robert Atwan, 1–8. New York: Ticknor and Fields, 1991.

Allport, Gordon W. *The Individual and His Religion.* New York: Macmillan, 1952.

Alter, Robert. *The Art of Biblical Narrative.* New York: Basic, 1981.

———. *The Art of Biblical Poetry.* New York: Basic, 1985.

———. *Genesis: Translation and Commentary.* New York: Norton, 1996.

Alter, Robert, and Frank Kermode, editors. *The Literary Guide to the Bible.* Cambridge: Belknap Press of Harvard University Press, 1987.

Andrews, Robert, editor. *The Columbia Dictionary of Quotations.* New York: Columbia University Press, 1993.

Andriolo, Karen R. "Myth and History: A General Model and Its Application to the Bible." *American Anthropologist* 83 (1981) 261–84.

Anobile, Richard J. *A Flask of Fields.* New York: Norton, 1972.

Arrington, French L. *The Acts of the Apostles.* Peabody, MA: Hendrickson, 1988.

Ash, Russel. *The Top Ten of Everything: 2006.* New York: DK, 2005.

Auerbach, Erich. *Mimesis: The Representation of Reality in Western Literature.* Princeton: Princeton University Press, 1953.

Bal, Mieke. "Lots of Writing." In *Ruth and Esther,* A Feminist Companion to the Bible, edited by Athalya Brenner, 220–38. Sheffield, UK: Sheffield Academic, 1999.

Balmer, Randall. "The Generation of Faith." In *Searching for Your Soul,* edited by Katherine Kurs, 192–99. New York: Shocken, 1999.

Barfield, Owen. *Poetic Diction: A Study in Meaning.* Middletown, CT: Wesleyan University Press, 1973.

Barnstone, Willis, editor. *The Other Bible.* San Francisco: Harper & Row, 1984.

Barton, John, and John Muddiman. *The Oxford Bible Commentary.* Oxford: Oxford University Press, 2001.

Bartowski, John P. "Debating Patriarchy: Discursive Disputes over Spousal Authority among Evangelical Family Commentators." *Journal for the Scientific Study of Religion* 36 (1997) 393–410.

Baugh, Albert C., editor. *A Literary History of England.* 2nd ed. New York: Appleton-Century-Crofts, 1967.

Baxandall, Lee. "Bertolt Brecht's 'J.B.'" *Tulane Drama Review* 4 (1960) 113–17.

Benayoun, Robert. *The Films of Woody Allen.* New York: Harmony, 1986.

Berg, Sandra Beth. *The Book of Esther: Motifs, Themes and Structures.* Society of Biblical Literature Dissertation Series 44. Missoula, MT: Scholars, 1978.

Berkove, Lawrence I. "The Trickster God in *Roughing It.*" In *Trickster Lives: Culture and Myth in American Fiction,* edited by Jeanne Campbell Reesman, 21–30. Athens, GA: University of Georgia Press: 2001.

Berlin, Adele. "The Book of Esther and Ancient Storytelling." *Journal of Biblical Literature* 120 (2001) 3–14.

———. *Esther.* The Jewish Publication Society Bible Commentary. Philadelphia: Jewish Publication Society, 2001.

———. *Poetics and Interpretation of Biblical Narrative.* Sheffield, UK: Almond, 1983.

Bewer, Julius A. *The Literature of the Old Testament.* 3rd ed. Revised by Emil G. Kraeling. New York: Columbia University Press, 1962.

"A Bible in the Hand Still May Not Be Read." *Baptist Standard,* Dec. 4, 2000. Online: http://www.baptiststandard.com/2000/124/pages/biblereading.htm.

Bloom, Harold, and David Rosenberg. *The Book of J: Translated from the Hebrew by David Rosenberg, Interpreted by Harold Bloom.* New York: Weidenfeld, 1990.

Boase, Elizabeth. "Life in the Shadows: The Role and Function of Isaac in Genesis—Synchronic and Diachronic Readings." *Vetus Testamentum* 51 (2001) 312–35.

Bosworth, David A. "Evaluating King David: Old Problems and Recent Scholarship." *Catholic Biblical Quarterly* 68 (2006) 191–210.

Brown, Raymond E. *The Critical Meaning of the Bible.* New York: Paulist, 1981.

Browning, Robert. *The Ring and the Book.* New York: Heritage, 1949.

Buttrick, George A. *God, Pain, and Evil.* Nashville: Abingdon, 1966.

———. *The Interpreter's Bible.* New York: Abingdon-Cokesbury, 1951–7.

———. *The Interpreter's Dictionary of the Bible.* New York: Abingdon, 1962.

———. *Sermons Preached in a University Church.* New York: Abingdon, 1959.

Carlyle, Thomas. *Sartor Resartus.* New York: Macmillan, 1927.

Carroll, Lewis. *Through the Looking Glass.* New York: Collier, 1962.

Chase, Mary Ellen. *The Bible and the Common Reader.* New York: Macmillan, 1952.

Ciardi, John. *The Collected Poems of John Ciardi.* Edited by Edward M. Cifelli. Fayetteville, AR: University of Arkansas Press, 1997.

Clines, David J. A. "Esther." In *Harper's Bible Commentary,* edited by James L. May et al., 387–94. San Francisco: Harper and Row, 1988.

Clough, Arthur Hugh. *The Poems of Arthur Hugh Clough.* 2nd ed. Edited by F. L. Mulhauser. London: Oxford University Press, 1974.

Confucius. *The Analects.* Chapter 6, Principle 18. New York: New Directions, 1951.

Connelly, Marc. *The Green Pastures*. MI: Farrar and Rinehart, 1929.

Cosby, Bill. *Bill Cosby Is a Very Funny Fellow, Right!* Warner Brothers Records, ©1963, compact disc.

———. *Fatherhood*. Garden City, NY: Doubleday, 1986.

Cracroft, Richard H. "The Humor of Mormon Seriousness: A Celestial Balancing Act." *Sunstone* 10 (1985) 14–17.

Craig, Kenneth M., Jr. *A Poetics of Jonah: Art in the Service of Ideology*. Columbia, SC: University of South Carolina Press, 1993.

———. *Reading Esther: A Case for the Literary Carnivalesque*. Louisville: Westminster/ John Knox, 1995.

Crenshaw, James L. "Jonah, The Book of." In *The Oxford Companion to the Bible*, edited by Bruce M. Metzger, 593–95. New York: Oxford University Press, 1993.

Crossan, John Dominic. *In Parables: The Challenge of the Historical Jesus*. New York: Harper & Row, 1973.

Crouch, Walter B. "To Question an End, to End a Question: Opening the Closure of the Book of Jonah." *Journal for the Study of the Old Testament* 62 (1994) 101–2.

Dekker, Sydney. "Eve and the Serpent: A Rational Choice to Err." *Journal of Religion and Health* 46 (2007) 571–77.

De Vos, Craig Steven. "Finding a Charge that Fits: The Accusation against Paul and Silas at Philippi (Acts 16:19–21)." *Journal for the Study of the New Testament* 74 (1999) 51–63.

Dickens, Charles. *David Copperfield*. New York: Sheldon, 1863.

Dozeman, Thomas B. "Inner-Biblical Interpretation of Yahweh's Gracious and Compassionate Character." *Journal of Biblical Literature* 108 (1989) 207–23.

Eddleman, H. Leo. *Acts 12: An Exegetical and Practical Commentary on Acts*. Dallas: Books of Life, 1974.

Eisler, Riane. *The Chalice and the Blade*. San Francisco: Harper, 1987.

Engar, Anne W. "Old Testament Women as Tricksters." In *Mappings of the Biblical Terrain: The Bible as Text*, edited by Vincent L. Tollers and John Maier, 143–57. Lewisburg, PA: Bucknell University Press, 1990.

Erlich, Victor. *Russian Formalism*. The Hague: Moulton, 1965.

Evans, G. Blakemore, et al. *The Riverside Shakespeare*. Boston: Mifflin, 1974.

Faulkner, William. "Nobel Prize Acceptance Speech." In *In Our Own Words: Extraordinary Speeches of the American Century*, edited by Robert G. Torricelli and Andrew Carroll, 179–80. New York: Washington Square, 1999.

Fewell, Danna Nolan, and David M Gunn. "Controlling Perspectives: Women, Men, and the Authority of Violence in Judges 4 & 5." *Journal of the American Academy of Religion* 58 (1990) 389–411.

———. "Feminist Reading of the Hebrew Bible: Affirmation, Resistance and Transformation." *Journal for the Study of the Old Testament* 39 (1987) 77–87.

Fowler, Alastair. *A History of English Literature*. Cambridge: Harvard University Press, 1987.

Fox, Michael V. *Character and Ideology in the Book of Esther*. Columbia, SC: University of South Carolina Press, 1991.

Freitheim, Terence E. "Jonah." In *Harper's Bible* Commentary, edited by James L. Mays, 728–30. San Francisco: Harper & Row, 1988.

Freke, Timothy. *The Laughing Jesus: Religious Lies and Gnostic Wisdom*. New York: Harmony, 2005.

Frontain, Raymond-Jean. "The Trickster Tricked: Strategies of Deception and Survival in the David Narrative." In *Mappings of the Biblical Terrain: The Bible as Text*, edited by Vincent L. Tollers and John Maiers, 170–92. Lewisburg, PA: Bucknell University Press, 1990.

Frost, Robert. *Robert Frost's Poem*. Edited by Louis Untermeyer. New York: Washington Square, 1968.

Frymer-Kensky, Tikva. "Patriarchal Family Relationships and Near Eastern Law." *Biblical Archaeologist* 44 (1981) 209–14.

Fuchs, Esther. "Reclaiming the Hebrew Bible for Women: The Neoliberal Turn in Contemporary Feminist Scholarship." *Journal of Feminist Studies in Religion* 24 (2008) 45–65.

Funk, Robert W. *Parables and Presence: Forms of the New Testament Tradition*. Philadelphia: Fortress, 1982.

Furnish, Victor Paul. "On Putting Paul in His Place." *Journal of Biblical Literature* 113 (1994) 3–17.

Gable, John B., Charles B. Wheeler, and Anthony Delano York. *The Bible as Literature: An Introduction*. New York: Oxford University Press, 1996.

Gallup, Alec, and Wendy Simmons. "Six in Ten Americans Read the Bible at Least Occasionally." *Gallup*, Oct. 20, 2000.

Garrett, Susan R. "Exodus from Bondage: Luke 9:31 and Acts 12:1–24." *Catholic Biblical Quarterly* 52 (1999) 656–81.

Gershwin, Ira. "It Ain't Necessarily So." 1935. Los Angeles: Warner/Chappell, 1979.

Good, Edwin M. *Irony in the Old Testament*. Sheffield, UK: Almond, 1981.

Gopnik, Adam. "Searching for Jesus in the Gospels." *New Yorker*, May 24, 2010, 72.

Gros Louis, Kenneth R. R., with James R. Ackerman. *Literary Interpretations of Biblical Narratives*. Vol. 2. Nashville: Abingdon, 1982.

Gunkel, Hermann. *What Remains of the Old Testament and Other Essays*. Translated and revised by A. K. New York: Macmillan, 1928.

Hamilton, Edith. *Spokesmen for God: The Great Teachers of the Old Testament*. New York: Norton, 1949.

Hartley, Sean. *Holy Moses*. Woodstock, IL: Dramatic, 1998.

Hauser, Alan Jon. "Jonah: In Pursuit of the Dove." *Journal of Biblical Literature* 104 (1985) 21–37.

Heller, Joseph. *God Knows*. New York: Knopf, 1984.

Helyer, Larry R. "The Separation of Abram and Lot: Its Significance in the Patriarchal Narratives." *Journal for the Study of the Old Testament* 26 (1983) 77–88.

Hendel, Ronald S. *The Epic of the Patriarch: The Jacob Cycle and the Narrative Traditions of Canaan and Israel*. Harvard Semitic Monographs 42. Edited by Frank Moore Cross. Atlanta: Scholars, 1987.

Heschel, Abraham. *The Prophets*. Vol. 2. New York: Harper, 1962.

Hickens, Zachary, et al. Survey in *English 350: The Bible as Literature* course. Brigham Young University: Spring Term, 2004.

Holbert, J. C. "'Deliverance Belongs to Jahweh': Satire in the Book of Jonah." *Journal for the Study of the Old Testament* 6 (1981) 59–81.

Holtz, Barry W. *Back to the Sources*. New York: Summit, 1984.

Hooke, S. H. "Fish Symbolism." In *Folklore* 72 (1961) 535–38.

Hussey, L. M. "The Wit of the Carpenter." *American Mercury* 5 (1925) 329–36.

Hvidberg, Flemming Friis. *Weeping and Laughter in the Old Testament: A Study of Canaanite-Israelite Religion.* Leiden: Brill, 1962.

Hyers, Conrad. *And God Created Laughter: The Bible as Divine Comedy.* Atlanta: John Knox, 1987.

———. *The Spirituality of Comedy: Comic Heroism in a Tragic World.* New Brunswick, NJ: Transaction, 1996.

Hynes, William J. "Mapping the Characteristics of Mythic Tricksters: A Heuristic Guide." In *Mythical Trickster Figures: Contours, Contexts, and Criticisms,* edited by William J. Hynes and William G. Doty, 33–45. Tuscaloosa, AL: University of Alabama Press, 1993.

Inge, William Ralph. *A Rustic Moralist.* London: Putnam, 1937.

Jacobson, Dan. *The Story of the Stories.* New York: Harper & Row, 1982.

Jones, Bruce W. "Two Misconceptions about the Book of Esther." *Catholic Biblical Quarterly* 39 (1977) 177–81.

Jones, Ernest. *Sigmund Freud: Life and Work.* Vol. 2. Edited by Lionel Trilling and Steven Marcus. New York: Basic, 1961.

Jonsson, Jacob. *Humor and Irony in the New Testament.* Leiden: Brill, 1985.

Jurich, Marilyn. *Scheherazade's Sisters: Trickster Heroines and Their Stories in World Literature.* London: Greenwood, 1998.

Kelly, Walt. *Pogo.* New York: Simon and Schuster, 1951.

Kennedy, X. J. *In a Prominent Bar in Secaucus: New and Selected Poems, 1955–2007.* Baltimore: Johns Hopkins University Press, 2007.

Kierkegaard, Søren. *Concluding Unscientific Postscript.* Translated by David F. Swenson. London: Oxford University Press, 1941.

Klauck, Hans Josef. *Magic and Paganism in Early Christianity: The World of the Acts of the Apostles.* Translated by Brian McNeil. Edinburgh: T. & T. Clark, 2000.

Kundera, Milan. *The Art of the Novel.* New York: HarperCollins, 2000.

Lacocque, Andre, and Pierre-Emmanuel Lacocque. *The Jonah Complex.* Atlanta: John Knox, 1981.

Laffey, Alice L. *An Introduction to the Old Testament: A Feminist Perspective.* Philadelphia: Fortress, 1988.

Landy, Francis. "Humour as a Tool for Biblical Exegesis." In *On Humour and the Comic in the Hebrew Bible,* edited by Yehuda T. Radday and Athalya Brenner, 99–118. Sheffield, UK: Sheffield Academic Press, 1996.

Laniak, Timothy S. *Shame and Honor in the Book of Esther.* Society of Biblical Literature Dissertation Series. Atlanta: Scholars, 1997.

Langtry, Lillie. *The Days I Knew: An Autobiography.* New York: George H. Doran, 1925.

Lanyon, Walter Clemow. *The Laughter of God.* London: Fowler, n.d.

Larkin, Katrina J. A. *Ruth and Esther.* Sheffield, UK: Sheffield Academic Press, 1996.

Larue, Gerald A. "Marriage and Divorce." In *What the Bible Really Says,* edited by Morton Smith and R. Joseph Hoffman, 75–98. San Francisco: HarperCollins, 1989.

Lawrence, D. H. *The Works of D. H. Lawrence.* Edited by David Farmer et al. London: Cambridge University Press, 1980.

L'Engle, Madeline. "Interview with Madeline L'Engle." *Literature and Belief* (1987) 1–14.

Lerner, Alan Jay, and Frederick Loewe. "I'm an Ordinary Man." In *My Fair Lady,* directed by George Cukor. Warner Brothers Pictures, 1964.

Levenson, Jon D. *Esther: A Commentary.* London: SCM, 1997.

Levinas, Emmanuel. *Ethics and Infinity: Conversations with Philippe Nemo.* Translated by Richard A. Cohen. Pittsburgh: Duquesne University Press, 1985.

Levine, Etan. "The Case of 'Jonah' vs. 'God.'" *Proceedings of the American Academy for Jewish Research* 62 (1996) 165–98.

Lewis, C. S. *A Preface to* Paradise Lost. New York: Oxford University Press, 1961.

———. *Reflections on the Psalms.* New York: Harcourt, Brace & World, 1958.

———. *The Screwtape Letters.* New York: Collier, 1961.

———. *Surprised by Joy.* New York: Harcourt Brace Jovanovich, 1955.

Lowth, Robert. *Lectures on the Sacred Poetry of the Hebrews.* Vol. 1. Boston: Buckingham, 1815.

Luke, Helen M. *The Laughter at the Heart of Things.* New York: Parabola, 2001.

MacDonald, Duncan Black. *The Hebrew Literary Genius.* Princeton: Princeton University Press, 1933.

Malul, M. "Aqeb 'Heel' and Aqab 'to Supplant' and the Concept of Succession in the Jacob-Esau Narratives." *Vetus Testamentum* 46 (1996) 190–212.

Mankowitze, Wolf. "It Could Happen to a Dog." In *Using Prose Readings for College Composition,* 2nd ed., edited by Donald Woodward Lee and William T. Moynihan, 43–49. New York: Dodd, Mead, 1967.

Marcus, David. "David the Deceiver and David the Dupe." *Prooftexts* 6 (1986) 163–71.

Marty, Martin. *Bible Mania.* Beliefnet, October 27, 2007. Online: http://www.beliefnet.com/story/58/story_5809_1.html. Reproduced from *The Christian Century.*

Mary Poppins. Dir. Robert Stevenson. Buena Vista Pictures, 1964.

Mather, Judson. "The Comic Art of the Book of Jonah." *Soundings* 65 (1982) 284–91.

Mays, James L. et al., editors. *Harper's Bible Commentary.* San Francisco: Harper & Row, 1988.

McDonough, Sean M. "Small Change: Saul to Paul, Again." *Journal of Biblical Literature* 125 (2006) 390–91.

McGeough, Kevin M. "Esther the Hero: Going beyond 'Wisdom' in Heroic Narratives." *Catholic Biblical Quarterly* 70 (2008) 44–65.

Medcalf, S. E. "Comedy." In *A Dictionary of Biblical Interpretation,* edited by R. J. Coggins and J. L. Houlden, 128–29. Philadelphia: Trinity, 1990.

Metzger, Bruce, editor. *The Oxford Companion to the Bible.* New York: Oxford University Press, 1993.

Meyers, Carol. "Esther." In *The Oxford Bible Commentary,* edited by John Barton and John Muddiman, 324–30. Oxford: Oxford University Press, 2001.

Miles, Jack. *A Biography of God.* New York: Random House, 1995.

Miles, John A. "Laughing at the Bible: Jonah as Parody." *Jewish Quarterly Review* 65 (1975) 168–81.

Milton, John. *Paradise Lost.* Cambridge: Cambridge University Press, 1936.

———. "When I Consider How My Light Is Spent." In *The Norton Anthology of English Literature,* 3rd ed., edited by M. H. Abrams, 1397. New York: Norton, 1979.

Mobley, Gregory. "The Wild Man in the Bible and the Ancient Near East." *Journal of Biblical Literature* 116 (1997) 217–33.

Moore, Carey A. *Esther.* The Anchor Bible. Garden City, NY: Doubleday, 1971.

Moulton, Richard G., John P. Peters, and A. B. Bruce. *The Bible as Literature.* 4th ed. New York: Crowell, 1896.

Moyers, Bill. *Genesis: A Living Conversation.* Garden City, NY: Doubleday, 1996.

Mukherjee, Bharati. *Jasmine.* New York: Ballantine, 1989.

Newport, Frank. "One-Third of Americans Believe the Bible is Literally True." In *Gallup*, May 25, 2007.

Niditch, Susan. "Judges." In *The Oxford Bible Commentary*, edited by John Barton and John Muddiman, 176–191, Oxford: Oxford University Press, 2001.

———. "Samson as Cultural Hero, Trickster, and Bandit: the Empowerment of the Weak." *Catholic Biblical Quarterly* 52 (1990) 608–24.

———. *Underdogs and Tricksters: A Prelude to Biblical Folklore*. San Francisco: Harper & Row, 1987.

Niehoff, Maren R. "Mother and Maiden, Sister and Spouse: Sarah in Philonic Midrash." *Harvard Theological Review* 97 (2000) 413–44.

Nietzsche, Friedrich. *Thus Spake Zarathustra*. Translated by Thomas Common. New York: Random House, n.d.

Noble, Paul R. "Esau, Tamar, and Joseph: Criteria for Identifying Inner-Biblical Allusions." *Vetus Testamentum* 52 (2002) 219–52.

Noegel, Scott B. "From Balaam to Jonah: Anti-Prophetic Satire in the Hebrew Bible." Review of David Marcus, *From Balaam to Jonah: Anti-Prophetic Satire in the Hebrew Bible*. *AJS Review* 22 (1997) 103–5.

Norris, Kathleen. *Amazing Grace: A Vocabulary of Faith*. New York: Riverhead, 1998.

O'Day, Gail R. "John 7:53—8:11: A Study in Misreading." *Journal of Biblical Literature* 111 (1992) 631–40.

Ostriker, Alicia. "Esther, Or the World Turned Upside Down." *Kenyon Review* 13 (1991) 18.

Parsons, Mikeal Carl. *Body and Character in Luke and Acts: The Subversion of Physiognomy in Early Christianity*. Grand Rapids: Baker Academic, 2006.

Paton, L. B. *A Critical and Exegetical Commentary on the Book of Esther*. New York: Scribner's Sons, 1908.

Peek, Charles W., George D. Lowe, and L. Susan Williams. "Gender and God's Word: Another Look at Religious Fundamentalism and Sexism." *Social Forces* 69 (1991) 1205–21.

Perrin, Norman, and Dennis C. Duling. *The New Testament: An Introduction*. 2nd ed. New York: Harcourt Brace Jovanovich, 1982.

Pfeiffer, Robert Henry. *Introduction to the Old Testament*. New York: Harper, 1941.

Phelps, W. William. *The Bible*. New York: n.p., 1892.

Piraro, Dan. *Houston Chronicle*. Jan. 27, 2007.

Plato. *Plato's Cratylus*. Translated by D. N. Sedley. New York: Cambridge University Press, 2003.

Potter, Charles Francis. *Is That in the Bible?* Garden City, NY: Garden City Books, 1933.

Price, Reynolds. *A Common Room: Essays 1954–1987*. New York: Atheneum, 1989.

Prickett, Stephen. *Words and the Word: Language, Poetics, and Biblical Interpretation*. Cambridge: Cambridge University Press, 1986.

Radday, Yehuda T. "Esther with Humour." In *On Humour and the Comic in the Hebrew Bible*, edited by Yehuda T. Radday and Athalya Brenner, 295–314. Sheffield, UK: Almond, 1990.

———. "On Missing the Humour in the Bible." In *On Humour and the Comic in the Hebrew Bible*, edited by Yehuda T. Radday and Athalya Brenner, 21–38. Sheffield, UK: Sheffield Academic Press, 1996.

Radday, Yehuda T., and Athalya Brenner, editors. *On Humour and the Comic in the Hebrew Bible*. Sheffield, UK: Almond, 1990.

Rauber, D. F. "Jonah: The Prophet as Schlemiel." *Bible Today* 49 (1970) 29–38.

Reasoner, Mark. "The Theme of Acts: Institutional History or Divine Necessity in History?" *Journal of Biblical Literature* 118 (1999) 635–59.

Ripley, Henry J. *The Acts of the Apostles with Notes.* New York: Sheldon, 1867.

Roberts, Keith A. *Religion in Sociological Perspective.* 2nd ed. Belmont: Wadsworth, 1990.

Roethke, Theodore. *Straw for the Fire: From the Notebooks of Theodore Roethke 1943–1963.* Arranged by David Wagoner. Garden City, NY: Doubleday, 1972.

Rogers, Will. *Greatest Exponent of Simple Homely Truths that Will Endure Forever.* New York: Union Associated Press, 1935.

Ryken, Leland. *How to Read the Bible as Literature.* Grand Rapids: Zondervan, 1984.

Samuel, Maurice. "The Comic as Fool." In *The Worlds of Maurice Samuel,* edited by Milton Hindus, 291–307. Philadelphia: Jewish Publication Society of America, 1977.

Sandburg, Carl. "Lincoln Was a Tall Pine." In *The People, Yes,* 147. New York: Harcourt Brace Jovanovich, 1936.

Sasson, Jack M. "Esther." In *The Literary Guide to the Bible,* edited by Robert Alter and Frank Kermode, 335–42. Cambridge: Belknap Press of Harvard University Press, 1987.

Schemesh, Yael. "David in the Service of King Achish of Gath." *Vetus Testamentum* 57 (2007) 73–90.

Schwartz, Regina. "Free Will and Character Autonomy in the Bible." *Notre Dame English Journal* 15 (1983) 51–74.

Scott, Bernard Brandon. *Jesus, Symbol-Maker for the Kingdom.* Philadelphia: Fortress, 1981.

Searl, Duncan. *Beagle: A Howling Good Time.* New York: Bearport, 2009.

The Second Shepherd's Play. In *Early English Drama—An Anthology,* edited by J. C. Coldewey, 343–63. New York: Garland, 1993.

Seeman, Don. "'Where is Sarah Your Wife?': Cultural Poetics of Gender and Nationhood in the Hebrew Bible." *Harvard Theological Review* 91 (1998) 103–25.

Sheen, Fulton J. *Life is Worth Living.* Garden City, NY: Garden City, 1955.

Short, Robert L. *The Gospel according to Peanuts.* Richmond, VA: John Knox, 1965.

———. *The Parables of Peanuts.* New York: Harper & Row, 1968.

Shutter, Marion D. *Wit and Humor of the Bible: A Literary Study.* Boston: Arena, 1893.

Silverstein, Shel. "Colors." In *Where the Sidewalk Ends,* 24. New York: HarperCollins, 1974.

Smith, Joseph. *Joseph Smith's "New Translation" of the Bible.* Independence, MO: Herald, 1970.

Smith, Morton, and R. Joseph Hoffman, editors. *What the Bible Really Says.* Buffalo, NY: Prometheus, 1989.

Smith, William Austin. "The Uses of the Comic Spirit in Religion." *Atlantic Monthly* 108 (1911) 186–91.

Southwell, Peter J. "Jonah." In *The Oxford Bible Commentary,* edited by John Barton and John Muddiman, 593–95. Oxford: Oxford University Press, 2001.

Stanton, Elizabeth Cady. *The Woman's Bible.* Seattle: n.p., 1895.

Stein, Robert H. *Difficult Sayings in the Gospels: Jesus's Use of Overstatement and Hyperbole.* Grand Rapids: Baker, 1985.

———. *An Introduction to the Parables of Jesus.* Philadelphia: Westminster, 1981.

Steiner, George. *After Babel: Aspects of Language and Translation.* Oxford: Oxford University Press, 1975.

Sternberg, Meir. *The Poetics of Biblical Narrative*. Bloomington, IN: Indiana University Press, 1985.

Stevenson, Robert Louis. "An Apology for Idlers." In *Essays of Robert Louis Stevenson*, 21–42. New York: Scribner's Sons, 1912.

Stinespring, W. F. "Humor." In *The Interpreter's Dictionary of the* Bible, edited by George A. Buttrick et al., 2:660–2. New York: Abingdon, 1982.

Telfer, Elizabeth. "Hutcheson's Reflections upon Laughter." *Journal of Aesthetics and Art Criticism* 53 (1995) 359–69.

Tennyson, Alfred. *In Memoriam*. In *The Norton Anthology of English Literature*, 9th ed., edited by Stephen Greenblatt, 1187–1235. New York: Norton, 2012.

Thatcher, G. W. "Galilee." In *A Dictionary of Christ and the Gospels*, edited by James Hastings, 633–34. New York: Scribner, 1908.

Tollers, Vincent L., and John Maier, editors. *Mappings of the Biblical Terrain: The Bible as Text*. Lewisburg, PA: Bucknell University Press, 1990.

Trible, Phyllis Lou. *Rhetorical Criticism: Context, Method, and the Book of Jonah*. Minneapolis: Fortress, 1994.

———. "Studies in the Book of Jonah." PhD diss., Columbia University, 1963.

Trueblood, Elton. *The Humor of Christ*. New York: Harper and Row, 1964.

Tueth, Michael V., S.J. "Comedy and the Christian Vision: A Comic Approach to Theological Questions." Unpublished manuscript, 1993.

Twain, Mark. *Extracts from Adam's Diary*. New York: Harper, 1904.

"The Unknown Dobro Player." Molly and Tenbrooks, Oct. 27, 2007. Online: http://www.mollyandtenbrooks.com/TheUnknownDobroPlayer.html.

Van Doren, Mark, and Maurice Samuel. *In the Beginning, Love: Dialogues on the Bible*. New York: Day, 1973.

Votaw, Clyde Webber. "Peter and the Keys of the Kingdom." *Biblical World* 36 (1910) 8–25.

Waldoks, Moshe, with Speed Vogel. "Meditations on a Joyful Year." *Parabola: Myth and the Quest for Meaning* 12 (1987) 58–67.

Walker, Steven C. "Jonah as Joke: A Glance at God's Sense of Humor." In *Enter to Learn*, edited by Gary Hatch and Danette Paul, 154–59. Provo, UT: Brigham Young University Press, 1999.

Webster, Gary (Webb B. Garrison, pseud.). *Laughter in the Bible*. St. Louis, MO: Bethany, 1960.

Wesling, Donald, and Tadeusz Slawek. *Literary Voice: The Calling of Jonah*. Albany, NY: State University of New York Press, 1995.

Whedbee, J. William. *The Bible and the Comic Vision*. Cambridge: Cambridge University Press, 1998.

Wheelwright, Phillip E. *Metaphor & Reality*. Bloomington, IN: Indiana University Press, 1962.

Whipple, E. P. *Literature and Life*. New York: Mifflin, 1899.

Whitehead, Alfred North. *Dialogues of Alfred North Whitehead*. Edited by Lucien Price. New York: Little, Brown, 1954.

Whitman, Walt. *Leaves of Grass*. Edited by Harold W. Blodgett and Sculley Bradley. New York: Norton, 1965.

Wilcox, Lance. "Staging Jonah." *Bible Review* 11 (1995) 20–28.

Wolff, Hans Walter. *Obadiah and Jonah: A Commentary*. Minneapolis: Augsburg, 1986.

Bibliography

Wordsworth, William, and Samuel Taylor Coleridge. *Lyrical Ballads and Related Writings.* Edited by William Richey and Daniel Robinson. New York: Houghton, 2002.

Yee, Gale A. *Poor Banished Children of Eve: Women as Evil in the Hebrew Bible.* Minneapolis: Fortress, 2003.

Zimmermann, Frank. "Problems and Solutions in the Book of Jonah." *Judaism* 40 (1991) 580–90.

The Zohar. Translated by Harry Sperling and Maurice Simon. 2nd ed. London: Soncino Press, 1984.

Zuver, Dudley. *Salvation by Laughter: A Study of Religion and the Sense of Humor.* New York: Harper & Brothers, 1933.

Subject Index

Scripture Index